Michael Marder

# Pyropolitics
Fire and the Political

With a foreword by Slavoj Žižek

Michael Marder

# PYROPOLITICS
Fire and the Political

With a foreword by Slavoj Žižek

**Bibliografische Information der Deutschen Nationalbibliothek**
Die Deutsche Nationalbibliothek verzeichnet diese Publikation in der Deutschen Nationalbibliografie; detaillierte bibliografische Daten sind im Internet über http://dnb.d-nb.de abrufbar.

**Bibliographic information published by the Deutsche Nationalbibliothek**
The Deutsche Nationalbibliothek lists this publication in the Deutsche Nationalbibliografie; detailed bibliographic data are available on the Internet at http://dnb.d-nb.de.

Cover picture: ID 19155633 © Ba-mi | Dreamstime.com

ISBN (Print): 978-3-8382-1972-1
ISBN (E-Book [PDF]): 978-3-8382-7972-5
© *ibidem*-Verlag, Hannover • Stuttgart 2025

Leuschnerstraße 40
30457 Hannover
info@ibidem.eu

Alle Rechte vorbehalten

Das Werk einschließlich aller seiner Teile ist urheberrechtlich geschützt. Jede Verwertung außerhalb der engen Grenzen des Urheberrechtsgesetzes ist ohne Zustimmung des Verlages unzulässig und strafbar. Dies gilt insbesondere für Vervielfältigungen, Übersetzungen, Mikroverfilmungen und elektronische Speicherformen sowie die Einspeicherung und Verarbeitung in elektronischen Systemen.

All rights reserved. No part of this publication may be reproduced, stored in or introduced into a retrieval system, or transmitted, in any form, or by any means (electronic, mechanical, photocopying, recording or otherwise) without the prior written permission of the publisher. Any person who commits any unauthorized act in relation to this publication may be liable to criminal prosecution and civil claims for damages.

Printed in the EU

לזיכרונם של שרה בת מלכה, רחל בת שרה ומוניה בן יוסף

# Contents

Foreword: *A Hologram of Our Present*
By *Slavoj Žižek* .................................................................. 11

Preface: *Pyropolitics Reborn* ............................................... 15

Kindling: *The World on Fire* ............................................... 21

Chapter 1.
*The ABC of Pyropolitics, or the 'Elemental Regimes' of Carl Schmitt* .. 33
    1.1. The Idea of Elemental Politics ................................ 33
    1.2. The Elements, *Nomos* and *Anomie* ........................ 37
    1.3. Through Air to Fire .................................................. 43
    1.4. Pyropolitics and Spatial Imaginary ....................... 47
    1.5. Toward a Pyropolitical Phenomenology ............... 50
    1.6. The Risk of Pyropolitics ......................................... 54

Chapter 2.
*Light without Heat, Heat without Light, and the Problem of Evil* ......... 59
    2.1. The Cold Light of the Enlightenment .................. 59
    2.2. The Two "Powers" of Fire ..................................... 61
    2.3. Dark Heat, or Evil from the Perspective of the Enlightenment .......................................................... 64
    2.4. The Substance, of Which Evil Is Made ................ 68
    2.5. Absolute Separation and Evil ................................ 70
    2.6. A New Synthesis of Light and Heat? .................... 75

Chapter 3.
*Pyropolitical Theology I: The Fires of Revolution* ....................... 79
    3.1. Flying Sparks ............................................................ 79
    3.2. A Flaming Ideal ....................................................... 82
    3.3. The Inflammations of Revolutionary Spirit ......... 85
    3.4. Hegel on Fire ............................................................ 89

    3.5. Revolutionary Alchemy ........................................................ 98

    3.6. Catching Fire, or How Revolutions Spread ................... 102

Chapter 4.
*Pyropolitical Theology II: The Politics of Sacrifice* ........................... 107

    4.1. A Theology of Burnt Offerings ....................................... 107

    4.2. Self-Immolation and Sovereignty .................................. 112

    4.3. An Interlude: Extremist Politics ...................................... 126

    4.4. On Holocausts, or Burnt Offerings at the Extreme ....... 129

    4.5. The Burning Question of the Inquisition ....................... 140

    4.6. Global Energy Production, or 'What Do They Salvage from the Great Fire of Life?' ............................................. 146

Chapter 5.
*The End of Heliotropic Utopias: When the Sun Sets on the City upon the Hill* ............................................................................................. 155

    5.1. Around the Sun(s) ............................................................ 155

    5.2. Heliocentric Unity and Its Discontents .......................... 159

    5.3. The Solar Fetish of the Empire ........................................ 164

    5.4. A Shining City upon a Hill: The Pyropolitical Sublime .. 169

    5.5. Westernisation, Nihilism, and the Setting Sun ............. 174

    5.6. Coda: Politics of Fire and Sexual Difference ................. 178

Chapter 6.
*Around the Hearth: Politics in the Kitchen* ..................................... 185

    6.1. The Power of the Hearth, or the Domestication of Politics ................................................................................. 185

    6.2. The Inner Fire of the 'Kitchen Cabinet' .......................... 190

    6.3. What's Cooking in the Melting Pot? .............................. 196

    6.4. In Search of Perfection: The Arts of Cooking and Politics ................................................................................. 201

    6.5. Revolutionary and Post-Revolutionary Political Kitchens .............................................................................. 207

    6.6. Consuming Ourselves: Pyropolitical Cannibalism ....... 213

Extinguishing: *The Politics of Ashes* .................................................. 217

Appendix .................................................................................... 233
   *Fiery Words: Against the Literal / Metaphorical Divide* .............. 233
   *A Shadow Sun* ..................................................................... 242
   *Burning Ourselves to Death* .................................................. 249
   *The Implosion of History* ...................................................... 254
   *Kant's Fire* .......................................................................... 259
   *A New Shape of Pyropolitics* ................................................ 269

Notes ........................................................................................ 273

# Foreword
## *A Hologram of Our Present*

*Slavoj Žižek*

While I cannot follow any of Bach's *Passions* without yawning, I find his solo violin and cello sonatas irresistible. Take the fugues of Bach's three sonatas for solo violin (especially that of N°1), in which the entire polyphonic structure is condensed in one instrumental line, so that, though we "effectively" hear only one violin line, in our imagination we automatically supplement it with other unheard implicit melodic lines and seem to hear the multitude of melodic lines in their interaction. It's a musical hologram at its purest. The actual condensation to one single line is thereby by no means simply suspended: the key element of the artistic effect is that we are all the time aware of how we effectively hear only one line.

The unique achievement of Michael Marder's *Pyropolitics: Fire and the Political* is that it is a book structured like a Bach fugue: the motif of fire serves as a prism, a single motif through which, like superpositions in quantum mechanics, all the antagonisms and threats of our predicament appear in their interconnectedness. Marder is breathtakingly imaginative in composing a list of all the modes and uses of fire, literal and metaphorical, a list that includes political theory, literature, theology, philosophy, biology, up to the analysis of current events like the "incendiary speech" of the New Right populists from Trump to his European counterparts. He is also far from focusing just on the two most obvious cases, namely global warming, which menaces to bring the entire surface of our planet to a boiling point, and the threat of nuclear warfare that could ruin all life on earth. He deals, among other things, with books and heretics burnt on Inquisition pyres, with self-immolations at protest rallies, with the sun, with phenomena ranging from the massive burning of oil and coal to forest fires in Amazonia and Australia to gigantic volcanic outbursts, from revolutionary sparks which ignite radical social changes to the terrorist bombings of cars and buildings...

The choice of fire as a prism through which to analyze the complex interaction of multiple crises is much more appropriate than the obvious culprit—global capitalism—because it avoids the temptation to "essentialize" economy into the ultimate ground. Fire serves as a kind of filter, which makes transparent the interplay of all our antagonisms and threats. But there is an additional reason for the choice of fire: Marder argues that geo-politics, or the politics of the Earth, has always had an unstable, at once shadowy and blinding, underside—pyro-politics, or the politics of fire, which is increasingly dictating the rules of the game today, and that, as a result, it is necessary to learn to speak its language, to discern its manifestations, and to project where our world ablaze is heading. To do this properly, one should relativize some of our most elementary oppositions, like the one between nature and society.

In a recent text, Marder analyzes the effects of "Lavender," an AI-based program developed by the Israeli army which has played a central role in the unprecedented bombing of Palestinians. Such digitalized destructiveness also produces as its outcome something which cannot be simply conceived in the old terms of "mutilated corpses" and "ruins"; rather, it is a specifically pyro-political event:

"Gaza is rapidly transformed into a dump, where high-rise buildings and human bodies, ecosystems (including the fragile riverine one, cutting between the north from the south of the Strip) and orchards are mutilated beyond recognition and reduced to organic-inorganic rubble. A solidarity with dumpified lives, places and worlds requires something other than compassion, so what could that be? 'I am biomass' is a speech act that identifies with a vanishing life, with life's vanishing into dumped massiveness. The affirmation says: I am decimated being and stymied becoming, yet not exactly nothing. Dumped, I resist the dump with the surreal power of not-nothing. It is quite a stretch of the imagination to think that one can easily identify with the victims of genocide in Palestine. But what if Gaza were a condensed and particularly blunt version of a planetary tendency, as neoliberal newspeak with regard to 'compassionate genocide' leads us to believe? If so, then the biomassification of life, which proceeds at an uneven pace elsewhere, is accelerated in Gaza at the cutting edge of the most recent technologies of devastation. Rather than compassion, then, what is required is the solidarity of the dumped, who dare assert, 'We are biomass.'"[1]

The "biomassification of life" is what a contemporary criminal use of fire does to us, albeit unevenly in different regions of the world. But Marder goes much further in undermining ordinary oppositions: in his overview of the existing literature on the modes of cognition, which do not involve any conscious self-awareness, not even the one that is sometimes attributed to highly developed animals, he convincingly argues that "plants are *res cogitantes extendentes*": "plants are constantly extending their cognition through the active extension of their bodies, and, with it, their functional cognitive apparatuses. And beyond that, plants also actively extend their cognitive process to the environment they are constantly engaged with and which houses a wide array of their biochemical substances."[2] Such an anti-Cartesian approach (rejecting the ontological distinction between *res cogitans* and *res extensa*) has nothing whatsoever to do with any New Age vitalist obscurantism: it remains firmly in the space of scientific materialism. And it bears on plants that relate to solar fire otherwise than today's pyro-politics would allow.

There is a book comparable to Marder's, namely Peter Sloterdijk's *Prometheus's Remorse*[3] which traces a line from the mythic beginning—Prometheus giving fire to humans—to the present threat of humanity's self-destruction through different forms of an all-encompassing fire (global warming, nuclear war…). I see the advantage of Marder's approach over Sloterdijk's precisely in what may appear as its weakness. While Sloterdijk follows a single straight line from the human use of fire to the entire earth caught in fire, Marder's book appears as a mess of examples—but this mess is our reality today, and one that contains fugal variations on the theme of fire that by far exceeds instrumental attitudes and their uncontrollable consequences.

Our predicament could be called "a six-crises problem": ecological crisis, economic imbalances, wars, chaotic migrations, the threat of AI, disintegration of society. Although the underlying cause of these crises is the dynamic of global capitalism, their interaction leads to chaos and unpredictability. Do these crises strengthen each other or does their interaction offer some hope—say, a hope that the ecological crisis will compel us to move beyond capitalism and war to a social order of global solidarity? Even more provocatively, we know that wars condition new scientific discoveries and that technological inventions propagate—so what if, after a new war, these inventions would help humanity to deal with the ecological crisis? For all those who want to orient themselves in this mess without falling prey to simplistic answers, Marder's book is an obligatory reading.

# Preface
## *Pyropolitics Reborn*

This tome is reborn from the ashes of the previous two editions of *Pyropolitics* (RLI, 2015, 2020) a little like a phoenix that has assumed the shape of a book. Truth be told, since I had first started my research into the immense theme of fire in the early 2010s, I have never quite abandoned it. In the interim period, other works of mine on this theme have appeared. In *Energy Dreams* (Columbia UP, 2017) I contemplated not alternative sources of energy but an alternative concept of energy, which would not require the burning of all that is in the unquenchable search for unlimited potentiality. In a much more pessimistic *Dump Philosophy* (Bloomsbury, 2020), I considered, among other things, the dump-term *biomass*, which, in addition to the massification of life and the enlivening of mass, designates all organic materials (whether living or dead, organismic or residual) that are suitable for combustion as energy sources. In *The Phoenix Complex* (MITP, 2023), I examined an entrenched psychological structure, modeled on the widely-known variation on the myth of the phoenix, according to which the acts of burning both "external nature" and ourselves are instigated by a deadly hope and even a certainty that the lives lost in the ashes would come back, finite existence being infinitely recoverable and reproducible. The current return to *Pyropolitics* happens via these and other detours and meanderings in the labyrinthine theme (or nontheme) of fire.

But it is not just the book that is reborn in this instance; pyropolitics itself has made a startling comeback ever since my initial forays into it ten years prior. Already at the time of preparing the book's second edition, it was clear that both political changes and the exacerbations of already existing tendencies had speeded up, even compared to the first decade of the new century. So, in 2020 I asked: "Who could have imagined still in 2015 the rapid rise of the populist right all over the world, from Brazil to the UK, from the US to Italy?" And I noted that "'far' right is no longer far; it is all too near, as it forms governments and coalitions across the political spectrum. Relying on the mechanism of collective incitement and excitement, fanning the flames of hatred toward outsiders and other 'others' while at the same time reigniting nationalist pride, these regimes have resorted to the arsenal of revolutionary pyropolitics. Their rapid and widespread ascent gives us a clear indication of how the world has burnt more intensively and more extensively over these last five years." Now, with far right on the rise also in France and Germany, to mention only the European configuration, the return of a *certain* pyropolitical intensity from the feigned technocratic coldness of the recent past is undeniable.

And then there is the return of open warfare to European soil, spearheaded by Russia's full-scale invasion of Ukraine in February 2022. Barefaced imperialism and rabid nationalism are combined in this pyropolitical explosion, which still covers itself, as with a fig leaf, with the discourses and images of a technocratic and neoliberal worldview. The outcome are the blatant contradictions in Putin's explanations for the invasion of the neighboring country: Russia having the courage to assert its sovereignty (in the old-fashioned way, by declaring war) and Russia having no other choice but to invade, given the pressures and threats posed by the encroaching NATO. A similar, if also drastically different, reliance on neoliberal newspeak in the bombings of Gaza by the Israeli military is evident in leaflets airdropped on the Strip's population, encouraged to proceed to evacuation routes "for your own safety," when, in fact, the officially designated safe zones are also bombed. It is in these incongruences that the still incomplete emancipation of pyropolitics from technocracy announces itself, in the movement of the tectonic plates of geopolitics caused by pyropolitical activity.

Harkening back to the beginning of the decade, Brexit and revamped US isolationism under Trump testify to the lightning-fast disintegration of synthetic political unities and processes (globalization, Anglo-Saxon postcolonial hegemony, European integration...) with pyropolitical incitement-excitement for a catalyst. The response of the global left to these watershed events has been inadequate, to say the least, in part because the left has disclaimed its own revolutionary pyropolitical tradition. In the vacuum left by the left, environmental movements have gained momentum, albeit with a distinct set of pyropolitical catalysts. Instead of incitement, they are nourished by indignation with the present state of the world and by the apprehension that a liveable future, too, is being stolen from us; instead of excitement, there is a feeling that it is simply impossible to act otherwise — or not to act at all — in light of ecological calamity.

At its dynamic edges, the global political scene is divided between, on the one hand, parochial populist regimes that despite their slogan "Me first!" form a right-wing International and that encourage unbridled deforestation, use of natural resources, and reliance on the most polluting methods of energy production, and, on the other hand, a loose but sizeable alliance of young people and others concerned with the severity of the ecological crisis. This polarity itself is far from new. Nearly one hundred years ago, the two movements (the nationalist and the environmentalist) were united under the aegis of the official regime in Nazi Germany. Contemporary populist nationalism is at the antipodes of ecological concerns, but the political affect shared across the dividing lines is the same—fear, whether of otherness or of extinction, of national differences dissolving in the hodge-podge of globalisation or of the conditions that make life possible being fatefully undermined.

Given this tacit unity of opposites, it stands to reason that the environmental movement does not forfeit, but merely transforms the pyropolitical incitement-excitement model, which is so evident in the rise of the new right. What serves as a call to action is the actual burning of the world in the mass combustion of fossil fuels and in the devastating bushfires and forest fires in Australia and in what remains of the Amazon, in Indonesia and California, Siberia and Iberia. It is this burning of past and present plant life that comes to consciousness and, in doing so, spurs protests, strikes, and other kinds of political organising. With vegetal matter, the earth and the sky are set on fire and filled with smoke, but so, also, is the consciousness licked by and engulfed in the flames of devastation. Fire alters that within which it rages; one cannot fit it into an objective and detached representation, to which one would remain cold and indifferent, least of all when what is burning in the swathes of forest and fossils aflame is time itself. The analogue of excitement, then, would be the feeling that you are burning together with and in the world—that your future is going up in smoke with it.

But what exactly is this world that is now burning up or burning out, without the chance of a phoenix-like rebirth? It is made of institutions (states, international organizations such as NATO, big corporations, and so forth) and discourses, forests and fields (cultivated so as to be converted into calories or construction materials, into biodiesels or paper), the earth and the sky (into which the unearthed and incinerated fossils are dumped), people's minds and hearts (on fire with indignation, anger directed against foreigners, or the desire for justice) … That is to say: the world aflame is as much outer as it is inner, physical and psychic, human and other-than-human, pertaining as much to nature as to culture. If the integration of the world's fractal dimensions in the long process of capitalist globalization (which began already more than half a millennium ago with the first colonial ventures across the Atlantic) has been swiftly supplanted by its seemingly total disintegration, that is because the deconstruction of opposites and, especially, of binary relations has never operated by "blurring boundaries," as fashionable theory has it, but by letting them be consumed by fire, in which they melted down. Fire itself carries out the ultimate act of deconstruction, conditioning and consuming both sides of the integration/disintegration polarity.

# Kindling
## *The World on Fire*

February 11, 2012. Tenzin Choedon, an eighteen-year-old Buddhist nun from the Ngaba region in the Sichuan Province of China, torched herself, while calling for the return of the Dalai Lama from exile and demanding political freedom for Tibet. A few months later, on July 14 of the same year, Moshe Silman, an Israeli trying to make ends meet on a meagre state disability program and about to be evicted from his apartment, set himself on fire during a social justice demonstration in Tel Aviv. February 20, 2013. Varna, Bulgaria. Plamen Goranov self-immolated as a part of anti-government protests that swept the country and eventually led to the resignation of Prime Minister Boyko Borisov. April 14, 2018. David Buckel, a prominent New York City environmental and LGBT+ rights advocate died in Prospect Park by self-immolation, meant to draw public attention to the disastrous consequences of continued reliance on fossil fuels. September 9, 2019. Sahar Khodayari burnt herself to death as she protested the impending six months in jail sentence for having tried to enter a stadium in order to watch a soccer game as a woman in Iran. February 25, 2024. Aaron Bushnell, a twenty-five-year-old American serviceman self-immolated in front of the Israeli embassy in Washington, DC, while shouting "Free Palestine!" in the midst of Israel's military assault of the Gaza Strip.

Fire, to which the six activists among countless others before and after them have delivered themselves, gave them a voice but spirited away their bodies: *la voix sans le phénomène*. It made visible the otherwise veiled oppression, injustice, and violence by instituting another regime of visibility, abysmal and unsustainable. Did this voice (the ideal medium of expression and self-expression) gain more power, as it resonated in international news outlets, in exchange for life itself? An impossible political phenomenology and an unfathomable economy of violence, to wit...

Momentarily shedding light on human suffering, fire speeded up and completed the work of destroying the abject victims of political, social, economic, and environmental brutality, driven beyond the threshold of despair. (Was this *our* lightning, the fleeting moment of truth, which Martin Heidegger had extracted from ancient Greece *via* the poetry of Hölderlin?[4] How many such "lightnings" are still bound to happen?) Rather than escape from the veritable furnace that fuels the growth of financial capital or the melting pot of a unified nation-state, as the case may be, the secular and religious martyrs who set themselves ablaze mediatised the true consequences of these merciless bonfires by throwing themselves there. In a brief and terrifying flash, the consequences of oppression became a public spectacle. What kind of a spectacle? Sublime? One, where the agents of self-immolation took phenomenality, the possibility of seeing and making sense, into their own hands, showing the rest of us the contours of an unjust world lit by black light and suffocating in the intolerable heat of suffering?

Perhaps, we've already had a premonition of this obscure phenomenology all along, and the acts of Tenzin, Moshe, Plamen, David, Sahar, and Aaron give it the most brazen form, which can strike as obscene only those of us who have the luxury of caring about and protecting our sensibilities. The world around us is disintegrating at such a vertiginous speed that any descriptions of its physical, social, economic, or political makeup yield but a series of nostalgic snapshots, similar to the black-and-white photographs of the yesteryear capturing the already outdated structures and processes. But — here is the twist — it is also building itself up through this disintegration. Neither the event nor the scale of the world's crumbling is new: in the nineteenth century, Marx and Engels linked it to the expansion of the capitalist model that caused all that was solid to melt into air. What is unique today is *how* world-destruction, which encompasses a globalising world-creation or world-integration and fierce ultranationalist or frankly neo-fascist resistance to these processes, is accomplished. Instead of evaporating into thin air, things are consumed by fire. For over a hundred years now, since the start of World War I in 1914, the world in its entirety has been burning. Does it, in this flaming up, come into its own, as "world"? Does it finally reveal its fragility and finitude, its material precarity made obvious in a piece of wood (the Aristotelian prototype of matter, *hylē*) about to be reduced to a pile of cinders and ashes?

When a physicist conceptualises matter as accumulated and temporarily held-back energy; when we quantify our diets in terms of caloric intake and measure fitness by calories burnt; when the quest for alternative sources of energy leads governments seriously to consider the prospect of burning *anything* whatsoever, to accelerate deforestation, and to spread plant monocultures for the sole purpose of transforming them into biofuels: when all this takes place, then fire comes to dominate our sense of reality. Life itself is an internal conflagration, a great fire in which all living beings are so many sparks, igniting other similar sparks in reproducing themselves. We would not swerve far from the ancient Greek take on the life-giving power of heat and its revival in nineteenth-century German thought (notably, that of Novalis) in making this assertion. But, while for the Greeks, the creative potential of fire had to do with its measured, controlled, periodic lighting up and extinguishing, for us all sense of measure has been lost as the blaze rages uncontrollably. As the worldwide fire grows, so does the destruction.

From the books and heretics incinerated on the pyres of the Inquisition to self-immolations at protest rallies, from the massive burning of oil to inflammatory speech, from global warming or heating to the melting pot, from the imagery of revolutionary sparks ready to ignite the spirits of the oppressed to car bombings in the Middle East—fire proves to be the *sine qua non* of politics. If, in physics, the dominant paradigm has shifted from the solidity of matter to the volatility of energy (which *is*, itself, matter), then, in the political sphere, there has been an analogous transition from the clarity of *geopolitics*, broadly understood as "the politics of the earth," to the explosive ambiguity of *pyropolitics*, or "the politics of fire." It is not that one elemental regime supplanted the other in a linear succession, putting an end to an era of stability tied to the soil and guaranteed by a sedentary, agricultural, telluric lifestyle. Indeed, as I wrote elsewhere, the earth itself presents only an illusion of stability; we would do well to recall that its core is fire as well, and that the earth can give way underneath our feet, for instance, in the situation of a landslide or an earthquake.[5] The fickle force of pyropolitics has erupted at cardinal points in human history, much like the lava spewed by a dormant volcano. The intensification of politics, with its threat or reality of war—be it civil, interstate, or worldwide—has always foregrounded the fiery core of the political, whereas its dulling down has tended to resort to the essentially economic, property-oriented logic of partitioning, exchange, and the demarcation of real and imaginary borders on the earth's surface. Peace dovetails with the economic interests of unimpeded trade, and, as such, it is yet to be thought in strictly political terms. "Cold" War is an exception that proves this rule, since the very designation implies the usually "heated" nature of hostilities.

The politics of fire comes to determine the rhythms and the arrhythmias of today's world, which, with the doggedness that would have driven Heraclitus to the point of madness, is literally burning itself up. Our conceptual vocabularies, however, are lagging behind this world-conflagration, geared as they are toward the analyses of geopolitics, or, at best, of maritime politics. The time has come to update the political lexicon so as to account for the elements that do not fit into the simple opposition of land and sea.

The word *pyropolitics* has no established genealogical line in political philosophy. It is a bastard term. In the early years of the twentieth century, French professor of common law, Ernest Roguin, used it derisively to refer to political anarchism with its penchant for the use of dynamite and lethal explosions to sow the seeds of chaos.[6] As we survey the term's episodic history, we may also appreciate the delicious irony of this sentence in a 1925 *Time Magazine* article, "Italy: Financial Improvement": "If Fascism has frequently indulged in pyropolitics to its moral discredit, it has at least vindicated itself on the practical side of its policies."[7] On this view, pyropolitics, comparable to pyrotechnics, is just for show; what matters the most, the essential issue, is the pragmatics of economic improvement, even if it is brought about by fascism... More recently, Hilary Hinds and Jackie Stacie dubbed the representations of feminists as bra-burners "pyro-political."[8] And then there is Nigel Clark's praise of fire as "our pre-eminent means of modifying the environment, of opening up pathways, of rendering the earth more fruitful, more homely, less hazardous."[9] Bio-politics, for Clark, is "first and foremost a 'pyropolitics', centred on the regulation, manipulation, and enhancement of fire,"[10] as though this deliberate use, associated with human technology in general, were assured and its consequences predictable. The exact opposite is the case: the apparently controlled deployment of fire, whether in "clearing" forested areas for pasture or in burning (fossilized or non-fossilized) organic matter to produce energy, leads to an uncontrollable global environmental disaster.

The examples are a handful, and for good reasons. If politics is a matter of the *polis* (originally, the Greek city-state and, now, more broadly, a political community), then it can only take place on earth where humans dwell, miscellaneous dreams of celestial or heavenly cities notwithstanding. As a physical support for the *polis*, the earth is preeminent, which is why we are under the illusion that all politics is ineluctably a geo-politics. Heedless to Immanuel Kant's warnings, we conflate the state with the territory it occupies. But, besides Kantian criticisms, doesn't this common-sense idea miss the forest for the trees? Does it not rob politics of what is most unique in it, of what is irreducible to the economic sphere in the Greek determination of *oikonomia* as the "law of a dwelling," or, less literally, "household management"? What if the political, on the contrary, disturbs every dwelling united around a carefully controlled fire of the hearth, unsettles everything and everyone it touches, debunks the myth of stability, and gives the lie to the much-vaunted permanence of the status quo?

Expressing this disturbance, *Pyropolitics* aims to create a semantico-discursive field that would draw toward itself, magnet-like, the instances when fires, flames, sparks, immolations, incinerations, and burning have made their appearance in political theories and practices. This field will be, as much as possible, free of hasty judgments of pyropolitical phenomena as "good" or "bad," "invigorating" or "dangerous," "progressive" or "dictatorial." Pyropolitics, along with the fire it feeds upon, precedes all binary oppositions, including the institution and the disruption of an order. These judgments and these oppositions crop up once pyropolitics is already in place, enabling the ongoing contestation of the meaning of human engagement with fire as benevolent, malevolent, or neutral. The tall task before us is to grasp the pyropolitical not as a conjunction of phenomena to be analysed but as a set of indicators pointing to what makes political phenomena visible in the first place.

That the regimes of political visibility may change is no news to us.[11] What is less obvious is that the medium of light is only half the story. It is not by chance that "the other half" of fire—heat—is forgotten; modernity has tended to divide the flame into two and to ignore its less than convenient, abstruse dimension. Unless intentionality (taken in its broadest sense as attraction to its object) connotes the warmth of love, phenomenology, both in its classical and in its more political variations, remains a faithful inheritor of the Enlightenment tradition, where the light of reason was severed from the ardour of *polemos* or the warmth of the good, with which it was interlaced in Antiquity. Even medieval *lumen naturale*, coupled with the supernatural *lumen gratiae* of divine revelation, was a far cry from its sterile and cold Enlightenment analogue.

The philosophy of Carl Schmitt, usually read as anathema to Enlightenment rationality, is one of the few approaches to the political that takes pyropolitics seriously. Although Schmitt himself does not extol the risk, danger, and instability of this "elemental" political regime, he nonetheless reluctantly assents to its unavoidability and its influence in the contemporary world. From the scant mentions of fire in his works, we may reconstruct the overall parameters of pyropolitics, as much as the centrality of mytho-poietic figures in the thinking of the political. Geo-politics, expressed in the *nomos* of the Earth, and pyro-politics, describing a certain experience of *anomie*, stand for the two contrasting poles, between which political theory and practice oscillate. Sovereignty, defined by Schmitt as the decision on the exception and traditionally associated with the fire of glory, is, then, the irruption of pyropolitical phenomena into the legalistic framework of geo-politics. The hubris of modernity, in turn, has to do with the attempt to dissolve sovereignty and political risk in the more or less deft management of public and foreign policy by demagogues and technocrats.

Modernity's predominant self-image, already made evident in its essentially anti-political stance (which might be the most cunning expression of the political), is that of the dispassionate light of reason refracted through the prism of critique. The modern fantasy of "light without heat" construes its exact opposite—"heat without light"—as the embodiment of evil. In the political sphere, terrorism falls into this last category, along with everything that appears senseless, absurd, or gratuitous from the perspective of pragmatic rationality. And yet, the mainspring of political evil is not the unintelligible, but the very split between the two aspects of fire: the light shining on the surface, on the one hand, and the heat penetrating into the depths of things, on the other. The deficient politics of pure light is responsible for the persistent and growing problem of "motivational deficit" in contemporary democracies unable to cope with the logic of terrorism that is driven by what we might call "motivational surplus." Nor is the bifurcation of heat and light limited to the political sphere alone. When the complex unity of fire is lost, we witness the proliferation of the staple oppositions of modernity—the bifurcations between the cold albeit transparent public sphere and the warm but obscure private realm; calculative rationality and the ethics of care; the mind and the heart; the masculine and the feminine, and so forth.

Revolutionary outbursts announce the return of heat — the other quality of fire, which, like the repressed in psychic life, cannot be brushed aside once and for all. The Terror, which followed the 1789 French Revolution and the 1917 Russian Revolution, issued from the failure of modern light without heat to deal otherwise than by resorting to the utmost violence with what it construed as the intense and overwhelming heat without light of political energy. Revolutionary fervour restored to the political both its inflammatory rhetoric and the burning of desire in the subjectivity of the revolutionaries. The quick and contagious spread of these fires from the vanguard to the rest of the *body politic* gave the impression of a wild blaze, which had to be hemmed in from all sides and contained, if not altogether extinguished, in the periods of post-revolutionary normalisation. The ruthlessness with which the new regimes consolidated themselves (for instance, in Stalin's "purges") borrowed from fire its unstoppable drive toward pure ideality, achieved at the price of levelling down and destroying all real differences and, indeed, actual human lives. Having secularised the Christian inflammation of the believers' souls with true spirit, revolutions faltered when it came to transferring these technologies of divine fire to the political realities here-below.

Certainly, pyropolitical theology is not limited to revolutions. In the notion of the holocaust (whether applied to the genocide of the Jewish people in World War II, or, more recently, the idea of a "nuclear holocaust"), there is a direct allusion to burnt offerings that, originally, were signs of a total devotion to God. The bond between fire and sacrifice seems to be unbreakable: Tenzin, Moshe, Plamen, David, Sahar, and

Aaron along with other agents of self-immolation, such as the *satī*s in India, made it their final act of affirmation. In seventeenth- and eighteenth-century Russia, collective suicides by fire, sometimes called "the second christening" or "christening by fire," were common among *staroobryadtsy*, who had voluntarily elected martyrdom. Suicide bombers, too, re-appropriate the ancient ritual of a burnt offering, though in that case self-sacrifice is a vehicle for the sacrifice of others to an idea or a cause. Finally, the heedless, utterly irresponsible tendency to dig up and burn all of the world's oil and natural gas reserves does not merely fuel the world's economy, which, by now, could have plausibly made the switch to other, more environmentally-friendly founts of energy; rather, it makes of the entire planet a burnt sacrificial offering to the gods of progress.

What brings together sources as diverse as the Indian Vedic tradition, Zoroastrianism, the pre-Socratics, and the philosophies of Hegel and Heidegger is the conviction that fire is the most ideal of material elements; it is this ideality that substantiates its proximity to spirit, while keeping a foothold in the world of matter. Fire is supposed to purge the bodies it consumes of their imperfections, seen as inseparable from their very materiality. The Inquisition was probably the most dreadful mass "purging" of heretics, as well as of their heretical printed doctrines, in the exemplary spectacles of *auto-da-fé*. The practice of burning flags, the leaders' effigies, texts, or even car tires and rubbish bins at contemporary political protests still clings, likely unbeknownst to its perpetrators, to the idea of purification by fire. The ultimate justification for the existence of matter here is that it is the instrument of spirit: consumed by the flames, matter sustains the burning life of spirit, for which it pays with its own integrity. Once material reality is completely destroyed, fire is reduced to mere embers and, finally, goes out altogether. Against the limitations imposed by finitude, nationalist pyropolitics deploys the proverbial eternal flame, typically commemorating the sacrifice of soldiers in a war. Its metaphysical hubris shines through in this image of an unextinguishable fire, freed from the constraints of matter.

The ideality of fire has played a distinct role in the formulation of utopias, most notably Campanella's *City of the Sun*, alluding to Plato's *The Republic* and older invocations of *Heliopolis*. The ideological construction of "America" as the shining city upon the hill, most emblematically by President Ronald Regan, has built upon this tradition, as did the self-representation of the Spanish, Portuguese, and British Empires as places, upon which "the sun never sets." In each case, the city and the empire serve as mediators between the light of divinity, freedom, or civilisation, and the rest of the world, which basks in this luminosity already refracted through the empire's privileged political instantiations. If, as psychoanalysis insists, sunrises and sunsets are apt symbols for penile erection and masculine sexual desire, then the ever-luminous polities dream up the state of a permanent excitation, an absolute potency that results from having swallowed up, incorporated, and subjugated the sun. (Hence, also, the styling of France's absolutist monarch Louis XIV as the "Sun King.") To swallow up the sun is, nonetheless, to interiorise not only its blinding light but also its unbearable heat. Heliocentric utopias are self-destructive, to the extent that they strive to contain the blaze of ideality in the material *body politic* of the sovereign, the country, or the empire. That is why, in a mélange of utopian metaphors, we might say that the sun is bound to set on the city upon the hill.

Besides fire's destructive potential, it is useful for preparing foodstuffs for consumption, that is to say, for cooking conceived as a basic cultural mediation of nature. This more constructive, down-to-earth function has a peculiar place in politics. Lenin's famous, though misquoted, remark about a simple cook's ability to run a communist state; Golda Meir's Israeli "Kitchen Cabinet" — still in existence today — which echoed the first ever such group created by the US President Andrew Jackson and referring to the inner circle of government ministers who gathered for informal policy meetings in the prime-minister's kitchen; the American immigration policy, known as the *melting pot* are three illustrations of the transformative and creative power of fire. Traditionally imbricated with the politics of sexual difference, the fire of the hearth, which does not burn whomever comes close to it, is not necessarily more "gentle," even if it displays a greater sensitivity to the materiality it preserves. This transformative fire welds previously distinct elements together and introduces an essentially economic, homely, administrative dimension into the political process.

Fire is embroiled in the theologico-metaphysical paradigm, and so is the explosive vision of politics emanating from it. But what would the politics of ashes look like at the dusk of metaphysics? What remains of light and heat when material existence as a whole is on the verge of being consumed and destroyed, without any hope for an eternal conflagration of spirit sustaining itself? How to make sense of the charred and smouldering remains — the traces of catastrophes found alongside those of hopes and revolutionary desires — littering the horizons of the political today? These are the questions that open the pyropolitical paradigm to another politics and another *ethos*, congruent with postmetaphysical thought.

# Chapter 1.
## The ABC of Pyropolitics, or the 'Elemental Regimes' of Carl Schmitt

### 1.1. The Idea of Elemental Politics

French philosopher Gaston Bachelard rightly deemed himself "justified in characterizing the four elements as the hormones of imagination."[12] If it is true that the elements are "the hormones of imagination," then contemporary political theory is in dire need of an intensive hormonal therapy. Earth, water, and, increasingly, clean air figure in it only as contested "natural resources," rid of the kind of potency that used to be associated with elemental thinking. And fire— which is, of course, not a resource—is all but absent from these discussions, even though it underpins both global energy production and its deleterious unintended consequences, chief among them global warming.

By contrast, the period that roughly coincided with and immediately followed World War II saw Carl Schmitt actively engaged in investigations into what we might call "politics of the elemental." In *The Leviathan in the State Theory of Thomas Hobbes* (1938), *Land and Sea* (1942), and *The* Nomos *of the Earth* (1950), to mention but a few prominent texts, he conceptualised political regimes as epic struggles between the primordial elements of earth and water.[13] In the course of these investigations, Schmitt concluded that all political communities and activities had presupposed a historically changeable image of the earth: first, disjointed and fragmentary; later on, consolidated into a coherent worldview. In England, Spain, Portugal, Holland and a few other countries that consolidated themselves into maritime empires, the next stage of mythic history hinged upon a collective reorientation toward the sea, a much more unstable element, where borders and divisions lost their definitive character and gave rise to increased uncertainty and to escalating strife. This, however, did not preclude the existence of the predominantly land-based empires, such as China, Japan, or Russia.

Depending on the type of collective orientation, the political coincided with a certain elemental sphere, replete with an appropriate mythical symbolism, distinct goals and military strategies, ways of organising space and demarcating the human place in it, waging war and maintaining peace. The world viewed from the standpoint of dry land was not the same world as the one experienced from the perspective of the high seas; the defence of sovereign territories was unlike the tactical-military supremacy over *mare liberum*; the constitution of the Leviathan diverged from that of the Behemoth. (Schmitt himself does not accentuate the economic groundwork of this contrast, but it is not surprising that the transition from land-based feudalism to capitalism coincided with the rise of political imaginary predicated on marine uncertainty, fluidity, and displacement. Colonial and industrial modernity is truly "liquid," as Zygmunt Bauman once put it.)

To be sure, this admittedly simplified schema of geopolitics and maritime politics, of which Schmitt himself was occasionally critical,[14] is reminiscent of ancient Greek, and, especially pre-Socratic, thought.[15] The first cosmologies in Greece, in Mesopotamia, where they are believed to have originated,[16] in India, and in the Buddhist Pali literature postulated, in various forms, the classical elements that, at minimum, included earth, water, air or wind, and fire. The Greeks and the Romans tended to interpret relations between the elements in terms of either harmony or strife: elemental frictions elevated contention (the political affect *par excellence*) to the status of an ontological, cosmic principle. Heraclitus and

Lucretius are the classic thinkers of originary discord, "the father of all and king of all," according to the pre-Socratic's famous Fragment 83, and "this war that has been waged since time everlasting, the contest between the elements," in the words of the Roman philosopher.[17] The external world is the place of bitter conflict, where elemental differences are fought out and, in the course of this cosmic battle, give rise to particular, differentiated entities. So, too, human reality, the mirror and the microcosm of the universe, is full of enmity. Power, governance, and sovereignty are the continuation of cosmology and cosmogony by other means, even where the relations between the elements that comprise the world are themselves construed on the basis of essentially human categories of kingship and war.

The mythology of the elements is the secret prehistory of political theology, a locution Schmitt reserved exclusively for the Judeo-Christian antecedents of the political imaginary. It stands at the crossroads of myth and metaphysics, that is to say, at the pre-conceptual inception of philosophy. Even so, the elemental prolegomena to thought are largely foreclosed to metaphysical grasp and may be finally retrieved only once the history of metaphysics has come to an end, as Heidegger claimed.[18] Schmitt's political philosophy may be similarly classified (if classify it we must) as postmetaphysical, an argument I advanced in *Groundless Existence*. This could well be one of the reasons why the anachronistic return to the classical elements in the German thinker's work is much more than a mere relic of his anti-Enlightenment theory of the political.

Regardless of this rapprochement, we should already note a crucial difference between the pre- and postmetaphysical paradigms. Whereas, for the ancients, ontology is inherently and eminently political insofar as it is marked by the ceaseless struggle between warring elements personified as divinities, Schmitt valorises the other side of the coin—the ontological nature of politics. If Schmittian ontology is existential-phenomenological in its attunement to the subjective experience of the political,[19] then a veritable gulf seems to have opened between the paradigms framing the history of metaphysics at either extreme. The initial questions we are faced with are: does the politics of the elemental, with its emphasis on the substantial, objective, and often clashing dimensions of the world, not contravene a subject-oriented approach to the political, spurred by Schmitt? Or, to put it differently, what is the relation between Schmitt's political *mythology* and his political *theology*?[20]

Taking care not to project subsequent developments in the history of metaphysics onto premetaphysical ways of thinking, one should be reluctant to describe the elements as the "substantial" and "objective" immutable givens, considering that these descriptors are themselves historically associated with modern philosophy. It should be also recalled that neither existentialism nor phenomenology advances an idealist version of the subject detached from the materiality of existence and encountering the world only in an *après coup*, after her "fall" into it. The notions of the lifeworld (*Lebenswelt*) and the environing world (*Umwelt*), for example, are paramount in phenomenological analyses that invariably demonstrate how we are embedded in the contexts of our existence. The same basic intuition applies to the inhabitants a political lifeworld, irreducible to merely imagined communities. In their materiality, political practices presume a particular milieu,[21] even if the elemental milieu of politics is far from being limited to the solidity of the earth.

The rapid changes in the political *Umwelt* come into a sharper focus as soon as we retrieve the thinking of the elements at the dusk of metaphysics. It is not only due to the impoverishment and the destruction of the earth that the social, economic, and political environing world becomes less and less auspicious for human dwelling and habitation. More accurately, we should say that the earth is no longer the principal arena where the world unfolds, and that the other, more ethereal elements gain ascendancy over it. The observation that thought, action, and existence are extraordinarily ungrounded today, should be related back to the fact that they no longer draw support from the earth (which is incalculably more than the property of landed aristocracy, the backbone of agrarian societies, or the "native soil," provoking sentimental attachment). Our situation today is that of *neither land nor sea*; updated for the twenty-first century, the central political elements are the dyad of air and fire.

## 1.2. The Elements, *Nomos* and *Anomie*

It would be all too easy to explain Schmitt's own recourse to mytho-poietic language with reference to the reactionary anti-modernism that stamps many of his political writings, or to dismiss it as a collection of fairy tales unsubstantiated by serious scholarship. But, after all, isn't the self-consciousness of myth *qua* myth the badge of honour distinguishing genuine enlightenment? Aren't careful analyses of political mythologies and theologies much more productive and intellectually honest than the rationalist fictions of contractarianism, full of self-congratulatory delusions regarding the complete overcoming of myth? Be this as it may, perhaps something other than anti-modernism is at stake in the articulation, prevalent in Schmitt's writings of the "middle period," of political subjectivity and its elemental milieu. Perhaps this articulation is a variation on the theme of the Hegelian subject-object synthesis, which Schmitt prefers to conceptualise as the unity of order and orientation, *Ordnung und Ortung*, that jointly constitute the totality of *nomos*.²² When orientation is lost, order crumbles almost immediately; when order collapses, one is unable either to find one's bearings any longer. *Nomos* is, at the same time, the end goal of and the prerequisite for political theory, not to mention for human life.

The scope of this hypothesis is admittedly limited, in that the unity of order and orientation singles out a particular element, namely the earth, to which a human being, "a terrestrial being, a groundling [*ein Landwesen, ein Landtreter*]" who "stands, moves and walks on the firmly-grounded Earth [*feste-grüdeten Erde*]" and uses it as "his standpoint [*Standpunkt*] and his base [*Boden*],"²³ belongs. *Nomos* is always and necessarily — one might say, tautologically — *of the earth*. It concerns the unity of order and orientation within the element, to which humans belong and which they seize, appropriate, and claim as their property, their most basic belonging, *dominium*. For terrestrial beings, all other elemental regimes have the air of lawlessness, or *anomie*, without the possibility of either establishing an order or orienting oneself in the absence of a clear base and a definite standpoint.

In contrast to the extra-legal regulation of the law by the earth itself, not all politics is a geopolitics. The *imperium* of the remaining elements is quite free of territorial *dominium*. When political activity departs from the firm abode of the earth, it may be extinguished in ungrounded abstractions and systems of legality, *or* it may undergo absolute de-territorialisation, but not in the manner of Deleuze and Guattari's nomads who still roam the stable surface of the planet. Without a firm attachment to the earth, the unity of order and orientation falls apart and each of its two components internally disintegrates. Operating outside the boundaries of geopolitics, political actors are no longer able to rely on the lines of law, Right, and legality. Instead, they entrust themselves to, or learn to operate, the much more subtle (and, by the same token, much more intense) differentiations, typical of the other elements.

What matters within this expanded horizon of the political is not that empires and hegemonic regional blocks encompassing enormous landmasses have risen and fallen but that geopolitics as an idea and as the elemental framing of practical politics is on a steady decline. This is why Schmitt states so pessimistically in his private notes collected in *Glossarium*: "This is the new *nomos* of the earth—no more *nomos* [*Das ist der neue Nomos der Erde; kein Nomos mehr*]."[24] The new *nomos* of the earth loses the outlines of *nomos* in the aftermath of its decoupling from the earth. The political sphere is rid of the solidity of substance, as much as of its "sphericality"—a quintessentially geopolitical and geometrical figure. From the vantage point of the politics of the earth, to which Schmitt remains sympathetic to say the least, the new *nomos* is a-nomic, if not anarchic, a harbinger of chaos unrestrained by sovereign authority.

The reaction to this ungrounding is two-pronged. For one, "America First!"- type nationalisms and neofascism develop, moved by a nostalgia for the presumed clarity of authoritatively stipulated moral rules and unambiguous national boundaries (the one a reflection of the other), coupled with disappointment with neoliberal globalisation. Internally, the actual regimes that arise as a result of this attempt at regrounding politics retain the anomie voters had opposed; externally, their leadership pursues its own vested interests in global economy, while taking protectionist measures with regard to domestic industry. The other, much more promising, kind of reaction to political and existential ungrounding is the new ecological movement, which may, likewise, be heavily nostalgic—for instance, over the loss of biodiversity or of the more "pure," uncontaminated nature. In Nazi Germany, the two prongs of the reaction were united in the official regime, both nationalist and ecologically concerned. In our world, they are at odds with one another, seeing that the populist nationalisms of the twenty-first century retain the nineteenth-century ideal of industrial activity and promote the use of fossil fuels, which environmental activists vehemently oppose, of course.

Returning to the trend interrupted by various reactions to globalisation, we might ask: after political activity has gravitated (or, better, levitated) to the other, non-terrestrial elements, is it not released from the dead weight of substance and given over to a wealth of existential determinations? And isn't the apparent dematerialisation of political practices a part of this dramatic ground-shift, explaining the human loss of grounding, firm foundations, footing, and standpoint on *terra firma*?[25] These hypotheses go a long way toward harmonising the pre-metaphysical mythology of elemental politics and its postmetaphysical resurgence in Schmittian thought.

As Schmitt acknowledges in his theory of maritime politics, the sea is much more unstable than the earth and, it should be added, the uncertainty only intensifies as soon as other elements come to define political action. The inaugural act of instituting the *nomos* of the earth implies drawing or redrawing the dividing lines on a local or global scale. Conversely, the *nomos* of the sea — much less, of air or fire — is inconceivable, despite all the international maritime treaties and regulations, because "[o]n the sea, fields cannot be planted and firm lines cannot be engraved."[26] Although non-terrestrial elements produce other kinds of traces, these are less stable than the divisions etched on the body of the earth. The deconstructive logic of the *arché*-trace, harkening back to Edmund Husserl's work on the concrete origins of geometry, needs to be rethought together with the automatic privileging of geopolitics.

We would be mistaken in assuming that the relative lawlessness of water, air, and fire prevents these elements from acquiring an acutely political character. Indeed, those elemental political regimes that no longer refer primarily to the earth institute new non-linear divisions, and, thereby, dramatically remould human ontology. While "man is neither fish nor bird, and certainly not a being of fire [*Feuerwesen*] — were one to exist,"[27] he is, nevertheless, thrust into these "non-human" elements by his own political activity. As a result, our *Umwelt*, the world around us, is de-familiarised and rendered uninhabitable. Everything in it, including ourselves, becomes unrecognizable, uncanny, foreign. Human beings no longer know whether or not they are "beings of fire"; at the extreme of the elemental transformation of the world and of the human, suicide bombers or self-immolating protestors endeavour to turn themselves into such beings and, literally, to set the world around them on fire.

Classical rules of engagement in a war have become irrelevant as part of a sweeping tendency toward a politics less preoccupied with territorial defences — especially there where human beings have been dispossessed and displaced — and more with the sheer assertion of political will. State and nonstate actors alike show complete and utter disregard for civilian casualties, but it is only the latter (pyropolitical nonstate actors) that are ready to substantiate this assertion with their own deaths. Their signature, forged of fire and a finite life or lives it consumes, is all the more symbolically potent, as far as its visibility and destructiveness are concerned. The disorder and disorientation it sows is not easy to overcome, precisely because it steps outside the confines of earth-bound politics, which is the bulwark of *nomos*. The case of the partisans, which Schmitt cites is quite telling: even if the aspirations of the radically dispossessed may (and will) ultimately revert back to the earth and to territorial claims, their desperate, "irregular" combat throws the tactics of professional military forces into disarray.[28] Loyal to their native soil, the partisan "bearers of the elemental powers of the [...] earth"[29] are, for all intents and purposes, a spoke in the wheels of geopolitics.

The condition of "irregular" fighters and their marine counterparts (e.g., the pirates, who operate outside the confines of *nomos* off the shores of Somalia) is, in fact, symptomatic of the global situation, where "world order" increasingly presents itself as world disorder because the "world" exceeds the boundaries of *terra firma*. In Schmitt's texts, the name of this excess is the sea, the watery element that lacks the inner measure, the sense of justice, and the *nomos*-generating unity of order and orientation typical of the earth. When it comes to the grand standoff of land and sea, Schmitt sides with the earthly element, pleading for "a new *nomos* of the earth" and suggesting that "[h]uman thinking again must be directed to the elemental orders of its terrestrial being here and now."[30] The politics of the earth is this politics of sheer immanence, of immersion in the "here and now," but so too are the remaining facets of elemental politics. Far from being absolute, the transcendence of each element is relative vis-à-vis all the others, despite the illusion that everything that is decoupled from the earth loses touch with the materiality of existence. We may not discover a new *nomos* in fire, but we cannot disregard *its* "here and now," simultaneously enlivening and threatening to devour life itself. Schmitt, for his part, certainly didn't.

## 1.3. Through Air to Fire

For Schmitt, human attachment to the soil is praiseworthy as one of the consequences of Catholicism, which, much more than a religion, is definitive of a telluric, earth-bound, *terrist* way of life.[31] Somewhat more mysterious are the circumscription of the non-terrestrial elements to the high seas and a certain forgetting of air and fire in the German thinker's robust political mythology. While the political regimes of the earth and of the water (the sea) boast a familiar structure, the politics of air is as hard to imagine as the politics of fire.

This is not to say that there are no clues in Schmitt's texts as to the shapes the politics of air and fire might assume. In principle, if each of the four elements is an "indication of the great possibilities of human existence,"[32] then what are the possibilities and the impossibilities of human existence ruled by air and fire? The decoupling of technology from its "terrestrial or maritime foundation" means that "today, it is conceivable that the air will envelop the sea and perhaps the earth, and that men will transform their planet into a combination of produce warehouse and aircraft carrier."[33] Aerial bombardments, outer space exploration, drones, and satellite telecommunications have changed beyond recognition the spatiality of human existence, not to mention our relation to the earth and the sea now observable (and, therefore, to some extent already dominated) from above.[34] They have indefinitely extended the Panopticon up. "The invention of the airplane," Schmitt writes in an earlier text, "marked the conquest of the third element, after those of land and sea [...]. It is easy to understand why the air force was called the 'space weapon.'...[A]ir [became] the new elemental space of human existence. To the two mythical creatures, leviathan and behemoth, a third would be added, quite likely in the shape of a big bird."[35]

More so than water, air is the element of "groundlessness" and uncertainty, of risk and unpredictability; in this, it better corresponds to the nature of the political. It is that in which one falls or that on which one glides in a mimetic approximation of birds. The fate of Icarus looms large over human efforts to dominate this element. Its riskiness stamps political epistemology as well, with thinking *of* air veering dangerously on the side of vacuous speculation. Schmitt himself recommends caution to all those who venture in their theorising beyond the solidity of the earth, lest they give in to "ruminations in which serious thinking is too tightly bound to speculation that partakes of pure fantasy, and so leaves too much to the imagination."[36] Politics of air, which may tempt us to think in the clouds, conjures up a charge Aristophanes levelled against Socrates and the Athenian Academy in his well-known comedy at the very inception of the metaphysical era. Still more complicated is the situation of thinking that turns toward the element of fire, which threatens to burn and destroy whoever tries to tame and circumscribe it into an object of knowledge. And yet, theoretical ventures beyond geo-politico-philosophical milieu are worth the effort and the risk, because they hold the potential for disclosing a global transformation now afoot at a faster pace than in Schmitt's twentieth century.

The danger-fraught path of thinking, on which Schmitt has reluctantly embarked, leads him to at least one erroneous conclusion. In his periodisation of the politics of the earth, water, air, and fire, he lines up the elements in an ostensibly linear succession, a continuous chain. This progressive detachment from the originality of the earth has a number of side effects, ranging from a desperate yearning for the lost ground to the desire to see through the germination of a new constellation of power that would be conducive to a revival of the *nomos* of the earth. It is, however, unwarranted to comprehend the association of human activity with various physical elements in terms of a straightforward drift away from, a forgetting, or a suppression of the terrestrial origin (equivalent to the Heideggerian "forgetting of being"). Schmitt reveals one of the reasons for the simplification of elemental politics in writing (or, to be more precise, telling his young daughter Anima, who had listened to the text of what was later to become *Land and Sea* as an exciting bedtime story[37]) that "[a]ccording to an ancient belief, the whole history of mankind is but a voyage through the four elements."[38] It follows that, as latecomers on the historical scene, we now live in the age of fire, the furthest from the earth and, by implication, the closest to the end of the epochal journey of humanity.

But a linear drift away from the earth is emphatically not the sense of the Heraclitean Fragment 25, to which the German thinker is tacitly referring: "Fire lives the death of earth, and air lives the death of fire; water lives the death of air, and earth that of water." Without denying the difficulty of the fragment, it would be fair to say that the relation between fire and the earth, along with the other pairings of elements, is not that of a simple succession, punctuated by radical breaks, but that of survival; to live the death of another element is to lead its afterlife.[39] Interpreted politically, the first part of the fragment implies that in an age dominated by pyropolitics we live the death of the *nomos* of the earth and that, at the same time, something of international law grounded in *jus publicum Europaeum* survives its deracination.

Today's political ontology unfolds on the ruins of the grand geopolitical systems of the past — the totalising systems whose fault lines, coordinates of order and orientation, and *nomoi* survive the death of geopolitics (live the Heraclitean "death of the earth") long after the destruction of the context (indeed, of the world) wherein they used to be meaningful. The segregation walls and separation fences being erected everywhere from the US-Mexico frontier to the imposed Israeli-Palestinian border are symptomatic of the death throes of past geopolitics, to which state actors cling in reaction to pyropolitical "terrorist attacks" and other "national security threats."

Another hint regarding the non-successive ordering of elemental regimes lies in the co-origination of the politics of air and that of fire: "If one thinks of the technical-machinic means and energy necessary for human prowess to manifest itself in airspace, and of the engines that propel airplanes, it seems that the proper new element of human activity [*eigentlich neue Element menschlicher Aktivität*] is fire."[40] The energy needed for the politics of air literally to take off the ground resides in the fire (which, itself, requires oxygen for burning) of combustion engines, as much as in the more amorphous fire synonymous, in the best of humanist traditions, with the explosive potential of human spirit. Fire is not so much the final frontier as the animating and, at the same time, disruptive force behind all our actions and institutions.

Generally speaking, pyropolitics is so ubiquitous that it permeates all periods of human history, for instance, in the form of revolutionary "sparks" and explosions that overturned the *ancien régime* in France, Russia, and elsewhere. The myth of Prometheus, who stole the fire of the gods and bequeathed it as a gift to humanity, points out that, at the origins of technoloigy, power and control have been associated with this element since the earliest periods of human history. Byzantine secret weapon called "Greek fire,"[41] and also known as "sea fire," *pyr thalassion*, or "war fire," *polemikon pyr*, was said to burn even under water and to effectively sink enemy vessels; it allowed Constantinople to maintain a strategic edge over its foes. In other words, the politics of fire, already inherent in other elemental regimes, merely comes into sharper relief in the late twentieth and early twenty-first centuries. It finally becomes clear that pyropolitics is coextensive with the concept *and* the event of the political.

## 1.4. Pyropolitics and Spatial Imaginary

As I mentioned in the Introduction, it is virtually impossible to "outline" the contours of the politics of fire with the help of a precise definition. Schmitt's linear narrative of elemental regime changes proceeds as though this impossibility is due to the fact that pyropolitics is still too fresh, too precarious, too indeterminate to provide us with materials for an accurate historical or philosophical judgment. More importantly, the politics of fire stands out among other elemental regimes insofar as it is absolutely bereft of clear boundaries, not only on the epistemic but also on the political-ontological plane. What imposed itself as a limitation upon our understanding is part and parcel of the basic character of pyropolitics.

Each element presupposes a peculiar awareness of space and a concept of spatiality appropriate to it, depending on whether collective existence orients itself inland, faces the sea from the edge of the country's shore, views national territory from the vantage point of marine expanses as a mere shoreline, or begins to observe land and sea from above, from a groundless, suspended, and detached aerial perspective, afforded by satellite technologies. The alterations in our representations of spatiality are explicable in terms of what Schmitt calls *Raumrevolution*, "space revolution," whereby "all important changes in history more often than not imply a new image of space [*Raumbildes*]."[42] Fire, on the contrary, seems to bear no relation to spatiality. What "new image of space" does it furnish? How to experience the other elements and ourselves from its standpoint? Or are these questions themselves misguided, concealing the fact that fire portends the most consequential *Raumrevolution* yet—the revolution that, in Hegelian terms, involves a spatial negation of space? For Hegel, only the principle of pure ideality would be capable of such a negation, and fire encapsulates this principle within and beyond Hegelian thought. The dematerialisation of political practices, removed from the concreteness of the earth, further corroborates its radical *Raumsrevolution*.

The dissolution of perceptible outlines in the political "domain," which consequently becomes less of a "sphere" or an inhabitable *domus*,[43] largely depends upon the distension of the figure of the enemy, which Schmitt chillingly described on the concluding pages of *Theory of the Partisan*. In that work, a transition from the "real enemy" to "absolute enmity" is tacitly conditioned by the decline of the politics of the earth, to which the partisan clings when it is already too late to resuscitate *terrist* attachments on a global scale. "Another limitation of enmity," Schmitt remarks, "follows from the telluric character of the partisan. He defends a piece of land with which he has an autochthonous relation."[44] It is not by chance that the "character of the partisan" is at once telluric and reactive.

Initially, it was the enclosure of the earth that delimited politics, which is to say, bracketed hostilities by situating them against a common horizon and on a certain terrain; friends and enemies found their respective places in relation to this third—geographical or geometrical—neutral element, which held the promise of their reconciliation.[45] In the absence of the terrestrial horizon, against which the silhouettes of friends and enemies came through in all their concreteness and "reality," the figure of the enemy is distended and uncanny. Pyropolitical enemies are, at the same time, everywhere and nowhere; even in defending their native soil, they bear little relation to the earth (from which they are "unchained"[46] by their very tactics), or, for that matter, to any other spatially bound element. Their non-belonging to the terrestrial fold awakens "absolute enmity," the enmity "so frightful that perhaps one no longer should speak of enemy and enmity, and both should be outlawed and damned in all their forms before the work of destruction can begin. Then, the destruction will be completely abstract and completely absolute."[47] Before the material annihilation of the enemy, a more thorough (because abstract and ideal) eradication takes place: the enemy is destroyed as a figure and as a concept. Far from making actual enemies disappear, their figural and conceptual extermination renders them potentially omniscient. Uncontainable by figural contours and conceptual representations, they elude the nets of recognition. Absolute—unlimited, unrestricted—enmity bubbles up in this relation to the unrecognizable. It accompanies the threat of a total annihilation that inheres in unbracketed "nonconventional" warfare, endangering not only any given national territory but also vast regions of the world and the planet as a whole.

The spatial negation of space, as the culmination and consummation of absolute enmity, is one of the ways in which metaphysical ideality boomerangs to and impacts the very human history that has birthed it. The technological expression of this impact is the ultimate means of destruction to have come out of World War II, the atomic bomb. While the explosion in general is a symbol of pyropolitics, the atomic bomb is a singular case, since its destructive potential threatens the entire earth. A weapon capable of devastation so thoroughgoing as to reach planetary proportions has broken with the politics of the earth, with the sense of measure and moderation inherent in it, and with the *nomos* tethered to this politics. Atomic and hydrogen bombs are uncontainable by any lines of legality, friendship or enmity; they will always fall "beyond" the "new amity lines."[48] Why? –Because the line is a marker befitting the earth, which is currently overshadowed by the menace of total annihilation, and its linear *nomos*, which is irrelevant to pyropolitics.

Asking himself in one of his diaries what kind of "line" will be predominant after the atomic explosion, Schmitt responds: "No global line in the sense of *raya*, amity line, or the line of the Western Hemisphere [...] and, in general, no line whatsoever, but only space [*Keine globale Linie, im Sinne der Raya, Amity line oder Linie der westlichen Hemisphäre* [...] *sondern überhaupt keine Linie mehr, sondern ein Raum*]."[49] After the explosion, only space (or time equivalent to eternity) remains, seeing that the spatial negation of space has emptied that which is negated of all inner determinations, has erased all traces and lines engraved on the surface of the earth, and has flashed before our imagination the frightening and flaming image of ideality in the flesh, as it were. The erasure of the line is another piece of evidence for the waning politics of the earth, divided between the first and the last *nomos*.

## 1.5. Toward a Pyropolitical Phenomenology

Henceforth, the challenge is to find one's bearings in a concrete elemental order—to mark and to represent one's place within the environing context of an element—given the disappearance of those linear determinations that turn space into an inhabitable place. For a mode of thinking dictated by geopolitical modern consciousness, the effects of pyropolitics and our place in it are unrepresentable, if not sublime. As we will see in the next chapter, the fire of absolute enmity and of the atomic explosion burns without illuminating, without clarifying anything, without producing a cognitive schema, without giving rise to a new *nomos*. It is the fire of destitution, as opposed to institution, to use Reiner Schürmann's favourite distinction.[50] But fire is not only a destructive force; besides burning (up) whatever or whomever comes too close to it, its flames cast a glow on things, warm up those who are shivering of cold, bring about a transformation from one state into another... And the same effects emanate from pyropolitics, where the best and the worst are entangled, awaiting the differentiation and discernment, a criteriology that would emanate from fire itself in a return of the ancient *pyr phronimon*.

Tapping into what, without a doubt, is a facet of the quotidian discourse surrounding revolutionary or subversive activity, Schmitt deems the partisans to be the bearers of political sparks ready to kindle the fire of total politicisation.[51] To the extent that the previously apolitical, "neutral" civilians are entrapped in partisan combat—whether fighting or aiding and abetting guerrilla fighters—, politics, in the sense of an existential conflict centred on the friend-enemy distinction, becomes an integral part of their lives (more accurately, their lives become a part of the political). The situation of a total politicisation or mobilisation, erroneously associated with authoritarian regimes, is certainly dangerous. Surprisingly, however, Schmitt ascribes a protective function to the revolutionary spark that, besides maintaining a certain intensity of the political alive, keeps the partisan, *qua* political subject, sheltered, safe in its glow, *Glut*: "The spark that jumped from Spain to the North in 1808 found in Berlin a theoretical form that made it possible to protect him [the partisan] in its glow [*ihn in seiner Glut zu behüten*]."[52] The glow of revolutionary fire warms political subjects, providing them with a motivation to continue their struggle, and allows them to attain political subjectivity in the first place.[53] It does not grant protection to the partisans' physical lives (quite the contrary: their lives are now more endangered than ever!) but it does preserve their political existence.

Although fire lacks definitive contours, its burning permits those who gather around it to come to light, if only temporarily, to exhibit themselves in the outlines proper to them, and, therefore, to be. In the glimmer of revolutionary fire, be it as weak as that cast by a spark, partisans rise to the level of political subjectivity, denied to them by the status quo that seeks their neutralising criminalisation and delegitimisation. Pyropolitics, therefore, sets the parameters for political phenomenality, for the appearing of political actors in their fully political being. But aren't partisans defined, precisely, by their clandestine activities, by their non-appearance on a well-illuminated political stage, by their operations in the "underground," for instance, in the thick of a forest? How to explain this ostensible paradox?

Note, firstly, the kind of light that emanates from a spark. Its glow is sufficiently dim to keep the partisan unidentifiable from the perspective of a "regular army" and of the political state. Unlike classical phenomenology, on the one hand, fascinated with the eidetic and the physical light without warmth, and ethics, on the other hand, clinging to the warmth of interpersonal intimacy without light, pyropolitics combines both aspects of fire. Its shimmer is different from the light of phenomenology, in that it leaves plenty of room for the non-identifiable: the secrets, the shadows, and the *arcana* indispensable, according to Schmitt, to any political practice. And the warmth it emits is dissimilar to that of ethics (with the possible exception of the ethical thought of Emmanuel Levinas), in that it may, at any given moment, burn anyone who basks in it. Whereas pyropolitical luminosity is scarce enough to occlude the identities of those it illuminates, the degree of heat emanating from its fire depends on the intensity of antagonisms ignited between particular friend and enemy groupings. At the extreme, it can get out of control and grow into an immense blaze, when the figuration of the enemy is destroyed in the sentiment of absolute enmity.

Secondly, Schmitt's notion of the political refers not to a fixed entity but to the movement of politicisation, a process whereby the standoffs and oppositions in various areas of human activity, such as the economic, attain the existential intensity of friend-enemy conflicts. This dynamic core of the political is reminiscent of the transformative effects of fire. The Heraclitean *pyros tropai* (transformative fire, or, literally, "the turns of fire") underlies the praise Schmitt lavishes on the dialectical transition from quantity to quality in Hegel's *Logic*: "That is Hegel's *Hic Rodus* and the genuineness of a philosophy which does not permit the fabrication of intellectual traps [...]. The often-quoted sentence of quantity transforming into quality has a thoroughly political meaning. It is an expression of the recognition that from every domain the point of the political is reached and with it a qualitative new intensity of human groupings."[54] The metamorphosis of economic, aesthetic, and other antagonisms into political confrontations should be interpreted in terms of reaching a "boiling point," as Heinrich Meier has it,[55] the critical quantitative point where qualitative changes from one state—liquid or economic—to another—vaporous or political—occur. (Is it by accident that Lenin is said to have quipped that under communism a simple cook should be able to run the government,[56] for who, if not the cook, knows better the exact point, at which the transformations due to fire take place?)

When the most significant and, to some extent, mysterious dialectical transition is politicised, it gives us a preview of the fine differentiations proper to fire. Rather than engrave lines and traces in the solid substratum of the earth, fire institutes other ontological discernments between quantity and quality, the political and the provisionally apolitical. Just as in Heraclitus *pyros tropai* signal a constant transfiguration where "everything goes over into everything" and nothing retains its definitiveness,[57] so in Schmitt all spheres of human activity lose their identity and are politicised upon contact with the transformative fire of strong antagonism. The manifold of non-political spheres is gathered into a potential unity of the political, which is never actually integrated into a whole. The same goes for *pyros tropai* — the fire that presides over the passages of the remaining elements into one another and into itself.

## 1.6. The Risk of Pyropolitics

From the brief overview thus far it should be obvious that pyropolitics is fraught with risk, especially that of succumbing to the annihilating fire that burns without illuminating, without shedding light on that which it modifies. For all his caution and a generally conservative worldview, Schmitt believes that the risk must be assumed, not evaded, so that the political ontology of human beings would not dissolve in the sea of indifference, apathy, and neutralisation typical of liberal parliamentary democracies. On the subject of the latter, he writes: "Many norms of contemporary parliamentary law […] function as a result like a superfluous decoration, useless and even embarrassing, as though someone has painted the radiator of a modern central heating system with red flames in order to give the appearance of a blazing fire."[58] There where political oppositions fuel nothing else but endless parliamentary discussions and debates, the transformative fire of politics is reduced to a mere caricature, something given to sight without opening the field of vision or letting beings and events be seen. The red flames painted on a radiator give off an illusion of political activity but, at any rate, they neither shine forth nor emit heat. The unpredictable effects of fire are neutralised, but so, also, is life itself, which, since the evolutionary emergence of plants, is inconceivable in the absence of heat and light.

The "modern central heating system," with a fake fire depicted on it, is a fitting allegory of the modern political system that translates conflicts into differences of opinion and relegates the existential danger of friend-enemy formations to parts of the world "beyond the lines" of humanitarian order and universal human rights.[59] The heat of a radiator, in contrast to that of fire, is domesticated, fully regulated, employed for the domicile it warms up and provides with the comfort and convenience that a mechanical system has to offer. The fire, whence it emanates, is not extinguished but merely occluded, removed from sight, its unpredictable and at the same time luminous core evacuated from the dwelling as well as from the political regimes obsessed with risk avoidance. (Often, this occluded fire may be traced back to burning fossil fuels that replace the old-fashioned wood-burning fireplaces or stoves for mass societies.) By analogy, sovereign decision-making does not vanish; its source is only further concealed in the interaction of corporate business interests and lawmakers. What the painted fire represents is an untenable utopia of heat without either burning or light, the utopia of politics without risk and without the political.

The main reason for the criticisms Schmitt launches against liberal democracy is that the risk of not taking risks outweighs any actual danger lurking in a confrontation with the enemy. Complete risk-avoidance spells out an automatic and consensual termination of political existence.[60] This is tantamount to saying that—the distinction between the enabling-constructive and the disabling-destructive consequences of fire notwithstanding—the risk of pyropolitics is irrecusable. Still, in the end, Schmitt's conservatism has gained an upper hand, leading him to disown the politics of fire in his frequent self-identification as "the Christian Epimetheus,"[61] the prototype he adopts not from Hesiod's *Theogony* but from the German poet, Konrad Weiss. The exact opposite of his forward-looking and praxis-driven political brother Prometheus, Epimetheus is the philosopher *per se*, absorbed, as he is in Schmitt's depiction, in an "active contemplation" of already "completed events" in an effort to tease out of them "the dark meaning of our history."[62] Instead of risking the creation of an unknown future, he is beholden to the events' afterglow, shunning technology, broadly understood, and, along with it, the desire to control and manipulate things in the world.

Epimetheus, who distributes the gifts of positive traits to animals, while leaving nothing special in store for humans, keeps closer to the natural realm and to the affairs of the earth than his renegade brother, who has granted us fire, the arts, and technicity.[63] Given the choice between a personification of geopolitics, in the most basic and powerful sense of the term, and a figuration of pyropolitics, between Epimetheus and Prometheus, Schmitt opts for the telluric and *terrist* image of the god-fearing brother. (In fact, a good alternative title for *Roman Catholicism and the Political Form* would have been *The Doctrine of a Young Christian Epimetheus*.) In so doing, he rejects the politics of fire and the unmatched dangers and risks associated with it. But, in light of everything that has happened since Schmitt's death in 1985, do we still have the luxury of a choice between geopolitics and pyropolitics? Hasn't the politics of fire inexorably erupted on the scene of the politics of the earth and isn't the power of this eruption felt in every "suicide bombing," which is now a global phenomenon, as well as in the new instantiations of absolute enmity based on differences in religious creed? Wouldn't the most constructive response to this political ground-shift be a sustained rethinking of pyropolitical legacy, including its venerable revolutionary tradition, and an adaptation of this tradition to our contemporaneity (or, vice versa, of our contemporaneity to this tradition)?

Pining for the lost immediacy of the human relation to nature, Epimetheus wishes he could withhold fire from the morals. He glances back and is absorbed in a contemplation of the past he cannot revitalise. Yearning for the politics of the earth, with its contrived simplicity and innocence, the Christian Epimetheus looks back at the dramatic opposition of land and sea with a full realisation that both elements have been surpassed as the organising metaphors and mythic representations of the political. Reluctantly, he opens a veritable Pandora's box and bestows the gift and the curse of the politics of fire onto his contemporaries, in the hope that the new "meaningful proportions [*sinnvolle Proportionen*]"[64] of the world will, phoenix-like, issue forth from it.

# Chapter 2.
*Light without Heat, Heat without Light, and the Problem of Evil*

## 2.1. The Cold Light of the Enlightenment

After centuries of critique, the semantic surface of "the Enlightenment" is still the most self-evident and the least understood of its features. We hear nothing mysterious in this overused and incredibly polarising word; it is almost embarrassing to point out the insistent privileging of light in seventeenth- and eighteenth-century European thought, or, for that matter, in Western philosophy as a whole, which "since the time of its beginning [...] has been a philosophy of light, vision, and enlightenment."[65] The same emphasis on light recurs, with slight variations, in other European languages: the German *Aufklärung* (literally, "clearing up"), the Spanish *Ilustración*, the French *le Siècle des Lumières* ("the Age of Lights") or simply *les Lumières* ("the Lights"), the Portuguese *o Século das Luzes*, the Russian *vek prosvescheniya*...

In its fixation on light, the Enlightenment has faithfully repeated the movement of philosophical heliotropism, with its "opposition of appearing and disappearing, the entire lexicon of the *phainesthai*, of *alētheia*, etc., of day and night, of the visible and the invisible, of the present and the absent," "possible only under the sun [*tout cela n'est possible que sous le soleil*]."[66] The criteria of clarity and distinctness, applied to certain and secure knowledge in the early modernity by the likes of Descartes and Spinoza, were themselves the tropes of heliotropism, enlisting the sun to the service of philosophy. Sunlight soaked the fields of sensory vision, as much as of intelligibility; of metaphor, as much as of *eidos*.[67] The ethereal shining ground for the European Enlightenment has been readied ever since Plato.

But in the course of all the turns of the sun, throughout its tropes and tropisms, something gets irretrievably lost and no longer returns. A critique of philosophical heliocentrism, even one as nuanced as that deconstruction sets in motion, is still too blinded by light to be sensitive to the other dimension of the celestial blaze. It does not see (perhaps, because this is no longer a matter of vision, of *theoreia*) that the contrast of light and darkness is only half the Enlightenment story. What, despite a careful reading of the Greeks, escapes the modern sensibility is the *ur*-division between light and darkness, on the one hand, and light and heat, on the other.

Antiquity perceived in light and heat two manifestations of the cosmic fire (the cosmos *as* fire) that illuminated and emitted life-giving warmth. That is why, for the ancients, fire could be creative, as well as destructive. The Vedic tradition in Hinduism intuited in the god of sacrificial fire, the hearth, and the sun—Agni, from whose name, via its Latin adaptation, the verb "to ignite" is derived—a conjunction of shining truth and "the ancient vigour of life."[68] In the *Heraclitus Seminar*, Heidegger and Fink construed pre-Socratic *helios* as a "fire that apportions light and life."[69] An inheritor of the Heraclitean way of thinking, Plato depicted the sun as a force that simultaneously enabled seeing and was responsible for the generation of beings, their springing up into existence, by virtue of its abundant heat. The idea of the good, to which the celestial body stood in a precise analogy, was incomplete unless it interrelated what we now refer to as "ontology" and "epistemology," the conditions of possibility for being and for knowing. Early Christian theology, likewise, treated the two functions of fire as mutually complementary. "Fire," Origen wrote in a commentary on the Book of Exodus, "has a double power: one by which it enlightens, another by which it burns."[70] The shining of eidetic and divine light was deficient without the burning of the undying onto-theological fire.

The Enlightenment puts an abrupt end to a tradition, which it seems to have carried forth. It dissociates the two powers of fire from one another, fetishises light without heat in the form of impassionate rationality, or the ideal of objectivity, and rejects heat without light as myth, unenlightened obscurity, and ultimately evil. The darkness, against which the light of reason was to assert itself, is more than sheer obscurity: it shelters the supplement of heat, unrelated either to vision or to its privation, since, unlike darkness, heat is not the logical negation of light. Enlightenment nihilism, so astutely diagnosed by Friedrich Nietzsche, is an offshoot of rationality's aversion to the warmth of life itself. The core binaries of modernity—warm animal vitality and cold calculative intelligence, the intimacy of the hearth and the icy public realm, feminine affect and masculine nonchalance—are poor replacements for the non-binary and, indeed, non-oppositional division between light and heat. The Enlightenment ideal of an aloof, non-pathetic, neutral luminosity is as sterile as the universe it has constructed in its own image. Restitched on the basis of pure reason, with its fire that "shines without burning,"[71] the cosmos is no longer alive; it is no longer a warm and shining order it had been for the Greeks, which is why organic life is showcased within it as something anomalous. *That* is where we should seek the origins of nihilism.

## 2.2. The Two "Powers" of Fire

We, humans, are rarely capable of exposing our thought to the two "powers" of fire at the same time. To accomplish this feat, metaphysics has relied on an external guarantor of the powers' union, be it the idea of the good or God. The light that burns overwhelms the senses, as does a blinding image of the sun directly emblazoned on the retina. Associated with the glory or splendour of God in the monotheistic tradition, it is a pivotal attribute of the sacred. The flaming glory of the absolute monarch (think of the Sun King, Louis XIV, in this respect) is borrowed from its theological prototype. More so than other human inventions, the art of politics aims to remedy our incapacity to reconcile the two powers of fire.

In her patient meditations on the episode of Plato's cave, Luce Irigaray is mindful of the excess, the "too-much" of light mixed with heat: "It was too much. Too much for them to be given both light and fire at once. That light which floods out in such a burning stream was making them lose their way. A separation had to be imposed. Brightness on the one side, heat on the other."[72] The excess of givenness calls for a decision on what the subject would consent to receive: light or heat? We know which effect of fire modernity opted for. Eventually, a separation within the given paved the way to a differential valuation of its various aspects: from Plato to Hegel, heat, registered by our tactile sense, was ranked as a less ideal force than that proper to light. And everything harbouring heat, including the animal, the feminine, emotions, and life, was devalued or outright vilified along with it.

Can calculated suppression of heat in favour of light be sensed already in *The Republic*? For Plato, the sun's generative capacity, its stimulation of growth and life, is as significant as its illuminative capacity. Everything that lives strives toward the sun and the good not only because they shed physical and eidetic light but also because their warmth summons the living to the source of heat they will never reach (their "final" end). Having said that, Irigaray's observation remains valid, insofar as the separation of the ocular from the thermal is the uncritical prelude to any critique—a split in the phenomenon of fire that endows modern philosophy, ethics, and politics with trimmed-down heliotropism. It induces a partial amnesia of fire, whereby to concentrate on one of its aspects is to be distracted from the other.

A segregation of the two powers of fire is not without precedent in Christian theological commentary that forewarns the believers against the deleterious consequences of this rift. Origen, in one of his homilies, interprets Jeremiah 5:14—"Behold, I have made my words in your mouth as fire [*dvarai b'pikha l'esh*]"—in terms of the need to enlighten the parishioners and, at the same time, chastise them for their sins. (In a more disenchanted way, incendiary words coming from one's mouth would be dubbed *incitement*.) A mere rebuke and censure that "explain nothing obscure," "touch nothing of more profound knowledge," and "do not open more sacred understanding" are the sparks of a fire "that burns only and does not enlighten."[73] Conversely, "if when you teach you open the mysteries of the Law, you discuss hidden secrets, but you do not reprove the sinner [...], your fire enlightens only; it does not burn." The religious leader who follows the best course of action, then, is the one who "mixes the small flame of severity with the light of knowledge."[74] He disciplines the parishioners with heat and saves them with the light *of the same fire*.

Similarly, twelfth-century French abbot Bernard of Clairvaux decries the exclusive focus on burning *or* shining, *ardere* or *lucere*, splendor *or* fervor: "Merely to shine is futile; merely to burn is not enough; but to burn and to shine is perfect."[75] (Does this formulation not prefigure Kant's quip about the blindness of intuitions devoid of understanding and the emptiness of understanding bereft of intuitions—and so complicate the story of the Enlightenment's predilection for sterile light?) The useless, frigid light that does not burn is epitomised, following Bernard's imagery, in moonlight, that is, in the luminosity of an ostensibly disengaged "pure" theory and speculation. From this division stems the problem of theory's disengagement from practice. By choosing light without heat, the Enlightenment comes to believe that it has resolved the dilemma at the heart of fire, has minimised the risk of passionate flare-ups, and has eradicated the dangers of "non-rational" political engagement. It shines with borrowed light, which is lunar, not solar. Romanticism, too, with its embrace of moonlight, emblematises the other side of the Enlightenment, a melancholy nocturnal shining, deprived of its own energy. It is the apex of a disconnect between the two powers of fire and, consequently, one of the most apolitical theoretical attitudes imaginable.

## 2.3. Dark Heat, or Evil from the Perspective of the Enlightenment

A case-in-point of the Enlightenment politics of light is Jürgen Habermas's theory of communicative rationality. With the stated goal of "achieving understanding in language," Habermas advocates "a rationally motivated agreement among participants that is measured against criticisable validity claims."[76] To communicate in this sense is to reflect the light of reason from one participant in the communicative process to another, all the while keeping an eye on "validity claims" that would warrant a non-hallucinatory nature of such an agreement. A postmetaphysical version of perpetual peace reigns on the planes of rationality's infinite self-reflection. But outside these ideal and tautological boundaries things are far from idyllic. Here, we come face-to-face not so much with an enemy, who puts in question the existence of a community that builds understanding in language, but with evil, at least as the politics of light would construe it. Enemies can still resort to a modicum of communication, if only for the purpose of signalling their stance as each other's opponents. Evil, on the other hand, is non-communicative, totally idiomatic and idiotic, in the etymological sense of *idios*, "one's own", separated. Despite its belaboured praise of pluralism, communicative rationality renders evil absolute. But is absolute evil at all conceivable? And, if so, how?

As a rule of thumb, if evil is only *partially separate* from those basking in the light of understanding without heat, then it is a force of darkness, participating in a dialectical combat with the practitioners of Enlightenment politics. This evil is relative. Novalis, in fact, proposes that there is no other kind of evil: "There is no absolute evil, and no absolute affliction," since, though "[a]ll affliction and evil is isolated and isolating—it is *the principle of separation*—the separation is both annulled and not annulled by means of combination" and, therefore, affliction and evil "*only exist in a reciprocal relation.*"[77] In other words, the principle of separation already postulates the principle of aggregation or relationality, from which it distinguishes itself. It relies on the very thing it repels, and, as evil, owes its substantiality to the good. F.W.J. Schelling wholeheartedly agrees with Novalis's assessment, when he observes that "evil does not have the power to exist through itself; that within evil which has being is (considered in and for itself) the good."[78] In this respect, both Novalis and Schelling are in a good company, as virtually every Western philosopher has ruled out the possibility of absolute evil, isolated from being and from the good.

There is one caveat, however. The conventional account of evil assumes that the dividing lines pass between the reciprocally related elements of good and evil, or being and nonbeing, not between two autonomous powers of light and heat. Once the Enlightenment splits the phenomenon of fire in two, evil becomes absolute, absolutely separate and non-communicative: not as a force (or, ultimately, the impotence) of darkness but as heat detached from light. Regardless of the efforts to shed light on and to comprehend this form of evil, it will escape the grasp of rationally inspired and ocularcentric overtures, since heat can only be felt on one's skin, not contemplated with one's eyes through the "distance sense" of vision. Evil is, so to speak, something that touches and burns us without our being able to anticipate, or to pre-view, it.

The absolute evil of heat without light is both a catalyst for and a monstrous brainchild of the enlightened light without heat. Historically, as Reinhart Koselleck attests, Enlightenment thought evolved from Absolutism and coincided with the consolidation of the modern state-form.[79] The nascent political and intellectual infrastructures of Hobbesian modernity formed a united front against the possibility of civil war. "Following the paths illuminated by reason," writes Koselleck, "the State can be realized only through ending civil warfare and, having ended it, preventing any recurrence. Thus, like the political morality of individuals, the state also corresponds to reason. For reason, faced with the historical alternative of civil war or State order, 'morality' and 'politics' coincide."[80] Civil war, then, is the absolute evil from the political perspective of the Enlightenment; it is the unthinkable heat without light, which is detached from the light without heat of the state-form and its attendant reason. In Hobbes's political philosophy, to be sure, the divestment of heat is still incomplete, to the extent that the Leviathan assumes the form of "an Artificial Animal."[81] As the state mutates into bureaucratic machinery, artificiality free of animality hijacks the political sphere, drained of the last vestiges of life-giving warmth *and* life-threatening ardour that are incompatible with the state-form, which glows with sterile light alone. In any event, Hobbes regards civil war as the absolute evil, separated from the power of reason and "scarce sensible, in respect of the miseries, and horrible calamities, that accompany" it.[82]

If, as some contend, the creation of a global civil society is the corollary of globalisation,[83] then the threat of a global civil war is bound to reanimate some of the spectres that haunted Hobbes in the seventeenth century. A knee-jerk response is to inscribe terrorism within the framework of global civil war as "radical evil,"[84] epitomising the lightless heat of absolute violence. The pyropolitical accoutrements of terrorist actions that frequently resort to explosions, suicide blasts, and car bombings, apparently corroborate this transposition. Terry Eagleton, for his part, cautions us not to succumb to the temptation of labelling terrorism or Islamic fundamentalism as "evil." Its "lethal fantasies," he specifies, "are mixed in with some specific political grievances, however illusory or unjustified its enemies may consider them to be. To think otherwise is to imagine that Islamic terrorists, rather than being viciously wrong-headed, have no heads on their shoulders at all."[85] Although he is not a Habermasian by any stretch of the imagination, Eagleton leaves the window of communicative rationality open, even in the case of those who entertain and act upon their "lethal fantasies." To grant that terrorists are not acephalic beasts, that they have a head on their shoulders, is to accept that their actions have a modicum of light mixed with the scorching heat emanating from them. A pure politics of light without heat is as incredible as a pure politics of heat without light.

## 2.4. The Substance, of Which Evil Is Made

Instead of referring to political reality, the split between the two "powers of fire" betokens nothing more than the Enlightenment ideal and its obscure underside. Just as absolute evil without any relation whatsoever to being and the good is inconceivable, so it is equally absurd to insist on light entirely devoid of heat and on heat without a glimmer of light. I have already commented on how Novalis, Schelling, and Eagleton insinuated the light of being, reason, and the good into the thickets of the darkest heat. Their take on evil is consistent with the prevalent view — to which the Gnostics take a lonely exception[86] — that evil has no substantial reality of its own. To be realizable, evil must be adulterated with the good, if only with the view to attaining its goal (*its* good). According to the Jewish Kabbalah's *Book of Zohar*, its adulteration relies on the "spark of God [that] burns even in Sammael, the personification of evil." In and of itself, evil is dead, but "it comes to life only because a ray of light, however faint, from the holiness of God falls upon it."[87] Without the life-giving heat of God or of the good, evil is paralyzed and remains purely passive.

The Enlightenment forsakes this long and rich history of inoculating evil with a smidgeon of the good and, as a consequence of denying evil any share in substance or existence, precludes the possibility of comprehending it. Its insistence on a neat division between good and evil, light and heat, testifies to the Enlightenment's strategy of dissociation, or splitting, in the psychoanalytic sense of the word. Dark heat is the unconscious and assiduously repressed portion of the Enlightenment at war with itself, which means that civil war, terrorism, and other phenomena it deems evil are corollaries to a cleavage in the modern political "ego." The unintelligibility and nonsubstantiality of evil are the symptoms of Enlightenment's opacity to itself.

A commitment to the light of reason and of the state, nevertheless, mixes the standard of luminosity with the heat of a passion *for* reason. In "Faith and Knowledge," Jacques Derrida observes that the divorce between the two has never been accomplished; that knowledge presupposes our *faith in knowledge*; and that its light finds religion even there where overt religiosity is absent: "Everywhere light dictates that which even yesterday was naïvely construed to be pure of all religion or even opposed to it and whose future today must be rethought (*Aufklärung, Lumières,* Enlightenment, *Illuminismo*)."[88] Politically, the problem of motivational deficit in liberal democracies bespeaks a lack of faith in the default political arrangement, as well as the dearth of stimuli for playing by the rules of its game. Public apathy and inaction are the tell-tale signs for the waning ardour of the liberal-democratic principle, which tried to reanimate (or reignite) itself by spreading "the light of freedom" outside the North-Atlantic "West" in the first decade of the twenty-first century only to give up on this task and to become refracted in the century's second decade. Cold indifference to election outcomes is, itself, a symptom for the cooling down of the regime's animating force.[89]

To sum up: the sterile light of political and philosophical Enlightenment brands its disavowed other "evil." When evil is presumed to be a mere privation of light, which will be dispelled as soon as reason and freedom shine their lanterns in the previously unilluminated corners of the planet, the implication is that this kind of evil is relative. Here, the frame of reference is essentially Aristotelian: degrees of evil can be measured against the optimal amount of light, so as to be categorised as deficiencies and, in a more critical vein, as excesses. Too little light is a characteristic of the uneducated and illiterate masses, manipulated by leaders in tyrannical (usually theocratic) political regimes; too much accompanies the demands of total transparency, all-around surveillance, or panopticism.

But as soon as, thanks to political machinations, evil is completely removed from the field of vision and associated with the highly lethal lightless heat, it grows absolute, albeit not in itself but in the political discourse that utilises it for its own purposes, that is, for its own good. Such is the sense of "evil" in George W. Bush's expression "the axis of evil,"[90] referring to Iran, Iraq, and North Korea—incidentally, all countries with the real or imagined nuclear arsenals. Beyond light and darkness, it makes no difference that weapons of mass destruction have never been found in Iraq by International Atomic Energy Agency's inspectors. Absolute evil, to which the Bush administration painstakingly linked Saddam Hussein's regime, is not about the hidden and the unconcealed, the visible and the invisible, but about the burning of hatred. (Originally, Bush's speechwriter David Frum toyed with the idea of using the expression "the axis of hatred".) Absolute evil exceeds the Aristotelian notion of excess, so that the so-called rogue states and terrorism, with which they are often identified, acquire an overloaded meaning, "meaningfulness-as-excess,"[91] or, more precisely, meaningfulness in excess of eidetic light.

## 2.5. Absolute Separation and Evil

Our typology of evil would have been inadequate were it not to take into account the consequences of a non-binary opposition installed at the foundation of modernity. To the relative evil of darkness and the absolute evil of heat, we must add a third category that follows from the separation of heat from light, the separation that conditions the dissociation of theory from praxis, of ethics from politics, and of life from reason and the state. Among the basic causes of evil in the Kabbalistic worldview is the partitioning of the manifestations (Sefiroth) of God. Gershom Scholem explains: "[T]he quality of stern judgment represents the great fire of wrath, which burns in God but is always tempered by His mercy. When it ceases to be tempered, when in its measureless hypertrophical outbreak it tears itself loose from the quality of mercy, then it breaks away from God altogether and is transformed into the radically evil, into Gehenna and the dark world of Satan."[92] Thus, "the metaphysical cause of evil is seen in an act which transforms the category of judgment into an absolute."[93] What is in question is not the plausibility of an absolute separation but an *absolutising tendency* that sacrifices everything to an ideal, be it light or heat, mercy without justice or justice without mercy. This tendency is evil.

The surge of radical evil, according to the Kabbalah, was due to the uncontrollable inflammation of God's wrath that disrupted the balance and harmony of the Sefiroth. Though presumably neutral, the cool judgment of the Enlightenment, for which mercy was but a pitiful appeal to the affects (and so a kind of "moral pathology"), pursued a similar self-absolutisation. For all his adherence to reason within human limits, Immanuel Kant, in "Perpetual Peace," enthusiastically seconded the uncompromising Latin motto, *Fiat iustitia, et pereat mundus*, "Let justice be done, though the world perish,"[94] underscoring his anti-utilitarianism as much as his moral absolutism. The dispassionate light of critical reason proved to be more deadly than any theological fire. The burning wrath of God was not so dissimilar to the merciless tribunal of pure practical reason, which could with equal ease destroy the entire world on the altar of critique.

Not moderated by any external factors and influences, judgment and critique bring about a crisis of reason, which results from the immoderate negativity of separation and division. (Critique, judgment, crime, and crisis share the same etymology, stemming from the Greek verb *krinein* – "to separate, to divide".) The merciless light of relentless critique is "unstuck" from the warmth of life, reducing the living body to a "meaningless mass of sensations" and, therefore, to a figure of evil.[95] Edmund Husserl's *exposé* of the crisis of European sciences blamed scientific rationality for forgetting the lifeworld, with the structures of practical sense embedded in it, and for precipitating the calamitous departure of thought from existence. More pertinently to our argument, in the wake of Koselleck's reading of Hobbes, the crisis of reason is, necessarily, a crisis of the state-form. Despite his fanatical adherence to transcendental principles, Kant did not dare to extend the tribunal of critique to the state. Owing to this reluctance, he clandestinely saved a part of the world from perishing in the name of justice. As Koselleck puts it, "[c]riticism [...] became the victim of its ostensible neutrality; it turned hypocritical."[96]

It is not until Karl Marx's *Critique of Hegel's Philosophy of Right* (1843) and *The German Ideology* (1846) that critique is saved from hypocrisy and the institutional "embodiment of reason" is revealed as a potent instrument in class struggle. For Marx, the state is not a *kat'echon*, the restrainer preventing the apocalypse of chaos and civil war, but, alternatively, a political support mechanism for economic exploitation. The sham neutrality of the state-form belies the myth of cold light emitted by bourgeois reason. Beneath the frozen façade of rationality boils an intense class struggle, rooted at the same time in the logic of capital and in the intolerable living conditions of its victims. Bourgeois critique dares not shed its light onto this scorching heat, in part because thermal measurements are beyond the scope of its sensitivity, which Marx has enlarged.

Emitted in excess, light and heat are pernicious: the one blinds, and the other burns. The more each of them tends to absoluteness, i.e., to an absolute separation from the other, the more destructive it waxes. Remarkably, the difference between absolute good and absolute evil evaporates, which is why, having placed the absolute separation of the I from the Other at the beginning of *Totality and Infinity*,[97] Emmanuel Levinas has no other choice but to admit, as did René Descartes before him, that I can never know whether the Other's intentions are good or evil with regard to me. The Platonic sun blinds those who gaze at it directly; the sacred (or the Other) burns those who approach it too closely, foregoing all mediations. The archetypal Biblical warning pertaining to the sacred is sounded in Leviticus 10:1-2, where "Aaron's sons Nadab and Abihu put coals of fire [*esh*] in their incense burners and sprinkled incense over it. In this way, they disobeyed the Lord by burning before him another kind of fire [*esh zarah*: literally, "a foreign fire," or "an other fire"] than he had commanded. So fire blazed forth from the Lord's presence and burned them up, and they died there before the Lord." At any moment, fire can slip out of our control, become other, foreign to our intentions. Playing with it is always risky business, but so, too, are non-normative ethics and politics!

The trick is that one cannot abstain from playing with fire, ethically or politically, without annihilating the ethical and the political altogether. In the words of Koselleck that could have been easily uttered by Schmitt: "That politics is fate, that it is fate not in the sense of blind fatality, this is what the enlighteners failed to understand."[98] The forgetting of fire in the Enlightenment demanded that the political-revolutionary spark, a revolt against theocratic and other arbitrary forms of dominance, which had ignited it in the first place, be extinguished. All that was left behind was a pale afterglow. But this extinguishing did not make tumults empirically less frequent or less bloody. On the contrary, an isolation of light from heat polarised oppositions and rendered disorders more violent. For one, revolution, in the sense of a complete upending of the existing order, is a purely modern political phenomenon, which entails a conflagration of the collective will. Whether they are thought of as quasi-miraculous events exploding in the continuum of history, or as the beacons of universality shining a steady light on human actions,[99] revolutions are the linchpins of pyropolitical theology, which preserves a secularised and truncated version of Judeo-Christian God's fiery manifestations in modern theory and political practice.

In a less dramatic form as well, "the Age of Reason" extends sacred fire beyond its theological prehistory. Separation of church and state notwithstanding, the light of the Enlightenment is nothing other than refracted divine light, rid of its "sting." As soon as criminal responsibility supplants the notion of sin, the indifferent light of justice, predicated on the equality of all persons before the law, takes the place of the flaming, singular, and individuating judgment of God. The coordinates of Origen's theology are no longer comprehensible to us. An Enlightenment thinker would greet with a condescending shoulder shrug his statement "[...] *our* God is said to be *a consuming fire* [...] [*Deus noster ignis consumens est*]. Light is He without a doubt to the just; and fire to the sinful, that He may consume in them every trace of weakness and corruption that He finds in their soul."[100] The fire of divine judgment is replaced with the cold light of justice that, from the outside, shines on all in equal measure. The judgment of interiority ("weakness and corruption [...] in their soul") is narrowed down to the assessment of criminal intent. At least for a time being, the category of evil vanishes from political philosophy and the chasm between the two powers of fire widens.

## 2.6. A New Synthesis of Light and Heat?

At this point, a staple political, Leninist question "What is to be done?" imposes itself on us. How do we reintegrate the two powers of fire? And is their reintegration possible, let alone desirable, today?

Certainly, the gap between light and heat, law and life, will remain unfilled, and no special effort is required for its maintenance.[101] Law, judgment, and the entire biopolitical apparatus will be imposed onto life from a feigned space outside it. But what if we refrained, for an instant, from passing judgments *on* life and, instead, judged along *with* it, guided by its own light or *logos*? The ancient equivalent to this attempt at taking the side of life without foregoing reason was *pyr phronimon*, a discerning fire, which silently announced its judgments by materially analysing whatever it burned. For example, the knowledge that, according to Heraclituys, resides in heat has to do with this discernment that, at the same time, precedes and succeeds human intelligence: "What we call 'hot' [*thermon*] seems to me to be immortal and to apprehend all things [*noeein panta*] and to see and hear and know all things [*eidenai panta*], both present and future."[102] An antidote to the severing of light from heat and of reason/state from life is not the undifferentiated mess of chaotic matter, which is how anarchy tends to be caricaturised, but the divisions and concrete judgments of fire and of life itself.

Subsequently, Origen will recover for Patristic theology the pre-Socratic idea of *pyr phronimon*, the discerning fire. As opposed to the Enlightenment, which operates with an impoverished scheme of justice derived from an unacknowledged division *in* fire (between light and heat), Origen comprehends divine justice as a division, or judgment, *by* fire. God's fire discerns among the just and the sinners: in the hearts of the former, it burns as the fire that "opens the Scriptures"; in the hearts of the latter, it "is that fire which burns up the thorns of the evil earth, that is, which consumes evil thoughts in the heart."[103] Justice is the crux a non-public, inner illumination and of a ravaging blaze. The same fire burns in each in a unique manner, respecting the ancient principle of dispensation *to each his own*: in this respect, justice and life coincide. Guiding the just, the fire elucidates the Scriptures; inflaming the hearts of the sinners, it works as a purifying remedy, distilled from the discernments of divine justice.

In a commentary on the Song of Songs, the *locus* of fire shifts onto the sun with its double capacity transposed onto justice. Interpreting the word of the psalmist, "The sun shall not burn thee by day, nor the moon by night," Origen concludes: "So you see that the sun never burns the saints, in whom is nothing sinful; for, as we have said, the sun has twofold power: it enlightens the righteous, but the sinners it enlightens not, but burns, for they themselves *hate the light because they do evil*."[104] Whereas the condition *sine qua non* for true enlightenment is the love of light and its warmth, the hatred of light is the lot of the sinners congruent with their futile flight from divine radiance by way of evil actions. Evil spawns its own burning darkness. So, also, divisions and decisions by fire are not external to the ethereal flammable matter—the soul—on which judgment is passed. Pyropolitical justice is, at once, singular and universal, inner and outer, fiery and luminous. Bordering on ethics, it moves along the trajectory, which Kierkegaard intuited in his reading of the Biblical burning bush: "For the universal can very well subsist with and in the singular without consuming the latter; it is like the fire that burned in the bush without consuming it."[105]

To be perfectly clear, I am not advocating a revival of Origen's conception of justice in the twenty-first century. It is too late for a grand new synthesis of light and heat in political fire. To us, the words of Origen reek of the smoke rising from the Inquisition pyres, and Heraclitus is as enigmatic as ever. As John Donne has it, "The sun is lost"[106] — and that is not such a bad thing. Deconstruction has done much to cement this loss, in that it dismantled the systematic alignment of the discourse of reason with the sun and the king, or, in a word, with sovereignty.[107] I only want to emphasise that one can go about losing the sun in contrasting and, at times, mutually exclusive ways. Is it really lost if the light of reason is retained at the expense of the heat of faith? Or, if the absolute and objective standards of both powers of fire give way to the dispersed sparks of luminosity and warmth, to say nothing of a positive political revaluation of darkness?[108] Here, then, is the tangle of contemporary postmetaphysics, which lends its ambiguous name to Habermasian politics, to much of analytic philosophy, and to post-Heideggerian thought.

Assuming that the deconstructive variety of postmetaphysical thought has a propaedeutic value, its lesson is that fighting fire with fire will get us hopelessly entangled in a spiral of sovereign violence. In Shakespeare's *King John*, this fight is the prerogative of the king ("govern[ing] the motion of a kingly eye"), as the advice of the Bastard goes: "Be stirring as the time; be fire with fire; / Threaten the threatener and outface the brow / Of bragging horror [...]."[109] Life that is fully alive, sovereignty completely in control of the situation, absolute good and evil, the fire of a successful revolution — all these are the inventions of metaphysical onto-theology. We may have underestimated the scope of our lateness, which is, to resort to the language of German Romanticism, late for life itself. In that case, we must contend with life *qua* afterlife, and, instead of a new synthesis of pyropolitics, wade through the politics of ashes and cinders, surveying what remains of a charred, carbonised world.[110]

# Chapter 3.
## Pyropolitical Theology I: The Fires of Revolution

### 3.1. Flying Sparks

On December 14, 1825, a group of Russian military officers, most of them from the nobility, led three thousand soldiers in an unsuccessful rebellion against Tsar Nicholas I. Based on the month when the uprising took place, they came to be known as "the Decembrists" or *Dekabristy*. While some of the Decembrists were summarily executed, others were sentenced to a lifetime of hard labour in Siberia, with their spouses voluntarily joining them in exile. A national myth of self-sacrifice, endurance, and indomitable spirit, still widely revered in contemporary Russia, was generated.

In 1827, less than two years after the unsuccessful coup, the poet Aleksandr Pushkin initiated correspondence with those Decembrists who were his childhood friends and classmates, dedicating several poems to them, including, most notably "Deep in the Siberian Mines."[111] A line from that poem, which reads "Not lost shall be your woeful toil," was echoed, one year later, in the poetic response of the exiled Prince Aleksandr Odoevsky: "Not lost shall be our woeful toil, / A flame will flare from a spark / And our enlightened people / Shall gather under a sacred banner."[112]

These lines go a long way toward explaining the pyropolitics of revolt. Radical political action by a relatively small but stalwart group of people is a spark that should—so they hope—jump over to the masses, igniting a nationwide and, in certain cases, a global flame. Rather than spreading the dark heat of raw affect, or encouraging blind fervour for change, the fire of the revolution will enlighten the people it enflames, move them to action, and so overcome the theory/practice divide. Political enlightenment will further instigate the desire for liberation from tsarist tyranny, as Odoevsky states in the concluding verses of his poem: "We will forge swords from chains / And will kindle the fire of freedom again! / It will descend upon the tsars / And the people will breathe joyously!"[113]

Odoevsky's metallurgical metaphor is highly revealing: the fire of the revolution will melt the metal from which the chains of the *ancien régime* are made, and *from the same basic matter* it will create the weapons that will turn against that suffocating regime. Revolutionaries work with the materials they encounter all around themselves, converting, with the help of fire, the paraphernalia of oppression into the tools of liberation. The revolutionary tradition liquefies, recycles, and recasts the slogans and aspirations of the past, of other movements for radical change, however distant in historical time and in geographical space from those they inspire. One reason behind this remarkable continuity may be that the apparently scattered occurrences essentially belong to the event of freedom and equality that haunts world history. Another reason has to do with the contagious nature of fire that, through the instability and mobility of its sparks, is always ready to spread to another place and another era.

It is widely known that the Russian October Revolution of 1917, for instance, took as its model the French Revolution of 1789, which, in turn, emulated certain features of Ancient Rome. Less publicised is the fact that the October Revolution drew inspiration from the revolt of the Decembrists, so much so that at the turn of the twentieth century Lenin borrowed the line "A flame will flare from a spark" as the motto of the revolutionary newspaper *Iskra* ("The Spark") he edited. "It will not take much to set the working people aflame," he wrote. "All that is wanted is a spark, and the fire will break out. How true are the words, 'The Spark will kindle a flame!' In the past every strike was an important event, but today everyone sees that strikes alone are not enough and that we must now fight for freedom, gain it through struggle."[114]

Indeed, Lenin's pre-revolutionary speeches, as well as those he delivered between the February and the October revolutions, have the feel of someone who assesses the situation by surveying highly flammable materials and looking for the most efficient methods of setting them alight. Louis Althusser's theory of revolution as the "weakest link" in the political-economic chain could have, just as well, invoked the most combustible spot in the system, where the blaze would initially erupt. But before we move on to the psycho-chemistry of revolutionary fire within the *body politic*, it is worth giving some thought to the mobile and mobilising power of its sparks.

The French Revolution and the Decembrist rebellion both struggled against monarchical rule. With the Communist Revolution of 1917 they shared the goal of overthrowing an oppressive system of government and the realisation that the interests of the monarch and those of the people were irreconcilable (as Odoevsky implies in his poem, for the Tsar, the burning blaze of the revolt will reek of suffocating smoke, while the people will be able to "breathe joyously" in the same atmosphere saturated with its fumes). Revolutionary fire is, therefore, a more recent incarnation of *pyr phronimon* that discerns among and judges the wicked and the righteous, the oppressors and the oppressed, having divergent effects on them.

But the opposite must also be true: fire is indifferent to the materials it incinerates and reduces to ashes. For it, everything is internally or externally, actually or potentially, combustible. This explains its highly contagious spread, when the spark of a bourgeois rebellion jumps over to the discourse of Communist revolutionaries. It migrates across spiritual and physical space, time, and political regimes not because it stands for the same event, repeated *ad infinitum* on the streets of Paris and Cairo, Beijing and St. Petersburg, but because it does not rest. Not simply "quick," fire *is* time itself, and it does the work of time in an accelerated manner by breaking down and reducing things to their constituents. As Novalis formulated it with characteristic insight, "A problem is a solid synthetic mass, which is broken up by means of the penetrating power of the mind. Thus, conversely, fire is nature's mental power and each *body* is a *problem*."[115] Paraphrasing slightly, we should say that "each *body politic* is a *problem*," broken up by the power of revolutionary fire, and that the revolutionary movement itself is not exempt from such problematisation.

## 3.2. A Flaming Ideal

Fire does not only analyse things into their basic constituents but also recombines the matter, of which they are made, into new unities. Novalis is alive to this phenomenon: "On our self—as *the flame* of the body in the *soul*. [...] All synthesis is a flame—or spark—or analogon of this."[116] Our self as a synthesis of experience gathers into a fresh unity the data, into which the world has been analysed, burnt by our senses. That is why Novalis comprehends hearing, vision, and the other sensory capacities as so many fires, breaking the world down for the self that recombines them in a perceptual field. Revolutionary fire similarly melts the solid structures of the old regime in order to synthesise the new. Its destructive purification is, in the words of Jean-Louis Chrétien *"n'est que le prélude à une refondation et à une reconstruction,"* "but a prelude to a refounding and a reconstruction."[117] Instigating the analysis and synthesis of institutions, states, and regimes, it is the catalyst of political modernity.

The synthetic activity of fire is also fundamental to Schelling's philosophy of nature, where "all manifoldness of material in the world is reducible to its relation to that substance which in our atmosphere enchains the element of light, and whose general possession seems to be the world system's luminous body." That substance is fire. Accordingly, "all materials are either burnt up, or burning, or such as become combustible again."[118] Whether internal in the animal or external elsewhere, fire erases \ qualitative differences among the living and between the organic and the inorganic worlds. Its unity is that of an ideal, for which the "manifoldness of material" difference does not matter. A melting down of heterogeneity is essential for realising the ideal unity of nature and, in politics, for constituting a well-organised revolutionary subject.

Leon Trotsky's *History of the Russian Revolution* (1930) emphasises the noncohesiveness of the masses prior to the revolution. He complains that "the masses are not homogeneous, and moreover they learn to handle the fire of revolution only by burning their hands and jumping away. The Bolsheviks could only accelerate the process of education of the masses. They patiently explained."[119] More than pedagogic experiments, Bolshevik explanations aimed to kindle revolutionary fire and, through it, to melt the heterogeneous masses down to their common political denominator. The ideal unity of the revolutionary subject was supposed to have resulted from these inflammations, making sure that the proletariat was "tempered in the fire of events."[120] At the same time, revolutionary leaders had to learn how to balance multifarious circumstances with the simplicity of their revolutionary project, to juggle historical reality and political ideality, many contingencies and the one necessity that obsessed them. If Trotsky's case is of utmost interest to us, it is because he styled this balancing act pyropolitically.

When, in preparation for the revolution, the moment was deemed unripe, the Communist Party's Central Committee sent its delegates "to the troops and factories to restrain them from untimely actions." Disappointed, these delegates later reported: "We have to play the part of the fire hose."[121] Lenin outshone everyone in his aptitude for controlling the intensity of revolutionary fervour, following the infamous zigzag in a negotiation between the real and the ideal, cooling things down and firing them up again. Provided that fire performs the work of time by encouraging the destruction (e.g., oxidation) of finite beings, control over fire is control over time itself—its deliberate speeding up ("The Bolsheviks could only accelerate the process...") and deceleration ("the part of the fire hose").

The ideality of fire and the idealisation of the world, wherein it erases all material differences, put this physical element on the par with spirit; from the ideal to the spiritual, there is but a single step. Moreover, the Judeo-Christian tradition has consistently identified spirit with fire. In Luke 12:49, Jesus admits that he has "come to cast fire on the earth," a cryptic statement, with an exegetical genealogy outlined by Chrétien.[122] Master Eckhart represents the Father and the Son as "fire and heat," that is, as "extensions of one another,"[123] and goes on to associate fire with divine love and wind with the Holy Spirit—"the greater the love and spirit in the soul, the more perfect the fire."[124] As always, the elements of fire and air go hand-in-hand. Franz Rosenzweig also finds ideality in fire, especially that of "eternal life," an everlasting "flame eternally feeding upon itself."[125] Heidegger's definition of spirit as "flame" that "glows and shines" in *On the Way to Language*[126] arrives on the heels of this long tradition. Spirit as *logos* acts by gathering beings together into a simple unity that replicates the ideal synthesis of and through fire.

These and innumerable other theological and philosophical references to the flaming nature of spirit pursue distinct hermeneutical paths and strategic objectives. But they, nonetheless, agree on one thing: spirit spreads and perpetuates itself in space and in time as fire. Human spirits can be inflamed by a desire for the divine, as much as for justice, freedom, or the good, to the point of martyrdom and self-sacrifice. The revolutionary fervour that, in extraordinary circumstances, comes to animate the entire *body politic* is the secularised rendition of a flaming theological ideal.

An obvious theoretical hinge between "theological" and "secular" fires is Karl Kautsky's portrayal of Biblical Jesus as a revolutionary. As Chrétien reminds us, in *Foundations of Christianity*, Kautsky depicted Jesus as a rebel and hinted at the "proletarian character" of the early Christian community.[127] The burning fire Jesus casts on the earth is that of class hatred (*Klassenhass*)[128] setting its sights on nothing less than the overthrow of the Roman Empire. "And," Kautsky prefaces the citation from Luke 12:49, "it appears the saints are not to play a passive role in this process."[129] The early Christian community demands a fiery eradication of unjust political institutions, including not only the Roman Empire but also the entire patriarchal family structure.[130] In Kautsky's Jesus, then, a flaming spirit is in equal measure theological and political, destructive toward the injustices of the old world and creative of a new world, which he bequeaths to the downtrodden.

## 3.3. The Inflammations of Revolutionary Spirit

There is no smoke without fire, and there is no destruction without an emergent positivity. In the case of revolutionary political theology, that positivity is, in the first place, psychic. The world of ideal and ethereal flammable matter is populated by spirits, not in the sense of ghosts—though past revolutionary experiments unfailingly come to haunt the present and the future—but in the sense of the spirited part of the human psyche, the Platonic *thymos*. *Thymos*, which can bring our blood to boil at the sight of injustice, is much more than the political emotions of anger, rage, or indignation.[131] It is the site of an inflammation in subjectivity itself and a breeding ground for the highly mobile revolutionary sparks that can instantaneously jump from one subject to another. Self-immolators and, in a different way, suicide bombers substitute the flammable matter of their own bodies for a part of the psyche. Their ulterior motive may well be to transform the body on fire and its aftermath into fuel for a desired political change, mediated through intense political affect, such as fear. By contrast, revolutionaries know that bodies on fire are not as effective as burning spirits. Their blaze is more durable, since the psyche does not burn up as quickly as the body, even if it does not, by the same token, bear out the fantasy of the theological "flame eternally feeding on itself."

Like Lenin before him, Fidel Castro was an expert in controlling the inflammations of revolutionary spirit. He excelled in the calculus of revolutionary pyropolitics, monitoring the spread and the volume of the fire of struggle in the population at large. On the subject of the Cuban Revolution, he stated in one of his early speeches: "We are sure that only a handful of men can launch the struggle [...]; that the revolutionary movement, the group, following the rules that guerrillas have to follow, we are sure that that is the spark that would start the fire." And, he continued: "We were like a match in a haystack. I won't say in a cane field, because a match in a cane field is serious business. A match in a haystack!"[132] The small group of guerrillas he headed played with fire: it was a match in a haystack that got the revolutionary process on the way. Castro refuses to extend the analogy to a cane field (a burning field is "serious business"), not because guerrilla activities were merely an adolescent prank, a teenage rebellion against the established national and global order, but because the fire of the revolution had to be strategically restricted for it not to get out of hand. The same restriction had to be imposed on the hubris of revolutionary achievement, which is diluted in the humbleness of Castro's self-assessment, his self-identification with a match in a haystack rather than a considerably larger cane field. The fires on the ground and in the psyche needed to be hemmed in.

That is the first example of the Cuban pyropolitical calculus. The second occurs in the speech on the possibility of an American invasion, with Castro admitting: "[...] as far as we are concerned, we base ourselves on mathematical calculations, on numbers of men, on the volume of fire, and on a fire that burns hotter than that of arms: the fire in the hearts and the fire of the valour of an entire people!"[133] Compared to the United States, Cuba has a much smaller population, but, according to Castro's calculations, the intensity of revolutionary fire is greater on the island nation. Despite the original guerrillas being outnumbered by the soldiers of the regular army, their "fire in the hearts and the fire of valour" prevailed. Castro then proceeds to apply this ratiocination to a hypothetical standoff of the Cubans and the Americans. Mathematical calculations of volume and intensity pertain to the politics of spirit, which is more potent than the actual firearms. A flaming ideal does not vanish into thin air after the revolution but is tasked with protecting the new regime it brought into existence against external threats.

The return of the undying fire that, in times of danger and need, is ready to flare up again veers close to the fiction of an eternal life and its self-perpetuating flame. One of the permutations of political ideality is the project of a permanent revolution that, akin to the sun, which supposedly never sets on the British Empire, is the shimmering symbol of phallic power's unending erection.[134] Commenting on St. Ambrose's discussion of the incendiary flesh of Christ, Chrétien writes: "*Dire que Dieu est feu, c'est dire que Dieu est acte, et que cet acte éternel peut venir brûler le temps* [To say that God is fire is to say that God is act, and that this eternal act can come to burn time]."[135] An eternal theological or political act (remember that the Latin *actus* is a translation of the Greek *energeia*) ideally subtracts itself from the order of time, the order it can ignite and animate or incinerate and destroy in an effort to extirpate temporal existence. It subtracts itself by virtue of its ideality, its conflagration that levels finite differences. Self-sufficient, fuelled by itself alone, its fate is not tied to the combustible universe or to another element—air or oxygen. Master Eckhart's allocation of air, in the form of the wind that fans the fire, to the Holy Spirit incorporates the very material possibility of combustion into the Trinity.

In politics, the permanent revolution and the Empire it fights against are heirs to the theological unending act of self-foundation and self-legitimation. When at the end of his 1850 "Address of the Central Committee to the Communist League" Marx concludes that the battle-cry of the German workers should be "Permanent Revolution!" he simply calls for an independently organised worker's party that would not "be misled by the hypocritical phrases of the democratic petty bourgeoisie."[136] With the appropriation of the expression by Trotsky and his comrade Ryazanov, however, the self-assertion of the proletariat as a political force transforms the revolutionary blaze into an inextinguishable metaphysical principle. "Our motto must be the revolution *in Permanenz* (uninterrupted revolution)," says Ryazanov in a slight paraphrase of Marx. But, he explains, this will not be "'order' in place of revolution, but revolution in place of order."[137]

In spite of being overtly critical of the proposal, the Stalinist regime that consolidated its hold on power in post-revolutionary Russia exhibited none of the normalisation, which Ryazanov, Trotsky, and most of us usually associate with the word "order." The purges that sooner or later caught up with both revolutionaries and that imitated, on a vast scale, Robespierre's reign of Terror were energised by the deadly power of ideality. The pure act of a permanent revolution climaxed in the massive purging of party members, along with their families and acquaintances. The darkness of the gulag, summary secret trials, and countless death sentences were the consequences of ideality run amok. How could a revolution not go awry, if, splitting the powers of fire, it embraced a pure act divorced from understanding, the heat of a struggle—which is always the struggle for survival, including in situations where the fighters sacrifice themselves on the revolutionary pyre—at the expense of light?

## 3.4. Hegel on Fire

Fire destroys and creates, but the flaming passage from the analysis of the old to the synthesis of the new is far from assured. The art of fanning a revolution, which Lenin and Castro mastered, is formidable: it contends with the possibility that, at the blink of an eye, the blaze can get out of control. That these two revolutionary leaders were more successful than the rest in their undertaking is attributable to their untiring vigilance, to their practice of a measured kindling and extinguishing of political fire, as well as their fastidious accounting for the psycho-political volume of fervour. In a word, they followed the precepts of the reason of fire, *pyr phronimon*.

Lenin and Castro are, for all that, exceptional in the strategic manipulation of the fires they ignited. It has become something of a cliché by now to say that the revolutionaries are scorched by the fires they have kindled and that revolutions ultimately destroy *themselves*, ending in a bloodbath of Terror (Robespierre), the purges and the gulags (Stalin), or cultural annihilation (Mao). Such is the basic message of the film *Burnt by the Sun* (1994), directed by Nikita Mikhalkov. (The original Russian title of is more poignant—*Wearied [Utomlyonnyye] by the Sun*.) Revolutions are not immune to their own force of negativity; they are the first to succumb to it. According to Artemy Magun, negativity is in fact constitutive of the revolutionary moment, as much as of modern subjectivity and of modernity.[138] How does pyropolitics enhance our appreciation of this thesis?

To begin with, it is imperative to read Hegel's *Phenomenology of Spirit* in conjunction with his *Philosophy of Nature*.[139] *Phenomenology* expressly deals with the question of Revolutionary Terror with reference to the French Revolution under the heading "Absolute Terror and Freedom." The slogan of 1789 was "Freedom, Equality, Fraternity," but, Hegel objects, universal freedom has no positive, determinate content and it, "therefore, can produce neither a positive work nor a deed; there is left for it only *negative* action; it is merely the *fury* of destruction."[140] Freedom is an ideal, which cannot acquiesce to the actual existence it confronts in material reality. Having destroyed "the actual organization of world," it is left as the "sole object" devoid of content and as the only candidate for further destruction.[141] Upon unleashing the power of negativity outward, a revolution has no other choice but to internalise this destructive drive, such that absolute freedom would negate itself. A successful passage from "the old" to "the new" involves, therefore, three steps, instead of two: it must guide us from a past actuality through the empty universality of an ideal to a new actuality of post-revolutionary life.

Besides its immediate subject matter, *Philosophy of Nature* is useful for a dialectical analysis of the tragedy that befalls revolutions. There, fire is implicitly construed as the physical instantiation of absolute freedom; "it is," Hegel writes, "an active, unstable being-for-self which is in ceaseless process, and thus is liberated negativity."[142] "Liberated negativity" was, not incidentally, how Hegel described Revolutionary Terror that, through its unchecked freedom of destruction, equalised everyone by levelling its victims (which is not a mere turn of phrase, seeing that the guillotine rid them of their heads) who were accused of "corruption"—Robespierre's term for the very materiality of existence.[143] Just as fire equalises by reducing everything it ravages to the grey of ash, so the ideal of equality, envisioned by the liberated negativity of spirit, comes to signify an equal subjection to destruction, equality in and before death. With liberty and equality swallowed up by fire, all that remains of the French slogan is fraternity, the being-together of subjects engulfed by fire, a revolutionary community energised by a common political "cause." But this community, congeneric with the blaze that gave birth to it in what the Greeks used to call *pyrogenesis* or "springing-forth in fire," is as precarious and finite as the world it intends to burn up, because, in consuming its other, fire "consumes itself and thus passes over into neutrality."[144] Intense politicisation logically culminates in a neutralising and deadly depoliticization. Taken together, these extrapolations comprise the dialectical chemistry of revolutionary self-destruction in a nutshell.

As it bears on the political and, above all, on revolutionary movements, Hegel's dialectics of the elements is too suggestive to skim over in a single paragraph. Below, I propose a close political reading of the Hegelian philosophy of fire. But as we go over this material, one question should keep revolving in our minds: are revolutions without ideals (i.e., without a fervent invocation of the impossible ideality of absolute freedom, equality, or justice) conceivable? Can there be political action and effective motivation in the absence of our adherence to an ideal, be it as "neutral" as that of reason or universal communicability? In other words, is a cold revolution that does not scorch the old and weld the new a contradiction in terms?

The closest we have come to something of the kind are the lacklustre "colour" and "velvet" revolutions of the early 2000s in the post-Soviet space, as well as the technocratic, top-down revolutions foisted on, and soon thereafter rejected in, Southern Europe (principally, Greece and Italy) one decade later. Rather than adhere to any ideals, pro-European leaders in Georgia and Ukraine requested their countries' admittance within the already sclerotic fold of Western liberalism. (The fiery uprising that marked the start of 2014 in Ukraine adopted a totally different revolutionary approach to this problem.) In Southern Europe, the delegation of fiscal state sovereignty to non-democratically elected institutions, such as the European Central Bank, was advertised as the only solution to the severe crisis, gripping these countries. Is technocracy, today's alias of *Realpolitik*, the only alternative to the pyropolitical ideality of revolutions? And, more crucially still, is violence, instead of disappearing altogether from the contemporary political scene in the West, only better concealed in neoliberal programs that deprive citizens of basic healthcare, job security, housing, and minimum subsistence?

But let us return to Hegel and fire! In the chapter on "The Elements" in *Philosophy of Nature*, the German thinker classifies water and fire as "the Elements of opposition,"[145] because each opposes (and, to some extent, neutralizes) the other and because fire is also opposed to everything it consumes, as well as to itself. In the scheme of *Phenomenology of Spirit*, the external opposition of these elements fits the structure of consciousness, while the self-opposition of fire, its internalisation of negativity, parallels the rise of self-consciousness. Be this as it may, the designation "the elements of opposition" already insinuates that the two are privy to a certain political relation (or self-relation). This is in contrast to the more passive universality of air and the "abstractly universal individuality" of the Earth,[146] the irreducible substratum of geopolitics. Then, light, separated from the totality of fire along the lines of Enlightenment thought, presides over the foursome of the elements and "kindles" their process, "arouses and governs it generally."[147] But, as a kindling agent, light is, after all, an effect of fire and a stimulus for dialectical movement.

Referring to the "elements," Hegel does not imply the sense modern chemistry bestows upon this ancient notion. In a lengthy addition to §281, he points out that chemistry "presupposes the individuality of bodies and then seeks to tear apart this individuality, this point of unity which holds differences in itself, and to liberate the latter from the violence that has been done to them."[148] Chemistry is the science of ideality, analysing the organismic whole into its constituents to get at its essence, in the same manner that fire and Terror undo the bodies they burn. It avails itself of fire and extreme heat to trigger its reactions so as "to reach what is simple and thus destroys individuality."[149] In undermining life, even organic chemistry forges an alliance with the realm of death — the alliance, for which Rousseau despised this science as much as he admired that of botany[150] — and so blocks the passage to a new living actuality. Similarly with the revolution: the unleashing of murderous negativity thwarts the "reconstruction" of life on a revolutionary footing, all appeals to a permanent revolution notwithstanding. Putting *pyrogenesis* in the limelight, it forgoes *pyrobios*, which was the Greek word for "living in fire."

Heard with a Hegelian ear, *pyrobios* is not as bizarre as it sounds to Schmitt, for whom the human, as we have already seen, is "certainly not a being of fire." The animal life-process *is* "also the fire-process for it consists in the consumption of particularized existences; but it perpetually reproduces its material."[151] Speaking of a biological fire-process, Hegel alludes to 1) the internal heat generated by the animal; 2) a diet, predicated on caloric intake and the processing of nutrients; and 3) finite animal life, in which individual specimens ("particularized existences") are consumed, while the species is reproduced. The revolution is, analogously, a political life-process unravelling as a fire-process, consuming individual existences, and ideally reproducing itself under the aegis of an inflamed, purely active spirit. Revolutionary energy is a mode of liberating — indeed, of unleashing — the principle of animality in politics — and, accordingly, one way of reconciling biopolitics and pyropolitics.

We would be right to deduce from this set of allusions that, surveyed from the Hegelian perspective, Terror is a symptom of political immaturity. His dialectically inflected philosophy of nature stages the transition from plant life to animality with regard to the kind of heat that is appropriate to each life form and, more significantly, *the relation* to heat, whether outward in the vegetal case or inward in the animal. Tending toward the light and the warmth of the sun, the "plant is itself the movement of the fiery nature within itself:

it proceeds to ferment; but the heat which it gives out from itself is not its blood but its destruction. This animal process which is higher than that of the plant is its ruin."[152] A successful revolution would be comparable to an animal that lives off its self-generated heat, without being destroyed by it. Conversely, Terror, as the inability to come to terms with both ideality and materiality, to reconcile the two, is (strangely enough) vegetal; in it, the revolutionary movement "proceeds to ferment" and is destroyed by the excessive heat of an ideal unreconciled with the real. The conceptual connection between Terror and the principle of plant life further depends on the tethering of both to abstract universality encapsulated in freedom or in sunlight, as the case may be. In the dialectical system, neither Revolutionary Terror nor the plant can come back to itself, having reached its goal by mastering the ideality that overpowers it. Heat and light are purely external to them, and it is this externality that drives them to their ruin.

The continuation of the section on "The Animal Organism" in *Philosophy of Nature* intimates that animality is the first ideality *realised in actual existence*. Although the "animal as sensuous is heavy," Hegel admits, it manifests its subjectivity, its "utterance of sensation, of self-feeling" by voicing itself. Animal voice is more than a sound or a collection of sounds; it is "the spiritualized mechanism which thus utters itself."[153] The heat of animal life is, in turn, a sign of lived ideality. "With voice there is linked animal heat. The chemical process also yields heat which can rise to the intensity of fire, but it is transitory. The animal, on the other hand, as the lasting process of self-movement, of consuming and producing itself, perpetually negates and reproduces what is material and must therefore perpetually reproduce heat."[154]

Differently put, the animal is in a position to combine the heaviness and the dense materiality of its bodily reality with the subjective voicing of itself and self-generation of heat. This means that, on the one hand, the idea of a permanent revolution was an attempt to abide by the animal model in politics, moving past the limits of a singular and transitory revolutionary explosion, akin to the heat released in a chemical process in Hegel's example, toward a perpetual negation *and* reproduction of "what is material" in political life. On the other hand, Terror committed to a pure ideal, foregoing all bodily mediations. In fact, its adherents considered the body and the rest of the material sphere to be obstacles to a communion with untainted ideality—say, with Robespierre's Virtue. An obsession with the ideal in Terror forges an alliance with the inorganic realm at the expense of organic existence. And, since Hegel's plant grows on the conceptual verge between organic and inorganic natures, Terror mirrors the vegetal life-process more than that of the animal.

Whereas the animal dialectically, albeit still incompletely, overcomes the heaviness of materiality by introducing into it the capacity for an ideal self-expression (the voice) and self-animation (animal heat), Terror deliberately suppresses the body in order to get in touch with the world of spirit. It rages like fire that that "does not merely drain the body, leaving it tasteless and odourless, as indeterminate and savourless matter, but it destroys its particularity as matter."[155] As instances of indeterminate universal freedom, an immoderate, uncontrollable fire and Terror militate against life and propagate death—the "wholly *unmediated* pure negation" of individual beings.[156] An abstract ideal is the outcome of this pure negation.

What inflames revolutionary desire is really nothing, the Nothing that an ideal is, an empty abstraction of universal freedom, which is free from the constraints of *"particular individuality."*[157] Absolute freedom is primarily a freedom from being. Installed in the place that has been left vacant by the concrete personality of the monarch is the rule of nothing (praised as a precondition for democracy by Claude Lefort), which, in addition to destroying all otherness, is self-annihilating. Hence, the tragic and nihilistic end of revolutions. The revolutionary process unfolds in all its "abstraction and one-sidedness,"[158] unravelling towards a chaotic lack of differentiation, so long as revolutionary energy prompts a total analysis (death) of the *body politic* and of the actual revolutionaries.

Such is the sense of neutralisation, which Hegel postulates as the consummation of the burning, where "the element of determinateness, of difference, of individuality and particularity, which is present in everything concrete, is reduced to a unity, to an indeterminate, neutral state." The physical expression of neutrality is water, left over from "all chemical processes"; it pertains to the element whose "ideal identity" is sufficiently powerful to neutralise and extinguish the oppositional element of fire,[159] as much as to homogenise (dilute or remain after) the different substances. As we have seen, in the cultural sphere, neutralisation and depoliticisation are the fate of every political or revolutionary process that strives to universalise itself. Dialectically speaking, there is not and cannot be such a thing as a permanent revolution, any more than there can be such a thing as an inextinguishable fire. Explosive revolutionary energy is either dampened by contact with its very by-products, or else it fizzles out of its own accord, ending up in the indeterminacy of the ashes.

While it is still burning, fire is "materialised time or selfhood (light identical with heat), the absolutely restless and consuming Element; just as this Element destroys a body when attacking it from without, so too, conversely, does the self-consumption of body, e.g. in friction, burst into flame."[160] Hegel's fire is an intermediate phenomenon that materialises the pure ideality of time and, by the same token, dematerialises the things it consumes. World history, taking over time, and political regimes, standing in for the burnt objects, are versions of these extremes mediated by fire. Now, according to the Marxist theory of revolution, regime change happens when the growing internal contradictions of a political order become unsustainable within the parameters of that order. Class conflicts (say, between the workers and the owners of the means of production) are the political-economic equivalents of physical friction, leading to the "self-consumption of body" — liberal democracy or capitalism — that bursts into the flames of a revolution. The time of a revolution is temporality intensified, redoubled, and materialised in fire.

## 3.5. Revolutionary Alchemy

Rolf Helleburst's excellent study, *Flesh to Metal: Soviet Literature and the Alchemy of Revolution*, tests a promising hypothesis that the almost compulsive metallic and metallurgical imagery in the poetry and prose of Soviet Russia shored up an alchemical self-representation of the October Revolution.[161] One way to define alchemy is as "a branch of knowledge that deals with the possibility of changing one metal into another more 'noble' or more 'evolved', and of making an elixir that will cure intractable illnesses and prolong active life even to the point where an individual can become immortal."[162] Revolutionary theory and praxis tended to create a narrative of the transmutation of political regimes from the less to the more "noble" (more just, equal, and so forth) and celebrated the instauration of immortal ideals a new political order was said to embody. Evidently, the fire of revolution was the engine of this transmutation.

If, in traditional alchemy, the noblest metal is gold and the goal of alchemists is to transmute the less precious metals into it, the official Soviet discourse venerated steel and iron.[163] The primary materials of industrialisation, these resources were to serve as a standard for the construction of the postrevolutionary order and political subjectivity, which had to be "tempered" as though it were steel, in consonance with the title of the novel *Kak Zakalyalas' Stal'* (*How Steel Was Tempered*, 1936) by Nikolai Ostrovsky. What Helleburst called "flesh-to-metal narrative" required a melting down of the existing political order and psychic structure before distilling from them a nobler essence. The fire of the revolution superseded the alchemist's furnace, where matter was turned into ash in the process of calcination, purified, made volatile and vaporous by "sublimation" or "distillation," and, at last, fixed by "congelation," creating new solid materials.[164] The masses that, as Trotsky observed, were far from homogeneous had to be reduced to the alchemical *prima materia* or *massa confusa* that defied identification and was reminiscent of Hegel's abstract freedom, so that they could then be remoulded from an amorphous crowd of relatively few workers and numerous peasants into revolutionary proletariat. Fire's destructive and creative properties found a series of applications, be they political or not, in alchemy. "There is," Helleburst concludes, "no better metaphor for revolution than that of the blast furnace, where the destructive energy of fire effects a creative transformation of raw material into something different and radically improved."[165]

So close is the connection between alchemy and fire that, in *The Forge and the Crucible*, Mircea Eliade assigns to alchemical activity the very qualities Hegel reserved for the flame.

The alchemist, in Eliade's view, "contributes to Nature's work by precipitating the rhythm of Time."[166] Following alchemical beliefs, the perfection of metals, or their transmutation into gold, happens very gradually in the bowls of the earth, where they mature, gestating inside the ores.[167] Alchemy does not introduce anything new into the world, but only quickens the natural gestation and self-perfection of the already existing metals. The fire of the revolution, in which the revolutionaries and the entire population are tempered and to which they are sacrificed, fulfils the same function with regard to the perfectibility of human society. Revolutions may be conservative or progressive, depending on whether the ideal of perfection is believed to belong to the past or to the future. But, regardless of their temporal orientation, they effect a transmutation of the *body politic* in the furnace of drastically accelerated historical time.

French and Russian revolutionaries intended for their activities to lay the foundations for a better future, even though the prior political sense of "revolution" entailed a past-oriented restoration of "usurped rights and freedoms," as in John Locke's treatment of the Glorious Revolution in seventeenth-century England.[168] The glory of the Glorious Revolution did not fail to evoke the brilliance, splendour, and brightness of fire associated, first, with the *gloire* of God and, second, with the Dutch invader of England, William III, who was described as "glorious" in the revolutionary years of 1688 and 1689.[169] The fire/glory of the conservative revolution reawakens the perfection of the past; the furnace of a progressive revolution hastens the advent of the yet non-existent but already gestating ideal.

Significantly, Eliade draws his readers' attention to the fact that the desired transmutation was not limited to the external world of hard matter melted down, vaporised, and crystallised again under the influence of fire, but had to do with the psychic life of the alchemist her- or himself. "In short, the Western alchemist, in his laboratory, like his Indian or Chinese colleague, worked on himself—upon his psycho-physiological life as well as on his moral and spiritual experience."[170] The ascetic, totally politicised, often exilic, and invariably dangerous existence of revolutionaries was, in and of itself, an experiment in the creation of a better subjectivity that would be ideally generalised, passing over to the masses like wildfire. In the words of nineteenth-century philosopher and socialist Moses Hess, it was necessary to "touch the igniting flame [...] to the structures of the old society,"[171] referring not only to the economic and political but also, and above all, the psychological structures. Just as the postrevolutionary calendars in France and in Russia marked the objective change of an era, so the new names adapted by the revolutionaries—Lenin, Stalin, not to mention Molotov, Kamenev, Trotsky, and many others—testified to a subjective epiphany, announcing the advent of the New Man.

Alchemical self-cultivation is analogous to the ennobling of metals: both gold in its embryonic state and a more perfect subjectivity *in nuce* lay dormant in the bowls of the earth or of the psyche. Fire and a correct (generally secretive) procedure were needed to actualize the potentiality that was slowly developing of its own accord. The fire of the revolution was also meant to promote the formation of a political subject that was ripening amid the contradictions of the previous regime. In France, that subject was the citizen, a bearer of equal rights and duties before the law. In Soviet Russia, China, and Cuba, it was the "New Man,"[172] born, in an imitation of the phoenix, from the ashes of the capitalist system. This utopian figure had to be psychologically distinct from the previous specimens of humanity, and it was also to engender, in keeping with Trotsky's unabashedly Nietzschean vision, "a higher social and biologic type, or, if you please, a superman," one who is "immeasurably stronger, wiser, and subtler."[173] Forged in the furnace of the revolution, the New Man is the political variation on the alchemical dream of imitating nature and artificially creating "various forms of life, especially an homunculus."[174] The New Man was an amalgam of the phoenix and the revolution's homunculus, a subjective supplement to the objectivity of new political institutions and regimes.

### 3.6. Catching Fire, or How Revolutions Spread

The great French revolutionary Jean-Paul Marat realised that public indifference was an obstacle on the revolutionary road to freedom. "The greatest misfortune," he wrote, "which can attend a free country, where the Prince is powerful and enterprising, is that no party, no commotion, no faction agitate the minds of the subjects. All is undone, when the people are unconcerned for public affairs; on the contrary, liberty constantly springs up out of the fires of sedition."[175] This assertion is especially pertinent today, when, despite the rhetoric of inclusiveness and political participation, parliamentary systems everywhere count on a pervasive public indifference that silently approves their actions. Freedom only issues forth from "the fires of sedition," provided that the sparks of concern over public affairs light the revolutionary flame of care for the whole, that is, for the common good. (I should remark, in passing, that besides his political activity Marat was a scientist, who authored several treatises on the physical nature of fire. More specifically, he was an adherent of the phlogiston theory of fire, which, for him, referred to *"le principe inflammable des corps,"* "the inflammable principle of bodies," responsible for their burning.[176] Surely, his theoretical reflections on thermodynamics and the phenomenon of combustion fed into his revolutionary activity, framed in terms of "the fires of sedition.")

From the outset of this chapter, we have begun responding to the question of how political fires spread. It turned out that revolutionary sparks did not respect any differences between regimes, epochs, and geographical locations. The fire of revolt proves to be highly contagious: as Edmond Jabès writes in *The Book of Resemblances II*, "even the smallest little flame has the ulterior motives of fire."[177] Why is it that the entire *body politic* can, in a matter of a few years or even months, become *diapyros*, pervaded by fire? What accounts for its lightning-fast spread?

Let us concentrate on the Hegelian notion of fire as an "element of opposition." Fire feeds and lives off friction in an elemental conflict with what it consumes and in opposition to itself. Oppositionality is so engrained in its logic, that any attempt to oppose the spread of fire, to quell it, will only promote its further flaring up. This is the secret of revolutionary fire, which Kautsky, for one, has uncovered. Imagining the scenario, whereby republican Belgium comes to be ruled by the proletariat, he surmises that the "governments of Germany and France would rush to extinguish this fire, from which such threatening sparks would fly in the form of agrarian and industrial agitators to the flammable thatched roofs of the neighbouring lands. But precisely the attempt to put out the revolutionary fire could lead to its generalised flare-up."[178] In lieu of trying to contain fire by opposing it, perhaps one would need to fight fire with fire. Rather than the hardening of the status quo, a counterrevolution is in a position to stop the train of a revolution in its tracks.

Under the pretext of discussing patriotism, Johann Gottfried Herder's "General Philosophical Program" briefly exposes the modus operandi of political fire. There where the public is engaged in the affairs of the state, "one educates [*bildet*] citizens as a patriot. — That fire spreads, reproduces itself." Patriotism educates citizens to be concerned with the common good; once a critical mass of patriots has been produced, "society is not too cold." It is then that political action blazes forth: "Deeds ignite deeds."[179] Instead of being extinguished in their outcomes, deeds kindle the motivation for further actions. Unwittingly, Herder comes across the principle of revolutionary politics and desire that struggle to do all the more in the degree to which their objectives are accomplished.[180] Idealism married to maximalism, the spread of fire is potentially infinite across all the finitudes it inflames.

Fascinated with the spread of fire, the ancients believed it to be a living being: it moved, nourished, and was able to reproduce itself, similar to an animal. A smattering of this belief persists in the sermons of Master Eckhart, who groups fire together with other living creatures, proclaiming "*le feu produit du feu; pourrait-il réduire en feu tout ce qui est proche de lui, il le ferait* [fire produces fire; if it could consign to fire everything in its proximity, it would do so]."[181] Fire spreads by devouring and reproducing itself in whatever is near. The fire of the revolution replicates itself in the souls and spirits (desires, motivations, and aspirations) of human beings, whom it engulfs. The cardinal factor in this replication is the *spiritual nearness* of those who join in its blaze, supplanting the fire of God that spread in a community of faith. Still, the life of fire is contingent upon the death and destruction of the materials it burns — if not actual bodies, then the sinful or apolitical existence prior to the experience of conversion or dedication to the Cause.

The intrinsic paradoxes of revolutionary fire are further made apparent in the title of the second instalment of

Suzanne Collins's hugely popular *Hunger Games: Catching Fire*. To catch fire is literally to grasp it, yet the idiomatic expression means "to ignite," "to be set on fire," or "to be enthusiastic." If you catch fire, you are immediately caught *by* it, engulfed in the flames of love, desire, religious devotion, or the revolution. Both Collins's novel and its 2013 screen adaptation by Francis Lawrence oversimplify this scheme, insofar as they privilege the active dimension of revolutionary praxis and the expense of the subjects' passivity in the face of fire that subjectivates them in the first place.

In the course of the seventy-fifth "hunger games," participants notice a certain regularity in the pattern of hazards they face on the arena covered by the artificial dome, which emulates the sky: a tree is struck by lightning every twelve hours, in anticipation of yet another trial. That is the weakest link, or the most combustible spot, of the regime. Realising that the refrain "Remember who the real enemy is" invokes not the other contestants but the oppressive system that dictates the rules of the deadly game and of miserable existence, Katniss Everdeen decides to attack the political order in its Achilles' heel. During one of the lightning strikes, as she shoots an arrow with an attached electrical wire into the invisible dome roof, she provokes a series of short circuits in the stage for the games, the total surveillance machinery of the state, and the political regime as a whole. In combination, the natural fire of the lightning and the artificial fire conducted through electrical wires destroy the semblance of Capitol's invincibility and spark widespread riots throughout all the districts of Panem.

Besides conveying the naïve idea that contemporary systems of domination operate with strict regularity and have a single, weak, flammable spot that can cause the rest to come crumbling down,[182] *Catching Fire* misconstrues the thermodynamics of the revolutionary blaze. Understandably, the government of Panem is obsessed with control, which tends to boil down to the control over fire, including the light it emits opening the field of total visibility. But Katniss, who tries hard to bring the regime down, ultimately subscribes to a comparable fallacy. Whether in her spectacular flaming costume, in which she shows up before the games, or in her harnessing of the system's firepower, she is somehow able to dominate this dangerous and unstable element at will. A discerning reader or viewer begins to suspect that the revolution she spearheads is as superficial as the perfectly regulated fire built into her dramatic attire. Catching fire is both grasping and being scorched by it, without the luxury of a safety valve or a fire escape route. Collins's narrative is aloof to this risk; it is a utopia of liberation palatable to contemporary risk-avoiding, security-driven, essentially apolitical societies.

Panem is neither France nor Russia nor China, where the fire of revolutions scorched everything and everyone in its path, without sparing the revolutionaries themselves. Regrettably, in the heat of the revolutionary moment, political fire lost its capacity for discernment and was no longer the *pyr phronimon* of modernity but an indifferent flame of pure ideality. Its theological undertones put it squarely on the side of the politics of sacrifice, demanding that *body politic* be purged of every impurity if it is to be reborn from the ashes of the previous regime. This bond between fire and sacrifice, the seizure of fire and handing oneself over to it,[183] is not, however, limited to revolutionary politics. From self-immolations by protestors and victims of traditional cultural practices, through the concept of the "holocaust," to the great blaze of "global energy production," the mantra is the same: "Into the fire!"

# Chapter 4.
*Pyropolitical Theology II: The Politics of Sacrifice*

## 4.1. A Theology of Burnt Offerings

The Indian Vedas recognised in the god of fire, Agni, a personification of sacrificial practice. According to the *Rig Veda*, Agni is the male "child of waters," *apām napāt*, themselves figured as the feminine element: "The young women, the waters, flow around the young god, making him shine and gazing solemnly upon him. With his clear, strong flames he shines riches upon us, wearing his garment of butter, blazing without fuel in the waters."[184] In the Vedic drama, Agni betrays his mothers, the waters, by putting himself in the service of the supreme god, Indra, who draws him out of diffuse feminine bliss with the proposition, "Let us speak great words as men of power in the sacrificial gathering."[185] Agni then lends himself to sacrificial rites and becomes an "oblation bearer" in return for immortality.[186] Vicariously, everything and everyone he consumes in his flames partakes of the payment he receives from Indra, who makes him immortal; in communion with Agni, the material body is transformed into a spiritual one, which is no longer prone to the destruction. In Vedic sublime economy, material devastation in fire is a trade-off for spiritual preservation.

The spiritualisation of whatever fuels sacrificial fires inverts the physical order of things. A dead body consumed by Agni on the funeral pyre is born into another life with the ancestors; the flesh, broken down by fire, is made whole again ("may Agni who eats all things make it [a dead body] whole"[187]). Indeed, destructive, "flesh-eating" fire must go hand-in-hand with another flame, "the knower of creatures," or *Jātavedas*, which will cleanse the impurities, "quench and revive the very one you [Agni] have burnt up," and permit new life to spring forth, letting "plants grow in this place,"[188] thanks to the fertilising power of the ashes. Sacrifice is, therefore, conducive to an exchange of one state of being for another: of death for life, and of material burdens for spiritual goods. Here, fire plays the part of a universal equivalent — money or gold — as Heraclitus's Fragment 90 suggests: "All things are an equal exchange for fire and fire for all things, as goods are for gold and gold for goods."[189]

In Biblical text, the Hebrew word for "burnt offering," *'olah*, is indicative of spiritual ascent, as it literally means "what goes up" (in smoke). Incidentally, this word shares the root with *'aliah*, or ascension, which in contemporary Israeli political discourse refers to the immigration of Jews to the State of Israel. Political decisions are loaded with a spiritual "luggage," so that the citizens who emigrate out of the country are called *yordim*, "those who go down." Similar to *'aliah*, the smoke of the *'olah* elevates the corporeality of the burnt offering, raising it skywards. Cain was so jealous of how high the smoke from Abel's sacrifices was rising that he killed his brother. Later, a father was to make a fiery sacrifice of his son: the order God gives to Abraham in Genesis 22:2-3 is to "offer Isaac as burnt offering [*'olah*]" on Mount Moriah.

The authoritative Greek translation of the Hebrew scripture, or Septuagint, renders the word *'olah* as *holocaust*, from the Greek *holon* ("the whole") and *kaustos* ("burnt"). The reasoning behind this translation is that the sacrificed animal "was completely incinerated," as opposed to "the sacrifice of salvation or peace (*zevakh shelamim*), in which part of the animal was burned, the blood poured out on the altar or the earth, and the remainder consumed in a communal meal."[190] That is the theological prehistory of the two "Holocausts," one of them actual and the other hypothetical: the genocide of Jewish people in World War II and world annihilation through the use of nuclear weaponry in a future global war.

The rising smoke of a burnt offering elevated the entire victim of sacrifice to God. Yet, as Giorgio Agamben points out, Church Fathers resorted to the nomenclature of the holocaust "as a polemical weapon against the Jews," even as they continued to use it metaphorically as a sign of total surrender of oneself to God.[191] We must agree with Agamben that a citation from Tertullian is particularly telling in this respect: "What is more foolish, what more weak, than the demand by God of bloody sacrifices and the stench of whole burnt offerings [*holocaustomatum nidorosorum*]?" (*Adversus Marcionem* 5.6). But, instead of simply denouncing the barbaric practices of non-Christians, Church Fathers eliminated material fire from the ritual of sacrifice, while leaving its structure intact. Christ's death, whereby a part of God is sacrificed to God for the sake of humanity, instituted a purely spiritual transaction in place of the outmoded exchange of raw flesh for spirit.

The martyrdom account of the early Christian Polycarp highlights the impotence of fire in relation to the already spiritualised flesh of the martyr. After "a great sheet of flame blazed out" around Polycarp, who was about to be burnt at the stake, a miracle happened: "The fire took on the shape of a hollow chamber, like a ship's sail when the wind fills it, and formed a wall round the martyr's figure; and there was he in the centre of it, not like a human being in flames but like a loaf baking in the oven, or like a gold or silver ingot being refined in the furnace."[192] We will return to this scene of the martyr's "baking" in chapter 6, as we explore the transformative power of fire in cooking. Why does fire lose its sting and become subservient to the perfection of the martyr, who is refined in it? –Because Polycarp is already spirit incarnate, which is why it would be absurd to exchange his mortal body for a higher life with the mediation of fire. Instead, the flames continue the work of spirit that is long past the point where the destruction of impure material existence would be necessary. The prophesy of Daniel (3:17) comes to fruition here: "If we are thrown into a blazing furnace, the God we serve is able to deliver us from it, and he will deliver us from Your Majesty's hand."

The elevating capacity of fire was familiar to ancient Greeks, as well. In *Timaeus*, Plato writes that the elements "shift up and down toward their proper regions," depending on the respective size of their particles (58c). Fire is composed of the smallest and most mobile particles that make it highly volatile and drive it up (58d-e). Continuing this line of thought in *Eudemian Ethics*, Aristotle deduces that "by force [*bia*] and under necessity," "the stone travels upwards and fire downwards" (1.1224a). *Contra natura*, the stone moves away from its proper region of the earth, while fire migrates away from its own realm, situated in the ether above air. Given this elemental logic, Jesus's statement in Luke 12:49, "I come to cast fire on the earth," testifies to a spiritual force that overcomes the natural tendency of fire to migrate upwards. The most sublime of elements, fire is brought down to the lowliest: divine spirit is incarnated and burns in human flesh. But the earth itself is also elevated, or spiritualised, when fire is cast upon it, as though Christ's sacrifice were a burnt offering, causing the entire earthly domain (it, too, imaginatively transformed into a single organism, an animal) to go up in smoke, reaching all the way up to heavens.

Aristotle discusses the "natural motion" of elemental fire in depth in his *De Caelo*, or *On the Heavens*. There, it is said that fire and air move upwards in a straight line, leading "away from the centre," which is occupied by the earth (1.ii).

This physical tendency of the shooting flames, defying the force of gravity that pulls heavy material bodies down, came to be associated with spiritual elevation through fire. Christianity, in its turn, has deemed physical elevation insufficient, due to its insistence, since the time of St. Augustine, on the metaphorical or allegorical meaning of rituals. (Such metaphorisation was, evidently, a corollary to the inwardness of faith and the preponderance of the soul's interiority over the external inscription of the Law on the body, as the "circumcision of the heart" supplanted that of the flesh). Hence, Tertullian's contention that the most sublime material element is lowly in comparison to the world of spirit and is debased by contact with matter exuding the stench of charred bodies.

It is time to take stock of the economic and political dimensions of theological burnt offerings. The idea that fire is the universal medium of sublime commerce, wherein bodily materiality is swapped for the ideality of spirit, underlies the economy of burnt offerings. In the Vedas, the initial exchange of Agni's services for immortality imbues everything this "child of waters" engulfs with life everlasting, which he receives as compensation from Indra. The exchange is never equal; at times reeking of treason, it is implicated in an intricate game of power. Already in Hinduism, the kindling of sacrificial fire marks a transition from the matriarchal fluidity of Agni's progenitors to the rigid relations of power in the masculine. The elevating capacity of the flame in the Greek and Judeo-Christian traditions and its subsequent interpretation as the highest physical force verging on the world of spirit endow fire with what we might term *elemental sovereignty*. On the whole, power relations assume the form of transactions between a burning agent and the burnt subject, between the one making the offering and the one offered to God in the name of an ideal. In adherence to an edict issued by the Sun King, Louis XIV, the royal insignia of sovereignty (the lily, or *fleur-de-lis*) in seventeenth-century France were emblazoned on the bodies of runaway slaves in the overseas colonies and of other criminals at home.[193] Livestock branding with hot iron is of a piece with these material practices of pyropolitical power. A tame version of burnt offering, the branding of the flesh is a vestige of elemental sovereignty, facilitated by fire.

## 4.2. Self-Immolation and Sovereignty

If the lines of sovereignty are drawn between the burning authority and the burnt subject, then the acts of self-immolation assimilate both sides of the power equation, usually by breaking out of the position of absolute abjection and subordination. However horrific, the acts of self-sacrifice follow the economic and political protocols of burnt offerings; not only do self-immolators take elemental sovereignty into their own hands but they also undertake to exchange their finite corporeality for an eternal (or, at least, a higher) life. Often, though not always, undertaken as the final and desperate measure of opposition to the injustice and imperfection of the world here-below, the practices of self-immolation forge evanescent communities of fire in response to the real or perceived impossibility of continued existence. Permutations of elemental sovereignty are evident in the rituals of *satī* (widow immolation) in India; in collective suicides by fire (*gar'*) among *staroobryadtsy* (the followers of "old customs") in Russia; in attacks by suicide bombers; and in acts of self-immolation at political protests.

For Gayatri Spivak, the performance of *satī* condenses in itself numerous contradictions inherent in cultural, colonial, and conceptual systems. "This suicide that is not suicide," *satī* is the tragedy of attaching the absent subjectivity of the widow to the body of her dead husband and the delivery of both to a bed of fire.[194] While the British proscription of the ritual in 1829 is to be saluted, the colonial intervention was driven by the misplaced pride of cultural prejudice on the part of "white men saving brown women from brown men."[195] Conceptually, it fleshed out the paradoxes of free will, the choice of a widow to become a *satī* that put an end to all further acts of willing and that was framed within the semantic and political structures of patriarchal domination.[196]

After we have taken these fine points to heart, several questions continue to provoke disquietude: what are the outlines of a community constituted in fire that indifferently consumes a dead male and a living female bodies? How does this final act imagine perfection and elevation in the flames? What kind of sovereignty does it invest a self-immolator with?

The literal piling of bodies — male and female, living and dead — on the funeral pyre holds the clue to a community forged in fire. According to the religious doctrine subtending the ritual, fire is the "supreme form of purification and consequently of healing."[197] Agni reunites the dead man with his ancestors and, at the same time, revives his lost life in the form of plants or another incarnation it may assume. The living female body, on the other hand, is purified of its very femaleness, or nihilistically "healed," much like Socrates who said, after drinking hemlock, that he owed a sacrificial rooster to Asclepius, the god of healing. The promise of self-immolation (if that what it is) is that the ritual would release the widow from her incarnation[198] and thus allow her to join a community of higher beings in a future life. The *satī* is a vanishing mediator between the past of her union with the now defunct husband (as a token of that union, the fire used for the funeral pyre is taken from the couple's domestic hearth, where it was lit on the day of their wedding[199]) and the future of her belonging to a "better" community. Fidelity to a dead man coincides with the betrayal of living womanhood, reminiscent of Agni's own abandonment of his mothers, the waters, in favour of the masculine power wielded by Indra.[200] As a foretoken of nihilism, the already dead carries the still living through a euphemistic "fire-bath" (*agnisnān*)[201] toward a higher form of life.

Etymologically as well as conceptually, sacrificial fire is inextricable from the essence of the *satī*, her goodness (*sat*). Far from being the physical cause of her death, it is the same substance that during her life has manifested itself as virtue, reminiscent of Origen's "discerning fire"[202]: she burns with goodness. The self-immolator presumably returns to herself in joining her dead husband on the pyre: she becomes herself in losing herself, as being and nothingness merge into one. This ontological confusion is typical of the workings of ideology, which binds the subject to itself and compels us to identify with the very thing that harms us, to the point of recognising ourselves in and loving it. (A similar process of identification takes place, when some Muslim women embrace the *burqa* as an "enabling" cultural artefact.) Upon taking charge of her life, in keeping with the dictates of ritual law, the *satī* is not permitted to continue living; her first and last "free" act of burning herself with the dead other severely limits her singular sovereignty.

For all the variations among the narrative accounts of the custom, they tend to emphasise the voluntary and determined character of the woman's actions, as in a newspaper report in the *Samachar Chundrika*, according to which, in 1825, at the age of twenty-two, a "chaste and virtuous widow" of a man who had died of cholera, "being resolved to burn herself with the dead body of her husband, immediately sent to the

Government notices of her immolation, but permission not being easily brought her, she was obliged to wait for two days, and on the morning of the third day, after obtaining the sanction, she ordered a pile to be prepared, and resolutely mounting it, she ordered it to be set on fire, and thus burnt herself to the great surprise of the spectators."[203] The delay that failed to persuade the widow to change her mind, her "resolute" conduct, and the two orders she issued from her newly gained position of morally superior authority testify to the fleeting sovereignty and power she wielded right before her death. To this list we ought to add the "trials by fire", to which the *satīs* can be subjected in order to verify whether they are fit for their self-sacrifice. Having a part of her body, such as a finger, a hand, or an arm, burnt as a symbolic replacement for the whole, a widow would prove her fitness to be a *satī* (*satītva*) by not displaying any outward signs of pain.[204] Her sovereignty and perfection were intertwined in these "acts of truth," where spirit and fire (virtuous spirit *as* fire) triumphed over the sensuous materiality of the body.

A distinct set of self-incendiary communities existed in tsarist Russia between the seventeenth and the nineteenth centuries. Hellbent on following "old customs," *staroobryadtsy* did not accept the liturgical, lexical, and cultural reforms Russian Orthodox patriarch Nikon had initiated with the view to harmonising existing church doctrine with that of Greek Orthodoxy. Facing persecution and imprisonment, the leaders of this movement disseminated millenarian sentiments, predicting an imminent end of the world in 1666 and warning their followers that only a "christening by fire" (*ognennoye krescheniye*) or "the burning" (*gar'*) could save them from eternal damnation.[205] (After the world failed to end that year, its continued existence was explained through divine grace that allotted additional thirty three years—

equivalent to the age of Christ at the time of his crucifixion — for sinners to repent.)

A collective act, through which believers had hoped to achieve the promise of salvation, was one of self-immolation *en masse*. Crowds of destitute, illiterate peasants heeded charismatic preachers of the likes of the monk Dani'il, who in 1677 convinced nearly two thousand followers to attain martyrdom by undergoing a christening by fire.[206] Contrary to the communion of the living and the dead in the Indian practice of *satī*, the most radical among *staroobryadtsy* formed suicidal communities of the living who threw themselves into fire. Their basic belief was nevertheless nearly identical: fire cleansed the sins and brought out the goodness of those who entered it and, elevating their spirits, ensured that they would secure a place in the Kingdom of Heaven or in a better incarnation on earth.

The Russian *gar'* was the outcome of frantic behaviour by subaltern groups that had no other cultural tools at their disposal to express themselves due to their abject poverty and illiteracy,[207] a situation worsened by a theological and political interdiction of their cherished religious practices. Claiming elemental sovereignty for themselves, *staroobryadtsy* resorted to collective self-immolations in order to achieve the only self-affirmation available to them. A traveling preacher, heading one of the *gar'*s in the middle of the eighteenth century, proclaimed that "by birth, he was of the sky and shall return to the sky" in the form of smoke, together with his followers.[208] The ascension of spirit by dint of a fiery death contrasted sharply with the lowly social and economic standing of these millenarian communities and the blocked channels of their religious participation. At the same time, it was this negative theological-political space devoid of hierarchies and institutionalised power that gave rise to the specific form of sovereignty that flourished among *staroobryadtsy*.

For several reasons, I am tempted to characterise the sovereignty of collective self-immolators in Russia as anarchic. First, having rejected official state and church authorities, many of the *staroobryadtsy* lived without the guidance of priests, in a condition of *bespopov'ye*, priestlessness.²⁰⁹ Traveling preachers did not establish a new institution but were, at times, as illiterate as their followers and relied, almost exclusively, on personal charisma. Second, Russian millenarian communities subscribed to the idea of gender equality, seeing that "gender—just like other social categories dividing humanity—was something temporary."²¹⁰ Their revolt against patriarchy was key to their anarchism. Third, and relatedly, from the standpoint of religious and state authorities, *staroobryadtsy* were seen as a heretical movement that escaped centralised control and proliferated outside the law.²¹¹ The destruction of gender, political, and theological hierarchies potentially anticipated the blotting out of material distinctions among the self-immolators who committed themselves to fire. *Gar'* was an extreme exercise in anarchic sovereignty, practiced outside the official apparatus of power and rendering all too palpable the principle of equality that governed breakaway communities.

Lest we get carried away, it is imperative to avoid romanticising the elemental sovereignty of self-immolators. Russian philosopher Nikolay Berdyaev falls prey to just this glamorisation of *gar'*, a phenomenon "almost unknown among other peoples," which he attributes to the peculiarities of the Russian national character with its penchant for revelling in suffering and self-sacrifice.²¹² Along the same lines, in Dostoyevsky's *Crime and Punishment*, the painter Mikolka confesses to a murder he did not commit and, in the footsteps of Christ, takes upon himself the guilt of the other.[213] In his turn, Berdyaev relies on the work of nineteenth-century Russian theologian Aleksandr Bukharev, so as to link the self-sacrificial and self-immolationary attitude of *staroobryadsy* to the supreme sacrifice of Jesus: "God created the world and surrendered Himself to immolation" as Christ-the-Lamb.[214] Nietzsche's response to such glorification of self-immolation is easy to reconstruct: ultimately, nihilistic and unsustainable, a community in fire says 'no' to the world here-below and values an otherworldly ideal above physical existence. Elemental sovereignty undermines and destroys itself to the extent that its proponents reject life and the body, which they wish to spiritualise as a whole.

"Scorched earth policy" — the military strategy used by the Russian forces against the advancing French army in the Napoleonic wars and, in World War II, adopted by Joseph Stalin — capitalised on a comparable willingness of the populace to sacrifice for the common cause. As the native soil together with everything built and growing on it went up in flames, the earth itself was made into a burnt offering to the continued existence of the nation; in other words, it was implicitly sacralised and spiritualised in the shape of the smoke. At the same time, "scorched earth" diverges from *gar'* with regard to ideality, community, and sovereignty: it has more in common with suicide bombings that convert the bomber's own loss of life, or of what makes life possible, into an instrument for ending the lives of the enemy than with ritual self-immolations.

If the *satī* joined an already dead other on the funeral pyre, and if *staroobryadtsy* forged a community of living friends ready to accept martyrdom in a massive *gar'*, then suicide bombers immolate themselves together with their enemies. In *The Business of Martyrdom*, Jeffrey William Lewis submits that suicide bombing, too, was a Russian invention, used by Ignaty Grinevitsky to assassinate Tsar Alexander II in March 1881.[215] Grinevitsky's suicide note was unambiguous: "Alexander II must die [...]. He will die and, with him, we, his enemies, his executioners, shall die too [...]. How many more sacrifices will our unhappy country ask of its sons before it is liberated?"[216] By sacrificing himself to the political cause of the *Narodnaya Volya* ("The People's Will") left-wing group of which he was a member, the regicide took a sovereign decision on matters of life-and-death at the expense of his own life. The fire of the blast created a community of death among enemies, razing the distinctions between the executioner and the executed. Even if suicide bombings did not originate at that moment in history (St. Petersburg at the end of the nineteenth century), their rationale was consciously delineated at that time.

Grinevitsky thought of his impending death as a sacrifice ("How many more sacrifices...?") despite belonging to a secular political organisation. Conceivably, the sacrificial side of political actions would be still more prominent in the case of contemporary Islamic "human bombers." As Ivan Strenski indicates, the Islamic sacrificial paradigm "normally" defines sacrifice as a "*giving of*" something alienable, such as one's property, rather than the "extreme *giving up*" of one's life.[217] But, in a state of emergency, when the existence of the *ummah* (or the Islamic nation) is under threat, the usual sacrificial regime no longer applies and certain "extremist scholars" justify the importance of self-sacrifice.[218]

At the intersection of these two types of sacrifice, we encounter contrasting readings of the *akedah* (or the binding) of Isaac, according to which Abraham is either a prudent worshipper of God, who tries to avert the disaster and to substitute a sacrificial animal for his son, or an absolute devotee, prepared for a total sacrifice, the ultimate holocaust.[219] The second interpretation is used to justify suicide bombings that, as sacrifices of oneself and the enemy other, are always and necessarily relations of substitution. They operate a complex exchange of the personal for the political; of individual life for the existence of a nation; of earthly suffering for heavenly rewards; and of crimes, in which bystanders are thought to be complicit, for their lives. The bomber's body torn apart together with those in close physical proximity to it (the Hebrew *korban* and the Arabic *qurbani*, meaning sacrifice, are both derived from the Semitic root *qrb* which signifies "closeness" or "proximity") is a medium of such an exchange, mimicking the work of fire itself.

Having said that, an external observer, let alone a theorist, cannot be expected to come up with an equation that would explain the motivations behind these actions. The exchange will remain indeterminate: "because the actor dies in the event, his motives are not fully retrievable."[220] The sovereignty of suicide bombers is not exhausted in their singular decision on life-and-death matters but, instead, extends to the excess of their motivations over cultural, psychological, socio-economic, and religious elucidations, regardless of all the suicide notes or remarkably uniform pre-recorded messages they might have left behind. It is this impenetrability of subjective motivations that is all too frequently mistaken for the heat without light of radical evil.

Reacting to Strenski's explanatory model, Talal Asad makes an important corrective to his analysis of *shahid*'s or *shuhadā*'s ("witnesses" to faith) deadly actions on the basis of sacrificial or self-sacrificial rites. To "take suicide bombing as sacrifice," he writes, "is to load it with a significance that is derived from a Christian and post-Christian tradition.

Although, in my view, this makes it inappropriate as an *explanation*, [...] as an *idea* it is an important part of the political imaginary of modern nationalism."[221] The conceptual knot tied in these lines is that of a political theology, in which a secularised non-Islamic (Christian) version of sacrifice in the name of a nation is deployed within the framework of Islamic fundamentalist politics. Could a fixation on sacrifice be too narrow, to the extent that it ignores the explosive pyropolitical nature of suicide bombings?

In the debate on the relevance of the idea of a burnt offering to a better understanding of Islamic human bombings, there has been much ado about the "offering" and virtually none about the "burning." Surely, the spectacular nature of such an attack has something to do both with the notion of *shahid* as a "witness" and with fire that is the preferred means of destruction here. The end of a *shahid*'s physical vision, the *terminus* of a living witnessing of the world, coincides with the beginning of the non-sensuous witnessing to faith. The spiritualising quality of fire gives the impetus to a transition from the visible to the invisible, from mundanely overlooked suffering to a newsworthy (often sensationalist) emergency, and from earthly affairs to the ideologies of heaven. After all, as per the *Qur'an*, spirits or *jinn*s are made of "a flame of fire" (55:15), whereas humans are "created from sounding clay" (15:26).

On the hither side of the "flesh-to-metal" narrative of revolutionary subjectivity, which we explored in chapter 3, suicide bombers aspire to transfigure their bodies into fire. In a statement, made in 2008, Hamas operative Umm Suheib warned: "I swear by Allah that I will turn my body parts into fire that will burn the occupation soldiers, if they move towards my house."[222] As a response to the impossibility of continued existence under Israeli military occupation, human bombers delivered their bodies *to* fire and endeavoured to turn the body *on* fire (from which destruction would spread, as though by contagion) into an instrument of justice. This is consistent with the theological view on the restitution of evil actions in Islam, and especially with the *sura* on women (*an-nisaa*) in the *Qur'an* that states: "Those who unjustly eat up the property of orphans, eat up a fire into their own bodies: they will soon be enduring a blazing fire!" (4:10). The figuration of injustice is a flaming excess that, from within, promises to consume the unjust subject. By implication, suicide bombers represent the return of fire, punishing the offenders and restoring the balance that has been disturbed by injustice. While the *satī* who committed herself to fire was reunited with her own element of goodness (*sat*), so suicide bombing is framed as the dispensation back to the unjust of the same fire they, themselves, have devoured.

In individual self-immolations at political protests, bodies on fire also strive to become the conduits of justice. Consider the report of the self-immolation of Changhui, a Buddhist monk at Tianning si, in 1914. Reacting to the fin-de-siècle sentiment that "the Way and the Virtue were declining every day," particularly after the fall of the Qing dynasty and the founding of the Republic only three years prior to his action, Changhui made a resolution "to cause the *Buddhadharma* to flourish, to turn people's minds around, to turn conflict into compassion and fortune, to defeat desire and anger before they appeared."[223] To this end, "he stacked up firewood like a small seat" next to the cloister wall, "sat erect and cross-legged on top, [...] lit the fire and transformed himself."[224]

There is no accurate rendition of the word *dharma* in English, which can mean, at the same time, virtue and justice as well as cosmic law and order, what keeps (from the Sanskrit root *dhr*, "to hold") the world upright and together. The closest equivalent to it in ancient Greek thought is, probably, *kosmos* itself—the brilliant and shining world order making beings what they are. Changhui wanted to assist with the balancing of *dharma* in the way that the practitioners of the Tong-len ("Sending-and-Taking") meditation practice do: carefully regulating their respiration, they breathe in the suffering of the world and breathe out justice and peace.[225] In the same vein, the Buddhist monk affirmed that he would "turn conflict into compassion and fortune," albeit with the help of another element. Whereas a Tong-len practitioner shifted between the prevailing injustice and the desired peace through air, Changhui did so through fire, which reflected the light and the heat emanating from *dharma*. Through the flaming "transformation" of the monk, the world transforms itself.

Granted: the conduct of a self-immolator is strictly individual, but it welds together, if only for a series of brief moments, a community with the spectators and with the ideal of justice. (As Bachelard poetically declares, "Death in a flame is the least lonely of deaths. It is truly a cosmic death in which the whole universe is reduced to nothingness [...]."[226]) The self-immolator's action strove "to turn people's minds around" with the help of a sublime spectacle that could not leave the observers detached, cold and unaffected. The fiery "transformation" of the body was received as an omen of its spiritualisation and its participation in the firmness of *dharma*. "His enlightened mind was so strong," the report of Changhui's self-immolation continued, "that he was determined to show that death was like returning home. Fire shot forth from his whole body, every joint was burning but he was completely without pain, not moving an inch. If he were not completely endowed with true liberation and had attained great sovereignty, how could he remain upright and steady, not moving from his position and departing in such a manner as this?"[227] The witness ascribes the uprightness and steadfastness of the body on fire to the strength and sovereignty of the enlightened mind, which has freed itself from its enchainment to the flesh. The advanced state of the monk's mind brings it closer to *dharma* not because the mind controls and dominates corporeity but because its hold first makes the body and the material world what they are. Bodily immobility serves as a tangible substitute for the fortitude of an enlightened mind, which, in its turn, is a metonym of *dharma*.

It goes without saying that the Buddhist practice of self-immolation is also entwined with Buddha's teachings, the most pertinent of them being the *Ādittapariyāya-sutta*, "The Fire Sermon." The theme of the sermon is that "all is burning," including the senses, sensory organs, their corresponding objects, and the impressions of these objects in us. "Burning with what? With the fire of lust, with the fire of hatred, with the fire of delusion; I say it is burning with birth, ageing and death, with sorrows, with lamentations, with pains, with griefs, with despairs."[228] Instead of this fire, which engulfs and corrupts everything, the fire of the self-immolator and that of justice are lit. The imbalance of a self that lusts, hates, desires, suffers, and is deluded is traceable to the same cause as socio-political injustice.

Buddha's advice is to initiate a certain cooling down: to become dispassionate, detached, and, "through detachment [...] liberated."[229] Is this not what the testimony to Chang-hui's immolation describes? The mind's detachment from the body, to the point of not experiencing pain anymore, is due to the cooling down of that fire which burns through everything in the world of finite becoming ("birth, ageing and death"). The physical fire kindled in the makeshift pyre serves, therefore, as proof that the fire of lust, hatred, and desire has been extinguished. Changhui's subsequent transition to the pure light and heat of *dharma* is intended as a passage for the spectators as well, whom he urges, very much in the spirit of *Ādittapariyāya-sutta*, to turn their minds and "to defeat desire and anger before they appeared."

As I made clear in the Introduction, self-immolations at political protests are not limited to Buddhist monks. My analyses of suicide bombings and self-immolations against the backdrop of certain Islamic and Buddhist bodies of writing respectively are, by far, not universal; they are something like hermeneutical sparks that, for a brief moment, fly next to the dark phenomena that otherwise offer resistance to interpretation. Also in the Introduction, I hinted at the possibility of another political phenomenology brewing in the actions of self-immolators. Faced with suicide bombings and with their motivations in excess of our attributions of causality, the sovereignty of reason and its propensity to explain the world suffers a setback.

When it comes to self-immolations at political rallies or in individual protests, the sovereignty of the observer's gaze is severely undermined and it is in this apparent limitation that another political phenomenology dawns. The fires lit in these circumstances change not only the physical state of things and bodies but also ideation by dint of a double aporia, the impossibility of being in and understanding the world "on fire." The "turning of people's minds around" that Changhui hoped for requires a "turning around" of our habitual phenomenology, which induces its subjects to grasp everything in the light of our own intentionality and egoic gaze. The unbearable spectacle exposes us to a fire that puts an end to the normalcy of vision and that, profoundly disturbing us, raises the demand for justice. It is certainly not the case that all self-immolators are as deliberate and calm in their actions as Changhui seems to have been prior to his flaming transformation. Most of them will have taken their lives after having crossed the Rubicon of despair. Regardless of this difference, the demand for justice remains constant, be it localised in the treatment of particular socio-economic, ethnic, religious, gender and other groups, or be it generalised to the cosmic level of *dharma*.

## 4.3. An Interlude: Extremist Politics

The elemental ontology of fire and its proximity to the ideals of spirit has much to contribute to theories of political extremism. To recap, fire can get out of hand if it engulfs everything—a being, a group of beings, or even the world—leading to the sacrifice of the whole, a *holo-caust*. Following ancient Greek and, particularly, Aristotelian cosmology, it is an element that "naturally" tends *ad extremum*, upwards, beyond physical reality and away from its centre, the earth. And, as we have seen, it can institute a phenomenology that not only displaces our habitual ways of seeing and interpreting reality but also foils both vision and interpretation. So, how are these "extreme" qualities of fire applicable to politics?

Ronald Wintrobe points out three forms of thinking about extremism: 1) a state where the "equilibrium position is located at a 'corner' rather than in the interior on some dimension"; 2) "a move away from the centre and towards the extreme in some dimension"; and 3) the use of "extremist methods, for example, bombings, inflammatory language, terrorist activity, and so forth."[230] A shadow of pyropolitics lurks behind all three definitions Wintrobe has supplied. The movement of decentring in (2) is parallel to the tendency of fire to leave the realm of the earth behind, while keeping alive the possibility of being cast down onto earth again. The decentred state in (1) is the outcome of such radicalisation, more often than not suffused by despair and a sense that all other methods of turning the situation around are futile (being "cornered"). The extremist methods in (3) share the emphasis on fire ("bombings, inflammatory language..."). All this suggests that political extremism is, of necessity, pyropolitical.

It is also true that, today, the notion of "extremism" (which, having first appeared in 1865, is of a relatively recent coinage) has grown remarkably distended. Religious, nationalist, separatist, anarchist, eco-terrorist—this is but a preliminary sampling of the kinds of political groupings the authorities condemn for their extremism. What binds them together, for all the diversity of their aims and tactics, is that the powers that be define them as extremist and, consequently, thrust them to the forefront of pyropolitics. Whereas, in classical cosmologies, fire was an extreme element in relation to the earth, the contemporary agents of the politics of fire are extremist as regards the national and transnational authorities that decide upon the shape of geopolitics.

"Extremism" is now an essentially relative and increasingly relativistic concept used to delegitimise the forces of a substantial opposition to the status quo. The point, of course, is to cut through this relativity and to recognise in the dominant geopolitical actors themselves the kind of extremism that makes billions of poor people around the world ever more vulnerable and that calls into question the future of life on this planet. The *extremism of the* centre—of the earth suffused with fire; of the ineluctably pyropolitical geopolitics—is responsible for spawning all other extremisms, said to endanger global peace and security. From the margins of this skewed world-system, the avowedly pyropolitical actors question the monopoly on violence sanctioned by sovereign states and brazenly declare their own states of exception.

As for "the state of exception," pyropolitics can make a fruitful contribution to honing those political concepts that may be classified as extreme. The Latin *extremus* names the outermost, that which is outward, outside. Now, Schmitt conceptualises sovereignty as "a borderline concept [*Grenzbegriff*] [...], one pertaining to the outermost sphere [*äußersten Sphäre*]."[231] In other words, sovereignty is an extreme concept, and it can be exercised only from the extreme regions of the political field, never from its centre (unless, as I have suggested, the centre itself has become extreme). Its intensity grows exponentially as the political is decentred, shifting from the element of the earth to that of fire, which belongs to the outermost elemental sphere. The objective outcome of this process is the willingness of marginalised actors, who take sovereignty into their own hands, to resort to sacrifices, including those in which they give up their lives.

Most liberal and even leftist political theorists avoid the concept of sovereignty, associating it with authoritarianism and an outmoded idea of supremacy divested of all sense in a world of networks and diffuse, multipolar power assemblages. But the extreme does not simply vanish as a result of their wilful blindness; it is pushed into the far recesses of the unconscious, making it a perfect candidate for sudden eruptions or unexpected flare-ups. Above all, it impregnates the entire *body politic*. The loss of a single and indivisible pole of sovereignty does not mean that there is no more sovereignty, but that the earth with its polarities and modes of orienting ourselves is no longer the suitable element for thinking the extreme. The outwardness of *extremus* is no longer situated on earth (which, in the age of globalisation, has no outside) but, instead, in the far-flung elemental domain of fire. That is one of the reasons why the extremes of the political "right" and "left," the quintessentially earthly markers of orientation, cease to make sense within the pyropolitical matrix.

In *On the Genealogy of Morality* Nietzsche contended that, with the priests, everything became more dangerous owing to the birth of psychic interiority, hidden intentions, and everything we group under the heading "spiritual."[232] For us, the danger lies in the spilling outward of this poisonous interiority onto the actual earth, which goes up in flames in the name of global energy production. (More on this soon.) While pyropolitics contains certain heterogeneous, indeterminate, unfixed, conflicting, and contradictory possibilities, which are readily identifiable as extremist, the murderous and largely hidden extremism of the centre is unspeakably more treacherous than any of the groups assigned this label in official political and academic discourses. Provided that "extremists typically kill people in large numbers, as will be denoted in the definition of political extremism,"[233] those driving the world toward an irreversible environmental calamity are the undisputed champions of extremism. The real extremism is that of *abolishing* the extreme, burning up all limits and, inevitably, being burnt by the impossibility of doing away with these limits for good. It is, in a word, the extremism of a Western "lifestyle," unquestioningly adapted by those outside the West who can afford it.

## 4.4. On Holocausts, or Burnt Offerings at the Extreme

*Holocaust* is a very infelicitous choice of word to designate what happened to the vast numbers of European Jewry in WWII. Its religious undercurrent reinscribes the word in a theodicy that lends a higher meaning to the systematic mass murder carried by Nazi forces. But the linkage of *holocaust* to those events and the continued use of the word today are also symptomatic of the tenacity, with which the rhetoric of sacrifice—and, most of all, of sacred fire—persists in political discourses and in cultural memory. A hard look at the intricate history of the term will go a long way toward illuminating the kind of political theology that *holocaust* has been mired in since it came to translate the Hebrew *'olah*.

I have noted above that *holocaust* is a composite of two Greek words: "whole" and "burnt." Without requiring much conceptual work, this etymology suggests that the word is ill-suited as a designation for the genocide of the Jewish people, first, because (fortunately) their executioners have not succeeded in the project of total extermination and, second, because not all the victims were burnt in gas chambers. Such factual imprecision is, in and of itself, telling. Habitually, Christianity has advanced a figurative reading of *holocaustum* as an allusion to Christ's sacrifice, which did not involve actual fire. St. Thomas Aquinas, in *Summa Theologiae*, gives the most lucid expression to the supreme offering on the cross where nothing is really burnt yet where spiritual fire attains its maximum intensity. Recalling that the "altar of holocausts [*altare holocausturum*], upon which the sacrifices of animals were immolated, was constructed of timbers," he likens it to the wood of the cross (III.46.4.1). Like St. Augustine before him, he views this wood through a spiritual prism, as the sublimation of matter. More relevant still, he favours the same substitution in the case of fire that consumes the wood: "instead of material fire, there was the spiritual fire of divine love in Christ's holocaust [*Loco autem materialis ignis, fuit in holocausto Christi ignis caritatis*]" (III.46.4.1).

One of the projects in Patristics was to establish narrative and logical connections between the events narrated in the Old Testament—events that were, in retrospect, prophetic to the extent that they anticipated the coming of Christ—and those in the New, maintaining, at the same time, the radical novelty of the Christian scriptures. Hence, the ambiguous appropriation of the rituals and concepts from the Hebrew Bible by the Fathers of the Church. St. Clement of Alexandria re-read the Mosaic law allegorically, such that the command for "holocausts to be skinned and divided into parts" came to mean that "the gnostic soul must be consecrated to the light, stripped of the integuments of matter, devoid of the frivolousness of the body and of all the passions, which are acquired through vain and lying opinions, and divested of the lusts of the flesh" (*Strom.* 5.11). The purifying fire of the holocaust liberates the soul from bodily fallenness, uplifts it, and, in this blissful estrangement, makes the true knowledge of God possible. The hidden significance of the skinning of sacrificial animals in Jewish rituals is the division and separation between the soul that seeks light and the dense darkness of mortal matter, wherein it is imprisoned.

Many centuries later, the Bishop of Geneva, St. Francis de Sales will have substantiated the theological connection between the sacrifice of Isaac and Jesus's crucifixion. Although there was no immolation in the latter event, it was essential to demonstrate the continuity between that sacrificial death and the *akedah* of Isaac, whose burnt offering was narrowly averted. Just as "our Saviour's death is a true sacrifice, and a sacrifice of holocaust [*un sacrifice d'holocauste*], which he, himself, offered to his Father for our redemption,"[234] so Isaac, that "novice and apprentice in the art of loving his God," "is quite willing to be sacrificed, and to that end permits himself to be bound, and extended upon the wood, and as a tender little lamb, peaceably awaits death's blow from the dear hand of his good father."[235] His father prefigures the

Father, to whom free will ought to be sacrificed in the fire of sacred love.

As far as St. Francis is concerned, everything in this scene is already as spiritual and interior as it was in the holocaust of Christ: Abraham, who "binds his son in order to immolate him has already sacrificed him in his heart [*qui lie son fils pour l'immoler, l'a déjà sacrifié dans son coeur*]."[236] The flaming interiority of the heart takes the place of the body on a burning pyre. This interiorising movement, so typical of Christian theology, enables the transition from physical fire to the flames of divine love already in St. Augustine, who in his hermeneutics of the Biblical psalms happens upon the word *holocaust*. "But what is a holocaust?" he asks. "A whole consumed by fire [*totum igne absumptum*]: *causis* is burning, *holon* is whole: but a holocaust is a whole consumed by fire. There is a certain fire of the most burning divine love [*flagrantissimae caritatis*]: let the soul be inflamed with divine love [*animus inflammetur caritate*], let the same love hurry off the limbs to its use, let it not allow them to serve carnal desire, in order that we may wholly glow with the fire of divine love that will offer to God a holocaust. Such 'holocausts of thine are in My sight always'" (*Ennar. in Psalmos* XLIX.15). The fire in the heart and in the soul (*animus*) takes precedence over the physical combustion of a body, animated by divine fire to devote its whole being (*totum igne absumptum*) to spiritual love (*caritas*), as opposed to the desires of the flesh (*cupiditas*). "The whole," *holon* of *holocaustum*, is not only real but, above all, ideal.

According to Christian doctrine, the whole will not be on fire until psychic interiority, too, is set aflame, making of the mind and the body a joint offering to God. But there is little agreement on ways of achieving this glorious effect. Should the body be mortified and "divested of the lusts of the flesh" to liberate the soul in its strivings toward divine light and heat, as St. Clement recommends? Should the mind be directly inflamed with the "most burning love" of God, following St. Augustine? Or is it better to divide works of virtue, as St. Thomas does, into those that affect the body and those that pertain to spiritual desires, burning on the "altar of holocausts" and on the "altar of incenses," respectively?[237] It seems to me that it is among these divergent suggestions that we can start searching for clues regarding the persistence of *holocaust* outside the context of its original enunciation.

Suppose that St. Clement prevails, and the soul triumphs at the expense of its bond to the body. (The prescription for self-abnegation is by no means the saint's invention, as it actually predates Christianity and goes back at least as far as Plotinus, who deemed his finite body, of which he was extremely ashamed, a barrier to his unity of the soul with the One.[238]) Under these circumstances, the whole of what is burnt in a holocaust will never be whole enough, will never attain the absolute spiritual unity with itself, until all matter is incinerated and reduced to ash. This dangerous and nihilistic trend is consistent with the "Gnostic theory that matter is evil in itself," the theory both St. Augustine and St. Thomas vehemently opposed.[239] The extremism of this view hinges on the desire for a total interiorisation or spiritualisation of *what is* through, for instance, the holocaust of material existence. Nothing short of the ideal will do, and the ideal is that of cleansing the world of all matter, that is to say, doing away with exteriority as such.

In Christianity, the Jewish teaching stood for a symbol of exteriority: the exteriority of ritual *versus* the interiority of faith, the letter *versus* the spirit of the law... Therefore, Judaism occupied the place of matter vis-à-vis Christian spirit and, as matter, was a perfect candidate for destruction. That is, probably, the reason for the first reference to a massacre of the Jews as a holocaust, which, as Agamben reminds us, goes back to the twelfth century, when, on the day of the coronation of Richard I, the inhabitants of London are said to have burnt the Jews, *immolare judaeos*, for "so long that the holocaust could not be completed before the next day."[240] In contrast to other ethnic and religious cleansings, theirs was supposed to be a purging of material exteriority itself.[241]

What about the holocaust of divine love, celebrated by St. Augustine and St. Francis de Sales, then? Surely, it could not have been responsible for the kind of violence that stemmed from Gnostic nihilism—or could it? Again, the accent should fall on the *holon* of the holocaust. *On the one hand*, St. Augustine extends the possibility of salvation to the soul as well as to the body that, together, make up "the whole" to be consumed by divine fire: "May divine fire take us up whole, and that fervour catch us whole [*Totos nos divinis ignis absumat, et fervor ille totus arripiat*]. What fervour? [...] That whereof speaketh the Apostle: 'In spirit fervent.' Be not merely our soul taken up by that divine fire of wisdom [*divino igni sapientiae*], but also our body; that it may earn its immortality; so be it lifted up for a holocaust [*sic levetur holocaustum*], that death be swallowed into victory" (*Ennar. in Psalmos*, L.23). The lifting of the body along with the soul "for a holocaust" assures full resurrection, an eternal life in and as divine fire. Immortality must be earned; that is, the body as dumb matter, prior to its being engulfed with divine wisdom, must be sacrificially exchanged for an enlightened, illuminated, and burning body-and-soul totality. The image of the Augustinian holocaust is that of the spirit of divine love making the entire physical and psychic being of the believer fervent.

*On the other hand*, the whole will be still lacking, unless the fire of love is universal. For St. Augustine, the Jews *qua* Jews stand in the way of future universality, not the least due to the literalness of their laws, including those governing sacrifices: "As yet that Israel perchance doth not understand [*non intelligit*] what are the holocausts thereof which He hath in His sight always, and is still thinking of oxen, of sheep, of he-goats: let it not so think: 'I will not accept calves of thy house.' Holocausts I named; at once in mind and thought to earthly flocks thou wast running, therefrom thou wast selecting for Me some fat thing" (*Ennar. in Psalmos* XLIX.16). The Jewish lack of understanding concerning the nature of the holocaust (as a synecdoche for religion) disqualifies them from participation in universal love. In fact, "that Israel perchance doth not understand" means that it has not yet given itself, body and soul, to the "divine fire of wisdom." Philosophically, Hegel will draw the implications of this presumed immaturity that arrests the dialectical development of Spirit at the stage of abstract monotheism. As construed by St. Augustine, however, Jewish "non-understanding" spans both the literalness of offering "some fat thing" as a holocaust to God and a failure to integrate material and spiritual practices in the kind of redemptive fervour he prays for.

A red thread winding through St. Thomas Aquinas's discussion of holocaust, which was heavily influenced by the thought of sixth-century Pope Gregory the Great, is the theme of perfection. Only total devotion to God and, therefore, the acceptance of God's absolute sovereignty and authority would bestow perfection onto the victim: "There were three kinds of sacrifices. There was one in which the victim was entirely consumed by fire: this was called 'a holocaust, i.e. all burnt [*totum incensum*].' For this kind of sacrifice was offered to God specially to show reverence to His majesty, and love of His goodness: and typified the state of perfection [*perfectionis statui*] [...]. Wherefore the whole was burnt up: so that as the whole animal by being dissolved into vapour soared aloft, so it might denote that the whole man, and whatever belongs to him, are subject to the authority of God [*Dei dominio*], and should be offered to Him" (IIa.102.3.8). The totality of devotion translates the *holon* of *holocaustum*, demanding the best among living beings. In light of the specification that the holocaust "was the most perfect sacrifice," St. Thomas explains, "none but a male [animal] was offered for a holocaust: because the female is an imperfect animal [*femina est animal imperfectum*]" (IIa.102.3.9). By dint of the imperfection imputed to her, the female (animal or human) escapes the grip of total sovereignty, which reckons her bodily unfit for the ritual and spiritually incapable of an unconditional self-offering to God. *Mutatis mutandis*, the same strange escape route opens before the practitioners of Judaism.

St. Thomas takes it for granted that Jews could not reach perfection in their sacrificial rites that were too crude, too material, barely spiritual. Still, he adds that the divine permission to make burnt offerings carried a didactic or heuristic significance: "God did not wish these sacrifices to be offered to Him on account of the things themselves that were offered, as though He stood in need of them [...]. But, as stated above, He wished them to be offered to Him, in order to prevent idolatry; in order to signify the right ordering of man's mind to God; and in order to represent the mystery of the Redemption of man by Christ [*figurandum mysterium redemptionis humanae factae per Christum*]" (IIa.102.3.1). The three reasons St. Thomas cites for burnt offerings ultimately boil down to perfection by 1) warding off a relapse into the worse habit of idolatry; 2) creating a disposition of mind propitious to the right worship; and 3) materially prefiguring the perfect sacrifice (of Christ). The height of perfection, on this view, is indeed the holocaust of Jesus who "as man, was not only priest, but also a perfect victim [*hostia perfecta*], being at the same time victim for sin, victim for a peace-offering, and a holocaust" (III.22.2.co). The diverse types of sacrifice, the act of burning and accepting the fate of being burnt, the offering and the offered merge into one and the same figure of the Redeemer. Only then and there is the totality of *holon* gathered up in spiritual fire and in the elemental sovereignty it harbours.

Since no human being can replicate the absolute synthesis of Jesus, religious education is required to bring the believers as close as possible to the perfection of the divine holocaust. The propaedeutic itinerary leads St. Thomas back to Gregory the Great, who defined holocaust as a situation "when a man vows to God all his possessions, all his life, all his knowledge" (IIb.186.6.co). "Those are called religious antonomastically," St. Thomas explains, "who give themselves up entirely [*se totaliter mancipant*] to the divine service, as offering a holocaust to God. [...] Now the perfection of man consists in adhering wholly to God and in this sense religion denotes the state of perfection" (IIb.186.6.co). There is no *qualitative* difference between a Jewish practitioner privy to a material prefiguration of redemption in burnt offerings, an average Christian believer, and a Christian monk, who dedicates himself entirely to divine service. Each of the three is at a greater or lesser remove from perfection (recall that the figure of the feminine has been intentionally marginalised as an "imperfect animal"), with neither matter *simpliciter* nor a lack of understanding posing insurmountable obstacles on the path toward the ideal. Matter is no longer an evil to be eliminated; it breathes with the anticipation of spirit. And a lack of understanding is not a thorn in the side of universal love but a perfectible state prone to educability, the state that is fittingly as obscure as "the *mystery* of Redemption" (animal sacrifice as an oblique symbol for the holocaust of "the Lamb of God").

In his book on Auschwitz, Agamben recoils, almost instinctively, from the analogy between the Biblical burnt offering and the Nazi crematoria. "In the case of the term 'holocaust'," he writes, "the attempt to establish a connection, however distant, between Auschwitz and the Biblical *'olah* and between death in the gas chamber and the 'complete devotion to sacred and superior motives' cannot but sound like a jest. Not only does the term imply an unacceptable equation between crematoria and altars; it also continues a semantic heredity that is from its inception anti-Semitic." "That is why we will never make use of this term," he concludes.[242] Nevertheless, omitting the existing linguistic association, no matter how abominable, between this political atrocity and a highly emblematic theological term is inexcusable. It is one thing to refuse to call what happened in the Nazi extermination camps *Holocaust* (the word capitalised, at that) and it is something else altogether to dismiss the regrettable choice of word as a sign of bad taste.

As Agamben is well aware, the Jewish euphemism for those events is *sho'ah*, or catastrophe, which is similarly tinged with theological hues, since, in Biblical discourse, it "often implies the idea of a divine punishment."[243] Because one finds it unbearable to look meaningless suffering and victimhood in the face, a theological meaning is readily procured, at times with inapposite redemptive insinuations. The perversity of linking purification by fire to the "all-burning" sacrifice (to whom or to what? the idea of pure race?) of millions is nothing new; in fact, this perversity is innate to the religious tradition or traditions where the concept and the practice first gestated. When a flesh-and-blood animal had to be entirely dissolved in smoke—its body sublimated and elevated—, its earthly life was presumed to be subservient to the vitality of pure spirit. When matter was seen as identical to evil and its destruction (notably, in fire) interpreted as an act of liberation, then the same nihilistic worldview was generalised to terrestrial existence *in toto*. When, burning with the fire of spirit, one pledged one's entire life to God, the renunciation of vitality shared with other living creatures, be they human or nonhuman, was inevitable.

These instances of exchanging finite existence for the assurances of eternity were not preternatural in the economy of sacrifice. The uniqueness of *holocaust* was that in total conversions, destructions, and renunciations there was no safety valve for asserting the value of earthly life: *everything* had to go, as a "guarantee that our whole person has departed for the beyond."[244] But, upon a closer look, something or someone (for example, the "imperfect" female in St. Thomas) has always eluded the holocaust's totalising grasp, even if these local resistances have been ignored in the uncompromising nihilism of the all-burning. The more recent ideology that took it upon itself to carry out the holocaust of the "undesirables" was not of a piece with this tradition or traditions, but it was permeated, through and through, by the deadliest nihilism, which has been ripening in the West for millennia.

On a planetary scale, the possibility of total destruction is sometimes called "nuclear holocaust." This imagined event would be one of the most complete burnt offering of the world to... nothing. From Plato to Husserl, philosophers have carried out thought experiments imagining what would remain unaffected after all of material reality is obliterated. Since the twentieth century these exercises are no longer the figments of idle imagination, seeing that advanced technological capacities can turn these thoughts into reality in a matter of seconds. But, while a nuclear holocaust may lead to the entire earth going up in smoke almost instantaneously, a slower burning total "offering" poses a threat that is more palpable, though less dramatic or spectacular. Global energy production, in the manner in which it is carried out since the start of the Industrial Revolution, depends on reorganising all life — be it past, present, or future; in us or outside us — such that the living would serve as no more than fuel to be burnt without a discernible substantive goal or end. To whom or to what is this all-burning sacrifice made? Is not the search for "energy" — this at once new and very old modality of activity from Aristotle's *energeia* to Nietzsche's "will-to-power," which implies the power to burn anything whatsoever — strangely autotelic and self-sacrificial? But, before leaving the religious realm *proper* and analysing the pyropolitics of global energy, I would like to touch upon the issue of burnt offerings in the spectacle of *auto-da-fé*, or "act of faith," promulgated by the Inquisition.

### 4.5. The Burning Question of the Inquisition

In January 1639, Francisco Maldonado de Silva was burnt at the stake in Lima (now, Peru). Before being set on fire by the authorities of the Inquisition, with the books he had written tied around his neck, Maldonado de Silva spent twelve long years in jail, where he continued affirming his Judaism, writing books and essays, and participating in fourteen disputations with distinguished Christian theologians.[245] In his farewell address to the Jewish community of Rome, he declared himself a martyr for the religion, which "I vowed to defend to death, with my power and arguments, against the adversaries of His truth and to uphold His Law until the altar of fire [*aras ignis*] being now (I think) prepared for me, so that

God may accept me as a holocaust for our sins [*holocaustum pro peccatis nostris*]."²⁴⁶ Although the body of the "Judaiser" was burnt by the Inquisition, in his final missive he upended the institutional relations of elemental sovereignty by offering himself as an "all-burning" sacrifice and, in so doing, combining the power of burning with the condition of being burnt.

This minuscule fragment from the history of the Inquisition illustrates the subversion of its pyropolitical program, which had two chief objectives: purging the souls of the believers and bringing to light (and heat) the secret worship of those Jews, called *marranos*, who practiced their religious rituals under the cover of an imposed identity as Christian converts. Death at the stake was the most violent form of purging, which also included the destruction of prohibited books, burning some of the accused in effigy, public confessions to sins and transgressions, temporary exiles (*destierros*) of those found guilty of blasphemy, and so forth.

Between June 11 and November 22, 1488 alone, seven *autos-da-fé* were held in the city of Guadalupe.²⁴⁷ And, in 1490, over six thousand Jewish manuscripts were burnt in the Spanish centre of learning, the city of Salamanca.²⁴⁸ So great was the purifying power of fire that Pope Innocent VIII conceded to the Spanish Inquisitors the right "to exhume and burn the bodies of the already dead heretics [*hereticorum defunctorum corpora exhumare et igni*]."²⁴⁹ Despite the allegorical and spiritual senses of fire in Christianity, actual flames became the preferred means for purging religious, sexual, political, and other deviant practices that did not conform to the Church's ideal, to which the practitioners were sacrificed. It was this principle of conformity with the established doctrine that stood behind the fires of *auto-da-fé* that, in the words of

Andalusian priest Andrés Bernáldez, once lit, "will burn until [...] not one of those who judaised is left."[250]

Demanding unconditional purification was demanding the impossible, the hallmark of the most recalcitrant idealism. As though it was not enough to ban or to banish bodies of thought and living-breathing human bodies, the authorities ordered their material elimination. Meticulously staged in the cities' central *plazas*, incendiary spectacles had to make power itself visible through the light, heat, and smoke of the fires of the Inquisition, while, at the same time, exposing the psychic interiority of the victims through forced confessions and penances. But, inadvertently, they also illuminated the resistance and the elemental sovereignty of those renegades, witches, and heretics, of the likes of Maldonado de Silva, who declined to cooperate with the Holy Office of the Inquisition. The actions of nonconformists and the judgment passed on them were summarised in official reports with three simple words "impenitent, negative, convicted"[251] that demarcated the limits of Inquisitorial power over the defiant souls of the accused. By the eighteenth century these words were erased from the official accounts and replaced with the bland and uniform "died [...] showing signs of repentance [*murió ... con señales de arrepentimiento*],"[252] probably in an attempt to obfuscate resistance and to confirm the corrective potential of the punishment in line with the novel criminological approaches of the time.

According to the cover of a report on the *auto-da-fé* that took place in Córdoba on June 29, 1665, the ceremonies were intended as "celebrations of the New Testament of light [...] against the Old of shadows [*que celebran el Nuevo Testamento de la luz ... contra el Antiguo de las sombras*]."[253] In the course of the Inquisition, this murderous light, flooding what it declared to be the shadows, was combined with the heat of the flames that maintained the unity of fire intact. As, inspired in part by Adorno and Derrida, I made the case in chapter 2, secular and often militantly anticlerical, the Enlightenment did not break with the Inquisitorial mode of pyropolitical oppression but simply modified it so as to spread death through the frigid light of abstract reason, incompatible with the warmth of life itself. What changed was the regime of political visibility, as Foucault convincingly demonstrated in *Discipline and Punish*. The fires of the Inquisition were so enormous that "the smoke from the effigies, books, and burning bodies rose from the plaza and was visible for miles around [...]. The rising smoke carried the presence of the Inquisition far beyond Guadalupe itself, bringing the vision of heretical activity to Iberians far beyond the Marian shrine."[254] The modern Panopticon invested power with the capacity for seeing without being seen; the *auto-da-fé* made power visible through that which normally obscures clear vision, the smoke emanating from the fiery origin of light (and heat). And it made power visible, precisely, in consequence of the ascent of burnt matter skywards, as a sign of its sacrificial spiritualisation.

In a letter detailing a brief history of the Inquisition to date, Pope Sixtus IV cited as one of the primary reasons for setting up the institution the invisible presence of Jews, "apparently behaving as though they were Christians [*christianis apparenter*]," among Spanish Catholics.[255] To illuminate the truth behind these appearances, the Holy See delegated to the Spanish King Ferdinand II and Queen Isabel I, the authority to nominate the Inquisitors and set up a juridical process, replete with trials and witness testimonies. The questioning of the Inquisition is apparently born of the will to know whether apparent Christians were genuinely Christian; whether someone really blasphemed; whether a woman or a group of women indeed practiced witchcraft... The stated intention behind the process was *apurar*, a Spanish verb that means "to purify," "to exhaust," and "to clear up," "to verify," "to investigate minutely." Without a doubt, the Inquisition produced its own truth through torture and forced confessions. But the purifying-verifying mission it proudly undertook was in consonance with the zealous will-to-know, which was not so easy to execute, given the interiority of Christian faith. The spectacles of *auto-da-fé* were tangible repetitions of the inquisitorial *apuramiento*, with the desired ontological effect of "saving souls and conserving the purity of Catholic faith [*pro animarum salute et fidei catholice conseruanda puritate*]."[256]

There is plenty of evidence, as well, that the idealism of the Inquisition was, in large part, a subterfuge concealing crudely material and economic interests in the Inquisitors' personal enrichment. More often than not, the condemned had their property confiscated and, seeing that many of them were wealthy Jewish (or crypto-Jewish) merchants, their fortunes were sizeable. So blatant were the abuses perpetrated by the Office of the Inquisition that, in 1482, Sixtus IV wrote a missive deploring the exercise of its functions "not due to faith and the salvation of souls, but due to a love of profits [*non zelo fidei et salutis animarum, sed lucre cupiditate*]."[257] (This concern all but evaporated by 1513, the year Pope Leo X included the prosecution of usurers among the competences of the Inquisitors.[258]) Fire and gold, the two universal equivalents analogised by Heraclitus, were exquisitely interweaved at the time of the Inquisition.

It is no secret that inquisitorial authorities regarded fire as an element that facilitated, besides purification, renewal and rebirth. Even after suspects had been absolved of the charges levelled against them, effigies bearing their names were burnt,[259] at once as a warning against committing future sins and as a proof of their being cleared of suspicion and reintegrated into the community of faith. But the purifying power of fire also had its limits: it could not correct the ways of the atheists who lived "without King, without Law, without Capitan, without God, without temple [...]."[260] Franciscan friar Pedro Mateo de Lara, who penned these speculations at the end of his report on the *auto-da-fé* held in Córdoba in July 1665, confessed to considering atheism, with its thesis that "faith and Religion are a political invention that must serve the reason of the state," irredeemable.[261] For de Lara, atheism is "the most impure stain [*mancha impurísima*] that cannot be taken out either with the powerful water of Baptism, or with the active fire of torture [*el fuego activo del suplicio*], or with the clear air of our commerce, or with the disenchanted earth of a grave." Only hellfire can absorb this stain, "handed over to the flames after death."[262]

De Lara's mention of water, fire, air, and earth will be readily recognised as a citation of the classical elements, imbued with redemptive Christian connotations. More nihilistic still than "the active fire of torture" is that of hell, where "the most impure stain" of atheism rightfully belongs, or so de Lara conjectures. For, isn't what irks the Franciscan friar the fact that, over and above not sharing Catholic values, atheism does not belong to the same system of value coordinates, the same axiology, as the those accepted by other "heretics"? It does not revere a higher religious or political reality and does not prioritise the smokescreen of spirit over finite existence. The nihilistic fire of the Inquisition is impotent in its confrontation with that of earthly life, here represented by atheism, which has refused to bow before a deadly flaming ideality. By lifting the ideological curtain, illuminating the obscure core of religion as "a political invention," and bringing it down to earth, the unbeliever purifies the purifying and dematerialising force of the Inquisition. Such a purification of the purifier *is* "the most impure stain," the unsurpassable and intolerable blind spot of ideology.

## 4.6. Global Energy Production, or 'What Do They Salvage from the Great Fire of Life?'

Schelling's nineteenth-century *Naturphilosophie* contains some of the most pertinent preambles to the twenty-first century ideas and approaches to matter as a temporary repository of energy. Reflecting on the nature of oxygen and the synthetic activity of fire, which we have already sighted in his work, Schelling makes the process of combustion central to the existence of every organic and inorganic terrestrial entity. With a flare typical of a metaphysician, the German philosopher sweepingly generalises the principle that underlies the appearance of a mindboggling variety: "All variety is reducible to the notion of that which is *combusted*; some are conceived in reduction—(the phenomenon of this reduction is vegetation; at the lowest stage the vegetation of metals which are maintained by the inner glow of the Earth, at a higher stage the vegetation of plants)—others in permanent combustion (the phenomenon of this permanent process of combustion is animal life)."[263]

A continuous chain strings together metals, plants, and animals, nourished by the external or internal heat of geothermal, solar, or vital energy. Elemental sovereignty, residing in the relation between the burning and the burnt, assigns to any given entity its place in the chain: the passive gestation of metals in the ores leaves them no possibilities other than those of being combusted; the animal is a self-combusting, combusting and combusted, entity that has the wellspring of its animation in itself; the plant, as always, is slotted in the ambiguous place in-between the two.

Taken a step further, the Schellengian argument implies that the human is a unique animal that, besides being self-combusting, claims the sovereign right actively to burn anything in its environs in order to supply itself with energy. The dark irony of this stance is that, by kindling the entire world, the human lays bare the flammable essence of reality and makes the world what it truly is without the interference of the material forms that overlay the process of combustion, which is now concretised in the solid shape of a metal, now as a plant, and now as an animal. In thought and in deed, the world reveals itself as what it is just as it evanesces in the flames. Doesn't, at the behest of truth, destructive human activity release the potency of energy from its temporary imprisonment in matter, thus liberating the ontological kernel of "all variety" from its diverse phenomenal shells? Isn't the act of setting things ablaze in order to derive energy from them correspond to the truth of being as being combusted?

To his credit, Schelling concentrated on potentiality, rather than actuality, in his philosophical investigation. In his system, the centre of gravity was *combustibility*, as opposed to the manifestation of this principle in burning or being burnt. "It follows necessarily from this," he sums up his reduction of physical variety, "that no substance on Earth can come to light which *was* not either combusted or *would be* combusted, or was not *combustible*."[264] The tragedy of the twenty-first century is that we have taken it upon ourselves to actualise this potentiality and to burn everything that is combustible, including ourselves.[265] The extraction of energy by burning things predates not only our epoch but industrial modernity as well. There is, however, a vast difference between the fires kindled with a few branches in a prehistoric cave, the coal burnt in the English factories of the eighteenth century, and the contemporary combustion of biofuels. The early representatives of humankind set a small bit of the present or immediate past alight; rapidly industrialising Europe submitted the deep past of vegetal and animal life to fire; today's blaze envelops all modalities of time, so that the past, the present, and the future burn together in a process indistinguishable from the incinerated life, from its production and reproduction for the sake of being consumed as energy. Global environmental crisis is a consequence and a culmination of this raging conflagration.

What is more, human existence itself is not spared in the all-encompassing combustion of reality in what Herbert Marcuse once called "productive destruction under total administration."[266] Some of the signs of our embroilment in this paradigm are our concern with caloric intake and the desire to burn excess calories at a gym; the growing consumption of energy drinks and energy bars; or the (consistent enough) word "burnout" for the breakdown and exhaustion we experience when we run out of the mental and physical resources to be expended at an ever-accelerating rhythm of self-incineration. Individual burnout is a reflection of how humanity denies the possibility of a liveable future to itself, to say nothing of the nonhuman, animal and plant, species.

The predominance of energy production, be it as food or as fuel, over other concerns makes the remaining elements of air, water, and earth sterile and inhospitable to life, even as they are mobilized or upended in the unquenchable search for energy. Air pollution, affecting major cities from Beijing to Paris, is a direct effect of the worldwide bonfire, its fumes rising higher than those from the burnt offerings of old or the fires of the Inquisition. Smog is the contemporary smoke of sacrifice to the gods of progress, claiming the respiratory health of billions around the world. It is the face of a planetary burnout.

Russian philosopher Vladimir Bibikhin astutely observed that the race to procure energy at all costs makes this sought-after object both a means and a goal in itself.[267] Michelle Cederberg's *Energy Now! Small Steps to an Energetic Life* proves this point in a stunningly tautological advice to the readers: "Since physical fitness is a sure-fire energizer, double your efforts by drinking energizing water so you have energy for energizing exercise."[268] Isn't this what we are compelled to do, in the gym or outside its walls? Aren't we supposed to run on the energy treadmill indefinitely—or until the next burnout? There is, moreover, no goal other than procuring more energy; we no longer ask what it is *for*. We burn ourselves and our world for the sake of burning, and the spectacular blaze is the most sublime work of *l'art pour l'art*, for which the entire planet supplies raw materials. Cederberg knows, of course, that it is not water but fire that rules the day, and she foregrounds, as the unwanted effect of dehydration, the slowdown of the body's metabolism. In turn, deceleration "means your body will burn calories more slowly than it should and you run the risk of storing extra calories as fat." Therefore, "[d]rink more water and burn, baby, burn!"[269]

It is worth keeping in mind that "burn, baby, burn!" was originally a chant in the Watts race riots that swept over Los Angeles in 1965. Thirty-three years later, the chair of the Republican National Committee, Michael Steele, paraphrased the rioters' chant into what became a presidential campaign slogan "drill, baby, drill!" This phrase was then popularised by vice-presidential candidate Sarah Palin, who used it as shorthand for her push to increase domestic oil drilling exponentially, including offshore exploration off the Alaskan coast.[270]

Actually, the two slogans are one and the same: the emphatic repetition of the injunction to drill puts its seal of approval on the demand to burn not only oil but also the environment and the world. Fuelled by religious apocalyptic sentiments among those American conservatives who assume that the fate of the planet is sealed and Last Judgment is nigh, the drilling battle cry is undaunted by what "conventional" energy production means for the earth's future. But a deeper reason for this nonchalant attitude is the metaphysical (and Gnostic) hatred of matter, which presents itself to us in the guise of provisionally stabilised energy, or, in other words, in the guise of energy alien to itself. Under the influence of fire, energy becomes fully itself, as it is liberated either in explosive bursts or in a more sustained ardency described by Schelling. It passes over into the realm of pure spirit, of pure act (*actus purus*, or *actualitas* as the Latin rendition of the Greek *energeia*) that has shed its finite bodily trappings.

The conception of energy as bustling, sizzling, agitated activity is, nonetheless, myopic. Bibikhin reminds us of the counterintuitive Aristotelian notion of *energeia* as "being in the fullness of rest," as the "*energy of rest*" that simply and fully is.[271] We can barely register the sense of this definition, since we are too accustomed to thinking of energy as something perpetually ebbing away, diminishing in the measure in which it is liberated, and, like the sands of time, slipping between our fingers, leaving us more impoverished the more we burn it. For us, energy is, precisely, what can never be fully actualised, while in Aristotle's mindset it was the accomplishment of actuality itself, the final entelechy of potentiality (cf. *Metaphysics* 9.1050a). The contrast between the two "energies" is all the more glaring considering the role of fire in their procurement and expenditure. The modern view of energy as something spent and depleted is anxiety-ridden about the imminent extinguishing of its blaze. Giving in to such fears, we throw our world and ourselves into the bonfire more thoroughly; as, tacitly rehashing the Freudian "where the id was, there the ego shall be," Bibikhin comments on a poem by Osip Mandelstam: "where there was a world, there is now fire."[272]

The energy of rest does not set the world aflame but draws its resources from the quenching of incessant activity, the calming down of *kinesis*. The process need not resurrect any metaphysical entities (e.g., the unmoved mover) posited over and above the actuality of existence. It is enough to invoke the Eastern practices of meditation to get a glimpse of that energy which derives *from* the extinguishing of the fires of desire, of passions, and of the senses, as Buddha explains in "The Fire Sermon." The most pressing issue of energy is neither petroleum nor solar power, neither caloric intake nor physical exercise, but burning and extinguishing—burning *or* extinguishing—and the effects of each of these increases and diminutions of fire on life in its actuality and actuation. Does everything need to be offered up in a nihilistic holocaust of "world energy resources" for human existence to be preserved and for world population to continue growing, at the expense of everything and everyone else? What about the flows of energy, as opposed to its ignitions? Is the stoppage of activity a sure symptom of death or of the fullness of life? The very either/or choice between energy as burning and as extinguishing is indicative of the arrhythmia and an unhealthy division that has crept into the Heraclitean cosmos of periodic flare-ups and decreases of fire. The world-encompassing blaze of "energy production" is a tragic exacerbation of this rift.

Freud's *Civilization and its Discontents* famously paints the image of humans as "prosthetic God[s]," who compensate for the weakness of their physical faculties with the technological additions of telephones, telescopes, motorised boats, and the like to their sense organs.[273] We can now specify that the human is a prosthetic Agni, the god of fire, who sacrifices himself first to himself and then to nothing at all. Permanently preoccupied with the dwindling energy of our finite lives, we seek to surround ourselves with supplementary fires (the engines that transport us, the central heating systems that keep us warm, the electrical grid that connects us to information technologies, etc., etc.) from which we expect to receive a compensation for the weakness of our vitality. But these compensatory mechanisms are, as we know, never sufficient. Given the endlessly growing needs for fuel, the fight over limited energy resources is intensifying, even as global warming makes drilling for oil in the Arctic practically plausible. If quarrels over the appropriation of these resources ignite wars, that is because energy is thought of as matter to be burnt and depleted at the behest of spirit rather than the consequence of slowing down our race toward the abyss or the outcome of the circulation of life that increases thanks to its sharing with other human and nonhuman beings.

Instead of saving finite life, as the ancients proposed to do, we squander it all the more rapidly the more we burn our "life supports," polluting the elements of the earth, water, or air and hoping (unconsciously and against hope) for their physical and spiritual revival. The haste, constant activity, and boiling "energy" with which we are supposed to go about our business are equally empty and destructive. As Kierkegaard brilliantly put it, "Of all ridiculous things in the world what strikes me as the most ridiculous of all is being busy in the world, to be a man quick to his meals and quick to his work. [...] For what do they achieve, these busy botchers? Are they not like the housewife who, in confusion at the fire in her house, saved the fire-tongs? What else do they salvage from the great fire of life?"[274] What do *we* salvage from the great fire of life? Why do we intensify the blaze to the point where it becomes indistinguishable from a nihilistic fire of death? Is free, limitless, and democratically distributed solar energy the answer to our troubles?

# Chapter 5.
## *The End of Heliotropic Utopias: When the Sun Sets on the City upon the Hill*

### 5.1. Around the Sun(s)

It all revolves around the sun. Or, better, the suns. The contemporary image of Europe is divided along the following lines. On the one hand, there are the sun-soaked streets of Madrid, Lisbon, Athens, and Rome; on the other hand, there are the gloomy avenues of Berlin, London, and Amsterdam, illuminated by another kind of light—that of knowledge and the Enlightenment.

Southern Europe, in the eyes of North Europeans, is an idyllic place of leisure, warmth, and laziness, sold (and bought) as a convenient vacation destination, where the Northerners can partake of a siesta lifestyle for two weeks a year or less. On the beaches of Algarve or on the Greek islands, they can let go of their worries and temporarily lose their "bearish seriousness," as Nietzsche was fond of calling it. Still, Southern Europe is a far cry from the Homeric Island of Circe, where visitors forgot their native lands. As soon as they get a little tanned, or sometimes burnt due to their inexperience with beach-going, our contemporary Odysseuses will return home to their routine, reenergised for another year of work and solemn dedication to all sorts of rational pursuits.

This caricature has more than one grain of truth, mixed with the grains of sand and salt in the hair of sunbathers on the beaches of Alicante. It is, to be sure, not a truthful representation of Southern Europe but of the typical attitude toward it in other corners of the continent. The severity of the barely overcome economic crisis in Spain, Portugal, Greece,

Cyprus, and Italy is explained through the same ideological lens. The populations of "peripheral" countries are lazy, renounce hard work, and instead bask in the warmth of the actual sun, which they enjoy in abundance. They have been squandering the money of the German taxpayer, the average tirade continues, and should now suffer the consequences of their economic carelessness. It matters little to those who cling to such a view that the Portuguese, for example, must endure much longer working hours than the Germans, or that South European countries have provided easily accessible consumer markets for goods made in the heart of the EU. It matters even less that, in Europe, the sun of philosophy first rose in Greece before migrating to Rome. The prejudice is by now fixed: the physical sun shines in the South, whilst that of knowledge illuminates the North.

I cannot neglect to mention the philosophical horizon for the two suns of Europe. In his *Philosophy of Nature*, Hegel goes so far as to compare the subject formation of the Southerners to that of plants, which also strive toward the light and warmth of the sun. "The externality of the subjective, selflike unity of the plant," he writes, "is objective in its relation to light [...] Man fashions himself in more interior fashion, although in southern latitudes he, too, does not reach the stage where his self, his freedom, is objectively guaranteed."[275] Translated into colloquial language, Hegel's statement means that plants are driven by something outside of themselves, namely light, from which they derive their identity. Humans, on the other hand, build themselves up from within, as conscious and self-conscious beings with memory, decision-making capabilities, and other signs of intelligence. *But*—here comes Hegel's racist punch line—human subjectivity in "southern latitudes" is more plant-like and the human self is neither as free nor as fully developed as that in northern latitudes. Much as he opposes Hegel, Nietzsche would agree that the overabundance of light hardly leaves any time for gloomy rumination, or for dwelling on the soul's interiority (and this lack of time is a good thing, he would add, laughingly). The amount of light from the metaphysical sun of knowledge and the intensity of the physical sun are inversely proportional; the more we receive of the latter, the less we benefit from the former.

Tourism is a flagship industry in Southern Europe, which is why the region has been hankering after a confirmation of its status as the ultimate "sun destination." Spain's 1982 advertisement campaign with the logo designed by Joan Miró and the motto "Everything under the sun," *Todo bajo el sol*, has cemented the common association of the entire country with the beach and entertainment. Portugal's more recent program *Reforma ao sol*, "Retirement under the sun," has aimed to attract North European pensioners (and their pension funds) to an environment propitious to relaxation after a lifetime of work. But, so long as the different zones of Europe remain lit by two different suns, the talk of "two-track Europe" will be on the political agenda. It is not within the realm of the possible to prevent rain from falling over Benelux countries. But it is within the scope of political planning to develop knowledge-based economies in Southern Europe. Until that moment arrives, European *integration* will be an empty word.

The situation I have described somewhat flippantly is as much an upshot of a longstanding prejudice regarding the capacities of the "Northerners" and "Southerners" as a symptom of Europe's postcolonial malaise. One should not be surprised that the difference between the North and the South, with their respective kinds of light, has been interiorised after centuries of being projected onto the divide between the

European metropolis and the colonies. The colonial adventure, as we shall see, was not only geopolitical but also pyropolitical, as it bragged about having dominated solar light and heat themselves in an empire, over which "the sun never set." Colonization of the earth meant a colonization of the sun. Dovetailing with the absolutist "Sun King," the empire pretended to have figuratively swallowed up the sun—that is to say, light and heat: the conditions of possibility for seeing, making sense, and living—whose rays it then reflected or refracted around the world. Generally speaking, every absolute political and theological authority indulges in such behaviour, to the extent that it controls the power structures, wherein understanding, sensibility, and life are caught. The outward sign of having swallowed up the sun is the blinding shine of glory, rendering a god, a king, or a political unit nearly unrepresentable, sublime. This unrepresentability, due to a pyropolitical monopoly on light and heat, underwrites the relations of representation among the subjects and between the subjects and the sovereign: everyone and everything, be it the polity, the empire, or the world, assembled around the incarnate sun.

Despite maintaining a strong hold on those gathered around it, a glorious instantiation of authority is unable to keep *itself* together forever; it comes undone by the excess of internal heat and light. Contemporary Europe is trying to pick up the pieces of its imperial project, to reintegrate itself, even as it continues, schizophrenically, to rotate around two suns. Its current predicament aside, the pyropolitics of the sun has a long history and a slew of psychoanalytic undertones. A genealogy of heliopolitics will be my subject in this chapter.

CHAPTER 5. *THE END OF HELIOTROPIC UTOPIAS* 159

## 5.2. Heliocentric Unity and Its Discontents

Some millennia before it became a posh suburb of Cairo, Heliopolis (alternatively, On or Annu) served as the religious capital of Egypt. The "city of the sun," according its Greek designation, was the locale where numerous Egyptian deities were convened into a hierarchy, over which the sun god Ra presided.[276] Under the rays and the symbolism of the sun, theologico-political unity was forged, honouring "the One God who came into being in the beginning of time."[277] This formulation does not only anticipate Judaic monotheism; according to Freud, it *is* an earlier form of the Jewish religion, transferred by Moses-the-Egyptian to the tribes he led.[278] The important point, however, is that it was in connection with the sun god that the thought of "the One" first emerged in the Mediterranean basin.

Plato's decision in *The Republic* to position the sun over and above the sensible world, in analogy to the idea of the good, illuminating the rest of the eidetic sphere, is undeniably laden with a heavy Egyptian heritage. More relevantly for us, many early modern utopias embraced the sun allegory in imagining an ideal, flawlessly ordered polity. Tommaso Campanella's *La Città del Sole*, *The City of the Sun* (1602), derives its name from the official title of Prince Prelate, who combines theological and political sovereignty, and who is called either "the Sun," *Sole*, or "Metaphysician," *Metafisico*.[279] The city is *of the Sun*, because the Sun governs it as the epitome of reason and because it achieves its identity, as a city, insofar as it is entirely steeped in and appropriated by a single rational principle hovering above physical reality (hence, the reference to metaphysics).

Margaret Cavendish's 1666 *The Blazing World* is still more explicit in its defence of political and religious unity: just as "it was natural for one body to have but one head, so it was natural for a political body to have but one governor [...]; for there is but one God, whom we all unanimously worship and adore with one faith, so we are resolved to have but one Emperor, to whom we all submit with one obedience."[280] Identified with the sun that dominates the imperial palace and other signs of sovereign authority, the Emperor transfigures the world into a blazing whole, melting down all differences into the unity of a perfect state. A similar royal iconography will accompany the reign of Louis XIV, *le Roi-Soleil*, whose funeral in 1715 depicted the stages of his life as a celestial journey from sunrise to sunset.[281] The Sun King's apocryphal statement, *"l'état, c'est moi,"* "I am the state," produces political concord out of his shining and burning solar body, of which the subjects are supposed to partake as though it were the Eucharistic flesh of Christ.[282]

The dark underside of heliocentric totality is its belligerent stance vis-à-vis the rest of the political pluriverse that does not conform to its norms and does not appear in its light. The ironic opening of Cavendish's narrative relativises the blazing world with its sun that neither illuminates nor warms other worlds: "you must know, that each of these worlds having its own sun to enlighten it, they move each one in their peculiar circles; [...] we in this world cannot so well perceive them, by reason of the brightness of our sun, which being nearer to us, obstructs the splendour of the suns of the other worlds."[283] The sun and political sovereignty exercised in the orbit of a given political world are *not* the absolute conditions of possibility for seeing and living; instead, they are conditioned conditions and finite powers. The brightness of the sun sheds light onto a small cross-section of our reality even as it blinds us to what goes on in other time zones, let alone to the existence of other planetary systems with their own suns. Contrary to the thesis of *The Republic*, none of the political worlds (or their celestial guides) has a supreme claim over and against the others, which is why heliocentric utopias always cast the shadow of an *inter-world* war.

In Cavendish's masterpiece, one of the regal insignia of the Empress was "a spear made of a white diamond, cut like the tail of a blazing star, which signified that she was ready to assault those that proved her enemies."[284] *The City of the Sun* contains an extended apologia of war, fought against "enemies who are rebels to reason [*ribello della ragione*] and, as such, do not deserve to be called men."[285] Thomas Northmore's 1795 *Memoirs of Planetes*, sketching a utopian form of government, resorts to a strikingly similar just war theory. A war, in which one should be "most happily engaged," is one "of reason against insanity, or virtue against vice, of religion against atheism."[286] Thomas More's *Utopia*, too, permits the Utopians to wage war for defensive purposes, even though they "think nothing so inglorious as the glory won in battle."[287] Far from paradisiac refuges of peace, utopias transmit a feeling of besieged islands, where totalitarian tranquillity is ever on the verge of being disrupted by the chaotic and messy realities of the outside world (or worlds).

The heliocentric unity of the Sun King does not fare any better than that of various utopias, more or less contemporaneous with it. As Ellen McClure argues, the investment of royal authority with magnificent solar paraphernalia is a reaction, at once, to Galileo's discovery in 1610 of dark spots on the sun and to the potential weakening of monarchic power in the wake of the assassination of Henri IV, Louis XIV's grandfather, in the same year.[288] The integrity of the shining and burning body of the monarch is, at bottom, a barely veiled bid to reassemble the pieces of the already shattered political and cosmic order. Henri IV's successor is poetically depicted as a phoenix, born of the hot cinders of his father, from whom he inherited "*cette inclination solaire* [this solar inclination]."[289] And so, the Sun King himself is twice removed from the "authentic" *Roi-Soleil*, his assassinated grandfather.

Pierre Le Moyne's *The Art of Governing* takes pains to patch up crumbling cosmic and political orders by restoring to the sun its purity and disputing Galileo's observations. Vehemently disagreeing that the spots on the sun are a part of the celestial body, he writes that "*elles sont, ou de nos yeux que sa lumiere éblouit; ou de quelque corps jaloux qui luy fait ombre* [they are either from our eyes, blinded by its light; or from some jealous body that casts its shadow upon it]."[290] Le Moyne could not have conceded any imperfection to the sun itself or to the king himself, as both stand above "*[l]a corruption du Monde, la contagion des mauvais exemples* [the corruption of the world, the contagion of bad examples]."[291] But his solutions to the problem of spots on the sun scarcely promote his goal. If the first explanation applies, then the deficiency of the subjects' "sight" prevents them from fully recognising the absolute nature of royal sovereignty, ineffective without such recognition. If the second explanation is favoured, then there is another, more powerful political entity that can overshadow the glory of the king and deprive it of its absoluteness. In any of these scenarios, the immunity of the sun and of the sovereign to earthly corruption is not as important as what is outside their control, i.e., another power or recognition by the subjects. Le Moyne's protection of the sun and the king from empirical accidents fails.

Not only is the solar unity of sovereignty scattered *in advance* and must therefore reconstitute itself from ashes or cinders; not only is it in a state of perpetual war with other shining and burning instances of political power; but it also tears apart, from within, anyone or anything said to personify it. To distinguish between "the two bodies of the king" is to deal with the sundered source of power in a methodical and controlled way, by proposing that its earthly and finite instantiation does not entirely overlap with the transcendental principle it instantiates. Moreover, the assertion that a person or a community, whether "real" or imaginary, embodies the sun, having incorporated it without remainder, leads to the immediate splintering of the one into the many. The sun burns up the very unity it helps set up.

Such is the case of Daniel Paul Schreber, a German judge, who, upon suffering a neurotic breakdown, develops numerous solar fantasies, including one where "he can look into the sun unscathed and undazzled."[292] Freud's influential analysis of the Schreber case links his obsession with solar images to "nothing but another sublimated symbol for the father,"[293] and boasting about the ability to gaze directly at the sun — to a self-affirmation of the judge's filial lineage.[294] But everything in Schreber's story indicates that it is not so much about his identification with the father as it is about a doomed attempt at an immediate coincidence of the reflecting and the reflected or at recreating the full presence of the One, refracted into a multiplicity of rays that irradiate from it. Accordingly, as he relates in his memoirs, "I saw — if my memory does not wholly deceive me — two suns in the sky at the same time, one of which was our earthly sun, the other was said to be the Cassiopeia group of stars, drawn together into a single sun."[295] (He saw, we might say if our memory does not wholly deceive us, today's Europe.)

Schreber experiments with situations where the "material" and the "ideal" suns are fused together, where all distinctions between life and law collapse, and "the two bodies of the king" are consolidated. Indeed, madness itself is a repercussion of the failure to embody the sun, or the One, directly; it scatters the subject into the many, and this scatter is what defines schizophrenia, especially in the thought of Gilles Deleuze and Félix Guattari, who are right to de-Oedipalise Schreber and to locate solar power *within* his psychotic body: "Judge Schreber has sunbeams in his ass. A *solar anus.*"[296]

Here, Deleuze and Guattari allude to the title of Georges Bataille's 1927 essay ("The Solar Anus"), which, radicalising the psychoanalytic association of solar rays with phallic symbols, puts this staple figure of the Enlightenment (and of enlightenment) on the side of the intolerable and the obscene: "Human eyes tolerate neither sun, coitus, cadavers, nor obscurity, but with different reactions."[297] Nothing prevents the incandescent power and glory of the king and of a utopian city, standing for reason itself, from joining Bataille's list of obscenities. Heliocentric unity crumbles, falls to the ground, and rots inasmuch as it cannot be tolerated, either in and of itself or by those it illuminates. But before its downfall, Bataille tells us in the same text, the very announcement, by a madman or by a king, that "I AM THE SUN" produces "an integral erection [...] because the verb *to be* is the vehicle of amorous frenzy."[298] The copula, which is a basic mediation, is sexualised as the channel for the interpenetration of subject and predicate, or subject and object—"I" and "sun," "I" and "state." It allows for the buggery of power or of meaning (and, primarily, for their intercourse with themselves) before this raging "integral erection" finally falls to the ground.

## 5.3. The Solar Fetish of the Empire

At its inception, the colonial project involved the spread of fire from the metropolis to the newly conquered areas. In ancient Greece, the sacred fire perpetually burning in Prytaneion, or the public hearth, was carried by the colonists and kindled in far-away territories as part of foundation rites.[299]

The autochthonous nature of Athens was expressed in the belief that its Prytaneion was "unmoved" (*akineton*), in the sense that "she did not receive it (as a colony) from another city."[300] Like the Aristotelian "unmoved mover," the Athenian public hearth, embedded in its original place (which is also the place of the origin) imparted the soul of the *polis* to other areas that came under its control. Like a tree, it branched out and grew without leaving the spot where it germinated.

The initial and, for the time being, fragmentary notion of the world did not arise from dispassionate cartographic representations of land and sea but by transferring the light and heat of the metropolis elsewhere. Significantly, it was the same Greek historian Herodotus, who recorded the ritual of taking possession of a place (*khōra*) by lighting a fire there,[301] and who also reported, in Book 7 of *The Persian Wars*, the words of king Xerex upon the conquest of Egypt: "[...] and we shall extend the Persian territory as far as God's heaven [*toi Dios aitheri*] reaches. The sun will then shine on no land beyond our borders."[302] According to Xerex, there will still be lands beyond the borders of the Persian domain, but these territories will not enjoy the light of the sun that has become synonymous with Xerex's political rule.

Although the extent of the conquest is "as far as God's heaven reaches," the Persians are not yet engaged in building an all-encompassing political totality but merely wish to mark the difference between the sunny imperial realm and the dark expanses outside it. At the same time, the political determination of what should have been a straightforward astronomical fact proceeds *contra natura*, miraculously, by hindering an equal distribution of sunlight over the face of the earth and aiming to extend control over the physical elements, including the celestial fire of the sun. From early on, then, the imperial undertaking transcends strictly geopolitical categories.

In sixteenth-century Spain, King Charles V vaunted his empire as one over which "*jamás se pone el sol* [the sun never sets]," until the rebellion of the Netherlands put an end to this delusion of absolute control.[303] The sun that never sets is a brilliant emblem of sovereignty, a "beam of glory"[304] with radiance undiminished by the rhythms of planetary time. Following the precepts of Freudian psychoanalysis, the rising and setting sun, related to the figure of the phoenix with its cyclical deaths and rebirths, bespeaks the limited duration of male sexual excitation: "A short step further brings us to the phoenix, the bird which, as often as it is consumed by fire, emerges rejuvenated once more, and which probably bore the significance of a penis revivified after its collapse [...] earlier than that of the sun setting in the glow of evening and afterwards rising again."[305] Imperial power obviates the need for nocturnal rejuvenation, a periodic break that everything living requires in order to gather itself afresh for daytime activities. Instead, it acts out the fantasy of an ever-potent, undiminished erection in the shape of a never-setting sun, or, more abstractly, of pure phenomenality. It looms in excess of physical, natural limitations, in the words of British imperial administrator Sir George Macartney, as "this vast empire on which the sun never sets and whose bounds nature has not yet ascertained."[306]

In line with other metaphysical pipedreams, the heliophallocentric project of the empire wishes to obliterate time as periodicity, and, along with it, difference and finitude. The solar erection of imperial power constructs the world after its own image, so as to put an end, once and for all, to the political pluriverse and the possibility of conflict it holds. The globe is pacified on the condition that it bows before the phallic "beam of glory" — of a fire that does not burn out and the sun that does not set. In this unending political present, the empire does not see itself as separate from the sun, which it converts into a fetishistic supplement of its identity, eliminating distinctions not only between different parts of the world and "time zones" but also between the four elements. It harnesses the earth, the sea, air, and fire for the single purpose of generating a supernatural unity of empire, the unity greater than the sum of its territorial and maritime domains, aerial space, and heliomorphic parts. The subdued elements are the fetishes of the empire, compensatory devices for assuaging its castration anxiety (i.e., the fear that the sun/penis of its authority will *not* rise again), elemental substitutes for the male sexual organ that, nevertheless, commemorate the "horror of castration."[307]

As Patrícia Vieira has shown in her analysis of Portuguese colonialism, the empire was constituted around the disavowal of the true dimensions of continental Portugal by fetishistically mitigating political castration anxiety and, at the same time, erecting a "memorial" to it: "...on the one hand, the leaders of the New State were conscious of the true political, economic, and geo-strategic dimensions of the country as a peripheral European nation. On the other hand, they aggrandized Portugal by drawing attention to the size of its territory [...]. The empire thus functioned as a fetish that helped keep the illusion that the country was a great European power."[308] But what if, to extend Vieira's line of thought, geopolitical fetishes were only half the story? Doesn't pyro- or heliopolitical fetishism aggrandise the empire further, taking it beyond the confines of the earth, whose dimensions are no longer sufficient to fit all the imperial ambitions? Doesn't it function as a kind of fetish of the fetish, a phantasmal substitute of the substitute, which only exacerbates the logic of fetishism, assuaging and intensifying political castration anxiety?

If we contemplate the Portuguese case a little longer, we will realise just how momentous the solar fetish of the empire is. In the course of one of his sermons, seventeenth-century Jesuit priest and philosopher Antônio Vieira scrutinised the distorted proportions of the shadows that depended upon the sun's position in the sky. In his habitual style, mixing the figurative and the literal, he adverted: "*A sombra, quando o sol está no zênite, é muito pequenina [...]; mas, quando o sol está no oriente, ou no ocaso, essa mesma sombra se estende tão imensamente que mal cabe dentro dos horizontes. Assim nem mais nem menos os que pretendem e alcançam os governos ultramarinos. [...Q]uando chegam àquelas índias, onde nasce o sol, ou a estas, onde se põe, crescem tanto as mesmas sombras que excedem muito a medida dos mesmos reis, de que são imagens* [The shadow, when the sun is at the zenith, is very small [...]; but when the sun is in the East, or at dawn, this same shadow extends so immensely, that it barely fits on the horizon. The same applies exactly to those who desire and attain the rule of foreign lands. [...W]hen they arrive to those Indias, where the sun rises, or to these one, where it sets, the same shadows grow so much that they greatly exceed the measure of these kings, whose images they are.]"[309]

Across centuries, Vieira teaches a lesson on the internal undoing of the imperial solar fetish. In his elegant prose, in place of the sun itself, the shadows it casts on the earth denote the emperor's power, and the truth of this fetishistic substitute for political authority is but a distortion of the real dimensions of the figure whose shadow it is. The greater the empire, the farther it extends East and West, where the shadows are the longest, the greater the corruption of the image of the king, which overshoots the earthly orb. Even the sun's position at the zenith, at the very center of heliocentric power where Portugal is reduced to its "true" size of a small European country, fails to eclipse the shortest shadow — a fetishistic, ideological veil hiding the impotence of whoever casts it.

With regard to the shortest shadow, which has survived in the history of Western philosophy (most notably, in Nietzsche's Zarathustra), Alenka Zupančič suggests that such a shadow of a thing *is* that thing itself,[310] inseparable from its minimal representation. The predicament of the thing is also that of the phallus and of political power that project the threat of their negation, castration, or being deposed as though that threat were their faithful shadow, their innermost possibility. The "truth" of the thing, of the phallus, and of power is not the opposite of a fetishistic ideology extending their reach beyond all measure. It is, on the contrary, the doggedness of obscurity, impotence, and finitude in the midst of the brightest metaphysical reveries.

## 5.4. A Shining City upon a Hill: The Pyropolitical Sublime

The postcolonial era did not signal the end of heliocentric imperialism but merely its sublimation, cultural interiorisation, and further de-territorialisation or unhinging from the bedrock of geopolitics. Without a hint of irony, David Crystal writes, in *English as a Global Language*, that "English ha[s] become a language 'on which the sun never sets'."[311] Crystal repeats the words of British linguist Randolph Quirk, who recycled colonial discourse with the view to sealing the postcolonial linguistic and cultural hegemony of English by calling it "a language — the language — on which the sun does not set, whose users never sleep."[312] If language is the root of all meaning, then it illuminates the world, making it intelligible, just as the sun sheds light on sensible reality. Effectively, then, Quirk converts English, whose "users never sleep," into an ever-active force, spinning meaning day and night on a global scale, and chosen from among other languages to be something like the universal form of language (not *a* but *the* language). As for the impression that the sun never sets on English, it is presumed to corroborate the supernatural status of this *lingua franca*.

Because the United States could not earnestly imitate the example of Spain or Britain in proclaiming an actual global empire, it had to rely from the outset on the kind of spiritualisation, sublimation, and de-territorialisation of its influence that typifies the postcolonial period in Europe. So, for instance, early twentieth-century US politician, William Jennings Bryan wrote, quite tellingly, that "[i]f we cannot boast that the sun never sets on American territory, we can find satisfaction in the fact that the sun never sets on American philanthropy; if the boom of our cannon does not follow the Orb of Day in his daily round, the grateful thanks of those who have been the beneficiaries of American generosity form a chorus that encircles the globe."[313] A global spiritual empire, with which Bryan credits the United States, substitutes for the physical sun the alleged worldwide gratitude felt by the recipients of "American generosity." Tacitly, his narrative reverts to the country's foundations, with their distinctive mix of political and theological redemption in the allegory of a city upon a hill.

Before *Arbella* reached American shores in 1630, Puritan lawyer John Winthrop gave a sermon, in which he set the tone for the subsequent self-perception of the United States. He proclaimed, legendarily: "For we must consider that we shall be a city upon a hill. The eyes of all people are upon us, so that if we shall deal falsely with our God in this work we have undertaken, and so cause him to withdraw his present help from us, we shall be made a story and a byword through the world."[314] At first glance, the divine election that bestows on Winthrop and his fellow emigrants an exemplary status elevates them and the political community they build "on a hill," at a place where the earth itself strives toward the sky. Their elevated status, however, renders them totally visible from any point on earth, adding to God's internal scrutiny of their actions persistent judgment by the rest of humanity. The society to be built in the New World will be a transparent object of complete visibility, a pure community of conscience, requiring no enforcement aside from the all-penetrating gaze of others. There is a sense of exposure and vulnerability in this wellspring of "American exceptionalism" that equates divine election, with infinite responsibility it imposes on those elected, to an almost unbearable moral and political burden.

But the theological subtext of Winthrop's words narrates another story altogether. "A city upon a hill" evokes Matthew 5:14-6 — verses from the Sermon on the Mount with its address to the faithful: "You are the light of the world. A town built on a hill cannot be hidden. Neither do people light a lamp and put it under a bowl. Instead they put it on its stand, and it gives light to everyone in the house. In the same way, let your light shine before others, that they may see your good deeds and glorify your Father in heaven." The group of the chosen ones is the apotheosis of light and a precondition for seeing, not an object of sheer visibility. Clearly, the light its city sheds onto the world does not shine from physical heights, nor is it located anywhere within lived space, despite the hill being a protrusion of the earth. Spreading spiritual radiance devoid of heat, the polity of the elect is the most sublime fetish, unbound from the materiality of the sun and the earth, higher than any mountain, "superelevated," "higher than any comparable height, more than comparative, a size not measurable in height."³¹⁵ This is what St. Augustine had in mind when he envisaged "the City of God, which will shine all the more brightly when compared with the other [earthly] city."³¹⁶

While, in theology, the city upon a hill pertains to a community of faith lacking an earthly *dominium*, Winthrop and subsequent US politicians have gone to great lengths to paint future "America" as the City of God on earth, as spiritual light shining in the world. The phenomenology of American exceptionalism is such that an actual political regime proclaims itself to be indispensable for seeing and living in general, something that Margaret Cavendish, for example, could not accept. So potent is this proclamation that the meaning of the political is lost behind the luminosity of theological and moral frames of reference. "America" takes it upon itself to be the universal exception, invalidating any opposition a priori.

Having added the adjective *shining* to the proverbial city in both his inaugural addresses, Ronald Reagan intended to relieve it of the last shreds of political significance, even as the Cold War was raging on: "A troubled and afflicted mankind looks to us, pleading for us to keep our rendezvous with destiny; that we will uphold the principles of self-reliance, self-discipline, morality, and, above all, responsible liberty for every individual; that we will become that shining city on a hill."³¹⁷ Veering closer to St. Matthew than to Winthrop, Reagan defined the US not as an object of global vision but as the yardstick of illumination, where the "afflicted mankind looks to us," not *at* us. That light, moreover, was as sublime as the elevation of the shining city whose sovereignty proliferated well beyond its walls; it irradiated from freedom, graciously gifted by God and reflected around the world

## CHAPTER 5. *THE END OF HELIOTROPIC UTOPIAS* 173

through the American empire. A transcendent standard within the immanence of world history, the apolitical polity unwittingly imitated the beliefs of the Solarians, the citizens of Campanella's City of the Sun, "convinced that the whole world will eventually bring itself to live as they do."[318]

Pyropolitical unity, in the meantime, remains precarious. The sun of absolute monarchy had its black spots; the empire cast a distorted shadow on the earth; and the shining city on the hill concealed an obscure side of misery and injustice. Mario Cuomo's 1984 keynote address at the Democratic National Convention highlighted this dark side: "A shining city is perhaps all the president sees from the portico of the White House [...]. But there's another city; there's another part to the shining city; the part where some people can't pay their mortgages, and most young people can't afford one, where students can't afford the education they need, and middle-class parents watch the dreams they hold for their children evaporate." That is why, Cuomo concluded, "this nation is more 'A Tale of Two Cities', than it is just a 'Shining City on a Hill'."[319]

The Democrat's strategy was consistent with the tenets of pyropolitics: to dispel the charm of luminescent unity, it is necessary to de-idealise (or, more concretely, to de-fetishize and de-sublimate) it by foregrounding those material differences, such as the economic ones, that are levelled in and by fire. The fetish of the shining city, erected as a radiant example for the rest of the world to emulate, falls apart into two cities divided along class lines, which is exactly what the dazzle of a triumphalist moral-theological discourse obscures. As always, the truth of political power is not exposed under a light brighter yet than that of the ideal, but against the backdrop of the darkness, despair, and division that "cannot be hidden" by contrived perfection and its luminosity.

## 5.5. Westernisation, Nihilism, and the Setting Sun

More than a symbol, the sun has permitted humankind to orient itself, in time and in space, and so to come up with the first differentiations essential to any social or political order. Although the meaningful distinctions of *nomos* are engraved on the earth, the cues for their inscription come from the sky. As I wrote apropos of Kant's influential essay on orientation, where he suggests that "[t]o *orientate* oneself, in the proper sense of the word, means to use a given direction—and we divide the horizon into four of these—in order to find the others, in particular that of *sunrise [namentlich den* Aufgang]"[320]: "Orientation, which is admittedly a Western word, implies a predilection for the Orient, where the sun rises, and for a non-terrestrial element (the sun itself as the ancient heavenly blaze) that helps us get our bearings here on earth. Now, to seek orientation in the Occident is counterintuitive, because that particular direction has been associated with darkness, decline, and death as early as in ancient Egypt, where the default place for a necropolis has been on the Western bank of the Nile River. And yet, modernity has always sought its orientation in the West, from the discoveries of 'the New World' onwards. Perhaps, the most literal sense of dis-orientation, especially in the 'West' itself, is 'Westernisation,' that is, the loss of the Orient as the direction referred to 'in order to find the others.'"[321] Westernisation, *eo ipso*, inaugurates *anomie*, nihilism, and the defeat of heliocentric meaning, the ramifications of which are equivocal. Oswald Spengler's *The Decline of the West* should have been more appropriately entitled *The Decline Is the West*.

Since the first voyages to the Americas, European colonial powers saw in "the West" a blank screen, a virgin space for projecting their collective fantasies, deformed and enlarged, elsewhere. The same dynamic was replayed in North

America itself, where the "frontier" progressively shifted westward and signalled extreme danger as well as the life of "[i]nnovation, adaptation, and invention."[322] When, finally, US President James Monroe popularised the notion of *the Western Hemisphere* in 1823, the inversion of planetary political orientation was consummated by opposing "to the Eurocentric lines of a global worldview a new global line that was no longer Eurocentric and [that] called into question the global position of old Europe."[323]

For Schmitt, the gravitation of global power toward the West and the subsequent ascendance of American exceptionalism amounted to a certain denaturalisation and deconventionalisation, seeing that "the geographical and historical concepts of *West* and *East* are determined neither by nature nor by common agreements."[324] This is in contrast to North and South that "appear to be more exactly determinable. The earth is divided by the equator into northern and southern halves, which are not problematic in the sense of a division into eastern and western halves. We have a North Pole and a South Pole, not an East Pole and a West Pole."[325] Schmitt's unstated conclusion is that, in the absence of natural and social parameters, a hemispheric division of the globe, dictated by the fictitious "West," is the brainchild of *anomie* and nihilism. It represents the power of the setting sun, of death, of impotence, of powerlessness…

In chapter 2, I cited John Donne on the loss of the sun and touched upon the ambiguous impact of this loss on postmetaphysical politics. Insomuch as Donne beheld the beginning of the sunset, symbolic of modernity and the West, Nietzsche attended to its advanced phase in the end of Western metaphysics and the "death of God." The political closure of metaphysics is an inversion of imperial fetishism: in the global dusk, one senses that the sun will never rise over any empire, let alone over other human projects.

The bulk of the madman's announcement that "God is dead" takes place in the twilight of heliocentrism: "Who gave us the sponge to wipe away the entire horizon? What were we doing when we unchained this earth from its sun? Whither is it moving now? Whither are we moving? Away from all suns? Are we not plunging continually? Backward, sideward, forward, in all directions? Is there still any up or down? Are we not straying as through an infinite nothing?"[326] These questions absorb into themselves and condense the entire pathos of nihilism. The process of secularisation, coextensive with Western modernity, "wipes away" the horizon of intelligibility that God used to vouchsafe transcendentally. The "earth unchained from its sun" is a place where the previous coordinates of time and space no longer apply and chaotic nondifferentiation supersedes the routine signposts for human orientation.

The first markers to be abolished are "up" and "down," that is, the vertical axis of metaphysical transcendence. The earth's move "away from all suns" then means the dissolution of meaning in nihilistic darkness ("an infinite nothing") *or* the birth of a dim, non-heliocentric sense, which, Nietzsche confesses, is the still incomprehensible event: "For the few at least, [...] some sun seems to have set and some ancient and profound trust has been turned into doubt; to them our old world must appear daily more like evening [...]. But in the main one may say: The event itself is far too great, too distant, too remote from the multitude's capacity for comprehension even for the tidings of it to be thought as having *arrived* as yet."[327] This same indeterminacy plagues the non-heliocentric, aporetic, powerless power that is the political corollary of the postmetaphysical event. It can be the harbinger of

## CHAPTER 5. *THE END OF HELIOTROPIC UTOPIAS* 177

nihilistic technocracy *or* of a more modest political ontology, rid of phallic phantasies and fetishes, sublime ideality and dazzling glory.

Formulating his methodology in *The Decline of the West* (1918-23), Spengler helps himself to healthy doses of sun-related imagery. Spengler's overarching goal is to introduce into historiography a Copernican turn akin to the one Kant initiated in philosophy: to overturn the "*Ptolemaic system* of history," with its assumption that Europe is "the presumed centre of all world-happenings," in favour of a world-historical model where the relation between the West and the rest is not the same as the gravitational pull between the sun and the planets populating the solar system.[328] In keeping with the Nietzschean program of "unchaining the earth from its sun," Spengler undermines the European usurpation and monopolisation of historical spirit and disallows the "privileged position to the Classical or the Western Culture as against the Cultures of India, Babylon, China, Egypt, the Arabs, Mexico — separate worlds of dynamic being."[329] But he falls short of denouncing the internal hegemony of each civilisation with its own solar centre of semantic authority. As far as his work is concerned, the event of powerless power and of a dim, non-heliocentric sense is unfathomable.

Cold and nihilistic, Western sun manages to enchant those who are outside its direct sphere of influence by passing its light and frigidity for the shimmer of universality, which, as we have seen with reference to Hegel, is deadly. But the stratagems of the false universal are generally far from effective. Defining its particular interests as those of the global community, the West puts itself in the empty place of the universal, equates itself to the totality of which it is a part, and so legitimises itself as the (utopian) representative of the whole world. In the confusion that ensues, the categories, if not the processes, of Westernisation and globalisation start to overlap. And, conversely, the enemies of the West are decried as the enemies of the world, threatening its peace and stability with the violence of lightless heat, with which we are already acquainted.

The seduction of the Western sun has proven to be overpowering in the case of nineteenth-century Russian philosopher Pyotr Chaadayev. In an aphorism, Chaadayev confessed: "A Russian liberal is a pointless fly, fluttering about in a sunray; that sun is the sun of the West."[330] The space of liberal theory and praxis is a priori occupied—pre-occupied—by the West, the perennial "City of the Sun," which awakens in Chaadayev the stirrings of admiration *and* nihilistic despair. Russian liberals are superfluous, having arrived too late and from a relative outside on the sunny scene of liberalism. All they can do is let the rays of Western sun illuminate their pointless fluttering about. The futility of their movements recalls the sense of disorientation factored into Westernisation. To this disorientation, some prefer a relapse into the most rigid of traditionalisms that set life back within fixed heliocentric parameters. While Europe is divided along the North-South axis, in Ukraine and Egypt, Turkey and Russia, a power struggle between Westernisers and traditionalists results in inner clefts that make these countries rotate on a bewildering orbit around two suns.[331]

## 5.6. Coda: Politics of Fire and Sexual Difference

After mentioning the conventional gendering of pyropolitics, here and at various other points in this book, it would be unforgivable to gloss over the issue of sexual difference and its relation to fire. In psychoanalysis, fire is the elemental coil of desire, physiology, and the drive to control the natural environment and human others. In addition to the obvious association of desire with burning, Freud locates the struggle between an urge to extinguish an actual flame by urinating on it, on the one hand, and a restrained decision to let it burn, on the other, at the origins of civilisation. As he speculates in a footnote to *Civilisation and Its Discontents*, power over external fire, whose tongues were reminiscent of an erection as they shot up skywards, was the sublimation of a "homosexual competition" with this sublime, symbolic, fiery male. Women were excluded from the contest in view of their physiology: "her anatomy made it impossible for her to yield to the temptation of this desire." Men, however, could preserve a burning fire only through a heroic feat of renouncing their infantile desire. Controlling themselves, they would then subdue and control the fire.[332] Their power over others is, in the first instance, predicated on a self-overcoming, self-control, and tremendous psychic repression.

It follows from this initial observation that the contrast between the fiery masculine principle and the watery feminine is somewhat simplistic. Women, analogised to the "Earth-Mother," house an inner fire, similar to the earth that emits heat from its innermost core, allowing metals to gestate in the ores.[333] Men must reconcile the two functions of the penis, its fiery erection and watery ejaculation or urination, without reducing the one to the other.

When, in 1931, Freud picks up the interpretative thread he left off in *Civilisation and Its Discontents*, he is mindful of the fact that such a reconciliation would risk disavowing the difference between the two, in the manner of a child who disavows sexual difference by equating women to castrated men. "The sexual organ of the male has two functions," he writes in a short essay on "The Acquisition and Control of Fire." "It serves for the evacuation of the bladder, and it carries out the act of love which sets the craving of the genital libido at rest. The child still believes that he can unite the two functions. According to a theory of his, babies are made by the man urinating into the woman's body."[334] More infantile yet, the heliocentric fetishism of the empire, the sovereignty of the Sun King, and the radiant utopias of modernity believe themselves to be ceaselessly and autonomously productive or reproductive and, in their delusion of grandeur, forget about the other function of the male sexual organ. Theirs is the dream of preserving their magnificent political clout without the renunciation of desire that the acquisition of fire presupposes.

That is why it would be a mistake to label pyropolitics as a whole *promethean*. Freud is adamant that the "Bringer of Fire [...] had renounced an instinct and had shown how beneficent, and at the same time how indispensable, such a renunciation was for the purposes of civilisation."[335] Hence the punishment the gods allotted to Prometheus: daily, a vulture fed on his liver, seeing that "[i]n ancient times the liver was regarded as the seat of all passions and desires."[336] Essentially, such a punishment was self-inflicted, since the hero had to pay with the fire of his own desire, which could no longer be enacted immediately and so was painfully wasted at its source, for procuring the civilising fire. The absurdity of political heliocentrism is that, as the self-proclaimed pinnacle of civilisation, it shuns the psychic process that made civilisation possible, or, at the very least, passes the burden squarely onto those it subjects and dominates. The unfulfillable demand is one of the reasons for its downfall.

The elemental division between "watery" women and "igneous" men can also work the other way around, while still harking back to the disavowal of sexual difference. A common form of this disavowal is the infantile hypothesis that women are the *already* castrated men; a less prevalent form inheres in the theory of a seventeenth-century French doctor Pierre-Jean Fabre, who thought that "women are men in a latent state because they have the male elements hidden within them."[337] Faced with Fabre's theory, which he has unearthed, Bachelard inquires: "How better can it be stated that the principle of fire is the male activity and that this wholly physical activity, like an erection, is the principle of life? The image that men are merely women dilated by heat is easy to psychoanalyse."[338] The struggle is over a principle, a beginning that would have been unified and unbroken, the same shared by all, yet more developed in some. Whoever possesses the principle of life gains control over life itself, except that the elemental beginnings of vitality are dispersed into four "principles," only one of which is fire. The latency of fire in women translates the potentialities of Aristotelian matter that actualises itself in being formed, in attaining its realisation, in entelechy. Yet, as Fabre among others implies, their fecundity is not really theirs but is due to the incomplete masculine presence they harbour. This early modern myth adds to the theft of fire from the gods by Prometheus the theft of a birth-giving power from women by men.

The clandestine act of stealing fecundity from existence in the feminine is prominent in Irigaray's reading of Plato's Myth of the Cave. The *hystera* is "a place shaped like a cave or a womb,"[339] starting from which men will give *themselves* birth and move into eidetic daylight, without the participation of the mother. "At the zenith of transcendence," the "Idea, the Being, the Idea (of) Being mask the *dehiscence* of an origin that is never recognized as (product of) copulation. [...] The second birth, secondary origin, renaissance or reminiscence of truth will never, simply, defer the *hysterical tropism*. The discourse of reason, solar and paternal metaphor, will never oust the fantasy structure of the cave completely."[340] The dehiscence of the origin implies that everything begins with a split between the material and the ideal, the maternal and the paternal, a physical birth and a renaissance in the realm of Ideas. Moreover, having stemmed from self-control, self-abnegation, and the repression of desire, the second term in each dyad draws toward itself and incorporates everything that is valuable and laudable, leaving the first term behind, as though it were trash. "At the zenith of transcendence," in the intense glare of the Platonic sun, neither the dehiscence of the origin nor the mimicking of the first beginning by the second ("the fantasy structure of the cave") nor, again, the non-ocular, non-theoretical, thermal effect of fire come to light. The metaphorical theft of the solar blaze from the elements and of life-giving warmth from the mother will stay in the blind spot of transcendental vision.

The castrated, neutral light of reason that germinates from the second beginning grants castration a power more potent than that of an undying erection. Freud failed to notice this strange negativity: Prometheus did not renounce (castrate) a purely positive instinct but avoided extinguishing (castrating) the incendiary symbol of erection, negating its negation. Better than Freud, Derrida pinpointed, in *Glas*, the trick of a renunciation that accumulates more power than what it renounces by pre-empting the threat of loss: "He exhibits his castration as an erection that defies the other."[341] A powerless power may, at any moment, don this terrifying mask of a self-immunising castration. But it may do so only on the condition that it keep its allegiance to the second beginning, which does not know *that* it has misappropriated something from the first and is unaware of *what* it has misappropriated. It matters whether the extinguishing and flaring up of fire (and of heliocentric meaning) is part of its calculated displacement in the pyropolitical *fort/da* game or whether the destitution of phallic radiance is final and complete, because no longer related to specula, speculations, sight or blindness, light or darkness. If the latter, then—and only then—can we ask together with Luce Irigaray, "Is fire not joy? Is burning with you not grace?"[342] and append our own question to these: Full of grace, is this burning-with, still or already political?

# Chapter 6.
## Around the Hearth: Politics in the Kitchen

### 6.1. The Power of the Hearth, or the Domestication of Politics

In our explorations thus far, we have held onto the idea that fire cannot be conceived as an element of sheer destruction. Its positive, life-giving force derives, for instance, from the heat it emits as the sun, or celestial fire, stimulating the growth of plants. The "conquest" of the element allowed humans to keep warm in the depths of winter. For Indo-European consciousness, the very thought of dwelling has been inseparable from the hearth burning at the centre of a house. The *harmyá* of the Vedic hymns signifies "habitation," even though the original sense of the word is "fire-pit" (and, later on, "hearth").[343] In ancient Rome, the guardian spirit of the living quarters was *lar familiaris*, whose dancing image was stored in a niche by the hearth in poorer households or in a special shrine called *lararium* in wealthy domiciles.[344] Keeping a memory of this custom, Latin-based languages, such as Portuguese, still refer to a house as *lar* and to a fireplace as *lareira*.

There is no dwelling without an inner fire, around which the house is constructed and its inhabitants gather for nourishment and warmth. An animal or a human may be thought of as a temporary interiorisation and delimitation of a small portion of cosmic fire, metamorphosed into animating, vital heat. A house analogously circumscribes a bit of the immense blaze inside the four walls of the private sphere. The real provenance of the Roman *lares* that were, originally, "the spirits of the fields"[345] are the wide expanses of the outdoors, cordoned off from the rest of open space.

The hearth and the dwelling it embodies are the figures of inner fire, of a flame that has been captured, subdued, regulated, measured, and put in the service of life. In the Greco-Roman world goddesses Hestia and Vesta were assigned to watch over the hearth; in Celtic mythology it was the goddess Brigid, who took care of domestic fire.[346] The gendering of these divinities is, obviously, not accidental, given that women were confined to the private sphere, charged with the tasks of cooking and maintaining the warmth (not only of the physical variety!) of everyday existence, and, from a psychoanalytic perspective, could keep the fire burning without the urge of extinguishing it. What is perhaps more astounding is that the flame of the household was, once again, exteriorised, smuggled into the public realm, and transposed onto collective existence.

To document this move, we ought to return to *koinē hestía*, or the common hearth, which burnt at Prytaneion, the seat of Greek government and power, and which we have visited in the preceding chapter,[347] as well as to Forum Romanum that also housed governmental structures, among them the hearth-temple of Vesta. While the fire of Prytaneion supplied the heat and the light for Greek colonisation, the Forum "reproduced the design of the individual house, with Janus as the taboo-ridden boundary between it and the outside world and Vesta as the sacred centre, the source of life within."[348] In both cases, the status of Hestia and Vesta in civil religion is highly significant: the inclusion of the hearth within the public space bespeaks the domestication of the political sphere, such that the city becomes nothing but a large family of families, or a common household. What is henceforth staged on the political arena is the spectacle of civil society.

Already Aristotle forewarned his readers against confusing the political and the economic domains in the first lines of *The Politics*. "Those then who think," he writes, "that the natures of the statesman [*politikon*], the royal ruler [*basilikon*], the head of an estate [*oikonomikon*] and the master of a family [*despotikon*] are the same, are mistaken" (1252a, 5-10). For Aristotle, the difference between a large household and a small city is not merely quantitative; it is not measured in the number of members, but in the kind of the good pursued by each of these communities. The ultimate goal of politics is freedom among equals in the exercise of reason, as opposed to the household (the *oikos* of *oikonomia*, which is of course translatable as "house") where necessity rules both through the tyranny of "natural needs" and through the hierarchical relations of dominance and subordination. That is why the fire of the domestic hearth can never legitimately emblematise political coexistence.

A diligent student of Aristotle will retort that he describes the symbolic mainstay of public authority with reference to the common hearth, *koinē hestía*, from which high officials "derive their honour [*timē*]" (*Politics* 1322b, 25-30). But is "honour," which pertains to the burning or spirited part of the psyche, an undisputedly political term? Isn't *timē* an economic concept, which implies esteem as much as worth, value, price, or even compensation? If that is the case, then Aristotle provides a tongue-in-cheek commentary on a custom, which, by way of its connection to the hearth and to domestic fire, is excluded from the logic of the political and brought back to the socio-economic underpinnings of authority. After all, the Greek Prytaneion was not only the site for guarding fire (*pyr*) but also for storing grain (*sitos*),[349] which further accentuated its pecuniary function.

For the inhabitants of a Greek *polis*, the link between the common hearth and granary must have seemed entirely natural. The germinal power of seeds was intimately related to that of fire, which also propagated, as though by rapid self-dissemination, through what Pindar dubs the "seed of flame."[350] Even more overtly economic was the version of Hestia as the "treasurer" on the island city of Cos. There, with money deposited at her feet, she "stood for 'the collection of revenues', the 'depository of common wealth'."[351] The common hearth was, at best, a reference to the economic aspects of politics, which have become predominant millennia later, in our own largely technocratic ideal of the political as a good managerial practice.

Within a private dwelling, a hearth supplied heat and was a place for cooking food. Needless to say, cooking initially carried sacrificial connotations as well, and Hestia "took possession of the fat offered up on the *hestia*" as payment for her "unalterable virginity."[352] By abjuring the establishment of a household (or the hearth) of her own, she gained the right of admission into every household; the exception she took to family life insinuated her as a universal power and presence into the burning centre of every residences. (To Tibetan Buddhists, too, the hearth was sacred, sacrificial grounds, upon which the god *t'ablha* received a portion of uncooked food that was left untouched for him.[353]) Her subtraction from the prevalent marital order, equipped Hestia with everything she needed to institute the economy of sacrifice at a daily ceremonial meal, during which the city "fed those who held power in the name of the rest."[354] The fire of the sacred hearth, on which food was prepared, invested political representation with the requisite symbolism, imparting to the magistrates Hestia's exceptional universality and enabling them to eat and to speak on behalf of everyone else. Similar to the way it blended together sundry ingredients in a cooked dish, fire momentarily melted the distinction between the representatives and those they represented. Thus, daily sacrificial meals reaffirmed and celebrated a prominent part that stood for the whole or that opened its mouth, so as to eat or to speak, *in the name of* the whole.

The confinement of fire to a hearth, with the subsequent construction of the polity around a domesticated flame, takes the sting out of the political, replacing its incalculable risk with economic calculations and payoffs. On a more personal level, Bachelard masterfully explained the substitution with recourse to the taming of passion: "The haphazard passion becomes the deliberate passion. Love becomes family; fire becomes hearth and home. This normalization, this socialization, this rationalization, are often, because of the awkwardness of the new forms of expression, considered to represent a cooling down of the passions."[355] The same is true for political affect: in virtue of the citizens' feeling of belonging to the extended family that is the *polis*, they gather around a common hearth, their internal conflicts and quarrels mitigated and a certain degree of cohesion achieved. Homogenisation is the main course served in the political kitchen where the flame is carefully regulated so that previously disparate ingredients (or participants) would come together in a new blend, formally reminiscent of alchemical smelting in revolutionary politics and the solar unities of early modern utopias.

To sum up: the fire of the hearth incorporates difference into the domestic, familiar and familial, sphere. Already tamed in and of itself, it harnesses everything and everyone it touches to the interiority to which it belongs. More concretely, Hestia presided "over the intermingling and coalescence of disparate elements," in "what might be called *panspermia*, the term used for a ritual offering of many different types of grain that became indistinguishable when cooked over a fire."[356] The banquet in her honour followed strict guidelines, according to which "nothing was to be introduced from the outside and nothing was to be taken outside": only certain kinds of food were admitted and had to be consumed without leaving a remainder behind.[357]

The political reverberations of the culinary ritual hardly need explaining. Once *body politic* coalesces into a coherent whole, represented by *panspermia*, its integrity depends on the policing of limits and on pinpointing exactly what can enter and what can leave the "cooked" mix. So potent is the unifying power of the hearth that it spills over cultural boundaries and can be sensed not only in ancient Greece or Rome but also in Tibet, since, for Tibetan Buddhists, "the productive and reproductive functions of the house as a single unit of wealth" and "a single ritual object" accrete around the central hearth.[358] At its apogee, this power extinguishes cultural difference as such, casting it into a "melting pot," into which the United States sought to refashion itself in the course of the twentieth century. The American dream of creating *e pluribus unum*, "out of many, one," is a late product of Hestia's and Vesta's political kitchen.

## 6.2. The Inner Fire of the 'Kitchen Cabinet'

The ancients regarded inner fire as a manifestation of the spirited soul, or *thymos*, "the impulsive centre of the proud self,"[359] responsible, among other things, for the inflammation of revolutionary spirits. The bodily organ, corresponding to *thymos* and residing in the chest,[360] is the heart[361] — a flaming, hidden interiority that animates the organism. The interiorisation and economisation of the political dimension in a collective dwelling dominated by a common hearth follows to the letter the spatial position of the heart, concealed behind the ribcage in the depths of the body. (In English, both 'hearth' and 'heart' refer to the proto-Indo-European root *ker*, evocative of heat, burning, and fire.) The source of vitality, this inner flame, is not easy to disclose without seriously interfering with the integrity and the life of the organism that harbours it. In turn, the economic, essentially domestic, version of politics sneaks the qualities of private life into the public realm, rendering it all the more secretive and non-transparent. The *arcana*, which Schmitt deemed vital to the political,[362] might, in the end, be due to the conflation of the *polis* with the *oikos* and of pyropolitics with *koinē hestía*.

With these considerations in mind, I would like to turn to the phenomenon of a "kitchen cabinet." Coined during the tenure of US President Andrew Jackson, who suspended formal cabinet consultations in his first administration, this term had a strong resonance in the twentieth century, for instance, in the political practices of Golda Meir in Israel or Harold Wilson and Margaret Thatcher in Great Britain. A kitchen cabinet is "a closed and constantly informal circle of associates, friends and insiders," the composition of which "is a matter of speculation and [...] changes quite quickly according to circumstances."[363] Granted: this informal circle is not really a political cabinet in the original sense of the word, as Richard Longaker concluded in 1957,[364] but it is a hidden linchpin of crucial decisions, the space for transmuting raw ideas into policy initiatives. Paraphrasing Longaker, then, we can ask: Is the kitchen cabinet really a (political) kitchen?

It is only fitting that the coinage itself was as shrouded in mystery as the informal consultations Jackson conducted with his confidants. Born of Washington speculation and "slapped onto the administration by its foes," the label stuck to the advisors "slipping into Jackson's study by way of the back stairs through the kitchen."³⁶⁵ Although to historians this might appear as a minor fact, we cannot afford to ignore the foregrounding of the kitchen, especially because it is pitted against "the parlour": Jackson's official group of ministers and advisers was sometimes designated "the parlour cabinet" and the president of the Bank of the United States was concerned that "the kitchen [...] predominate[s] over the Parlor."³⁶⁶

The kitchen and the parlour are divisions of a house, which means that, regardless of how fissured, the political process migrates to the household. The *oikos* becomes the platform for decision-making that would affect everyone in the *polis*. But not all areas of the house are identical: the parlour is adapted for receiving guests and, generally speaking, opens the dwelling to the outside; the kitchen, on the contrary, is an intimate space where the fire of the hearth is burning and the nourishing heat and food for the family are generated. A clash between the two quarters, then, replicates a much deeper-running rift between the concerns of the mind and those of the body, the entertaining discussion or musical performances taking place in the parlour and the mouths full of food or gossip in the kitchen. Under Jackson, the Cartesian mind/body split matches the polarisation of the political process, mapped onto different parts of the domicile.

An inheritor of the ancient hearth, the kitchen is the living heart of the house and, much as the preparation of food that goes on there has been gendered and devalued, it has continued in secret to rule over the rest of the dwelling. The prejudice against the kitchen is rooted in the conception of cooking as a crude activity mired in the physical needs of the body and concerned with the processing of raw natural products. Jackson and his closest circle of associates, "the kitchenites," earned their nickname, precisely, based on "their reputation for unpolished manners."[367] If, ideally, politics is a spiritual enterprise, then the crudeness of manners or of manual labour, such as cooking, are incompatible with it. Unless we remember that, like politics, cooking is an art and an original one at that—the first *technē*, inaugurated by the fire of Prometheus! Resorting to the transformative and refining effect that fire brings to bear on raw materials, it is a way of "culturing" nature, which demands of its practitioners the mastery, timing, and regulation of heat. At its best, the art of the political relies on these very skills in its mediation between a merely natural belonging and citizenship, oppositional formations, and conflicting visions of the future.

From early nineteenth-century United States to mid twentieth-century Israel and late twentieth-century Britain, kitchen cabinets continued to thrive. Israeli Prime Minister Golda Meir was wont to convene a close circle of advisors at her residence on Saturday nights, in anticipation of Sunday's official cabinet meetings. Known as "Golda's Kitchen," this decision-making body brandished real power behind the scenes, while ministers were expected to rubberstamp the conclusions reached during the informal sessions.[368] Her guests did not pass through the cooking quarters, as did those of Jackson, but gathered in the living room of the Prime Minister, who frequently went "in and out of her kitchen to bring coffee and sandwiches for those present."[369]

The erasure of distinctions between the social and the political facilitated a re-imposition of traditional feminine roles—taking care of the hearth and of men's bodily needs— onto the most powerful figure in Israeli politics at the time. Care for life and bellicose foreign policy also intermingled, permitting "the metaphor 'Golda's Kitchen' [to] camouflage its function as a *war room*."[370] Coupled with Meir's supposed "anti-intellectualism,"[371] the relegation of her politics to the house was redolent of Jackson's "unpolished" character, which was similarly associated with the kitchen.

Given the link between the heart and the hearth, the allegedly crude, anti-intellectual, or unpolished predilections of Jackson, Meir, and other kitchen politicians will be taken by Enlightenment apologists as signs that, during the secret sessions, emotion prevailed over reason. For, who would seriously think that political kitchen's procedure for deliberation was predicated on dispassionate debate and rational argumentation and counter-argumentation? That hands-on political involvement "in the heat of the moment" precludes this normative imposition from the get-go is beside the point. What is more important is that, in contemplating the interiority of the heart, we have lost sight of another fiery interiority, which is undoubtedly more relevant to the political phenomenon (or, rather, the non-phenomenon) in question. I mean the stomach.

Philippe Hecquet, an eighteenth-century medical researcher in Paris, "explains the fire of digestion in the light of his theory of stomachal trituration, by recalling that a wheel can catch fire by being rubbed along the ground,"[372] implying that cooking both replicates and aids this digestive fire. Friction between surfaces, opposition, and contention are at the physical origin of combustion, "stomachal trituration," and the political kitchen. When it comes to digestion, nonetheless, Hecquet recognises that its fire needs to be moderated and that the "juices in our bodies are all the more perfect, the less they partake of those *creatures* of fire that chemistry produces, & physics presupposes."[373]

In the context of a cross-cultural history of ideas, Hecquet's revelation is akin to re-inventing the wheel, since, well before his time, Hindu thought had already postulated that "there is a fire in the belly (called the fire that belongs to all men) that digests all the food you eat by cooking it (again)."[374] A technical supplement of digestion, cooking moderates our inner fire and perfects our bodily "juices." But, as a deconstructive supplement, it comes *before* the thing it supplements, preceding the natural combustion that happens in the stomach. The kitchen cabinet is also the supplement of official political structures that adhere to and regurgitate the ideas first cooked there. It decreases the heat of formal cabinet discussion by absorbing the thermal energy of contention, much like the fire of the stove mitigates that of digestion. Dissimulated power resides in these inscrutable spaces outside politics *proper*.

The sheltering of the political process in the house and, especially, in the kitchen was indicative of a broadly economic construction of the political domain and resistance to the Enlightenment programme of a purely translucent public sphere. Unstipulated in any procedural regulations or protocols, kitchen cabinets were exceptional environments for making decisions, analogous to the extra-juridical or non-institutional lacunae Schmitt identified as propitious for the exercise of sovereignty. Here, however, the exteriority of the exception was one and the same as its interiorisation within the flaming heart of the house. The fire of the hearth, essential to the kitchen, gives off intimate light and heat that, instead of bolstering transparency and public lucidity, put into sharper relief the secretive and personalist aspects of sovereignty.

That the interiorisation of politics can wind on almost indefinitely is attested by the still more exclusive gatherings of Meir's "inner kitchen" that preceded the sessions of Golda's Kitchen. The former meetings were scrupulously isolated from the public sphere, as they "were never announced or talked about,"[375] in contrast the Saturday night discussions where minutes were taken. As a rule, the closer a group of associates inched to the hearth, the more it dwindled, the less visible was its political dynamic, and the more fateful the outcomes of the meetings. In this, the informal arrangement of the political kitchen, with concentric circles of proximity to the flaming core, replicates the spatial configuration of the sacred in Judaism, progressing from the outer temple wall to the innermost sanctuary, "the Holy of Holies."

### 6.3. What's Cooking in the Melting Pot?

Yet another figure of interiority related to the culinary arts is that of a pot, which, already in ancient China, symbolised the state. The Chinese *ding*, shaped as a tripod cauldron, carried cosmological significance, as it bounded the empty space inside it in the right proportion; hence, the expression *ding-zheng*, "making right."[376] A psychological corollary of this delimitation was the restriction of mental space, within which the correctness of a proposition could be assessed in a manner evocative of Kant's critique of reason. A political offshoot of the practice of *ding-zheng* was the demarcation of a territory for the exercise of good governance.

"Making-right," indicating fitness to rule, involved nine legendary cauldrons, "cast in remote antiquity by the sage-king Yu": "In the capital of a virtuous leader, they were immovably heavy, but under a wicked ruler they were light and easily removable."[377] The focus of cosmological, psychological, and political appropriations of the *ding* was, to be sure, on empty space and its proper distribution, management, and use. At the same time, the cauldron is neither a box nor any other container whatsoever nor a merely formal delimitation of space. Its function is to accommodate a new mix or a changed substance within its walls, heated by fire. Hence, the "Fire over Wood" hexagram for the cauldron may also denote "renewal" in light of the flame's transformative effect on what is cooked.[378]

The US immigration policy of the melting pot echoes both the Chinese state symbolism of the *ding* and the Greek ritual preparation of *panspermia* (the undifferentiated blend of various types of seeds), along with glaring allusions to the alchemical furnace. Intended to create a more or less homogeneous body of citizenry, the policy encouraged cultural assimilation on the part of recent immigrants. James Davis, US Labour Secretary from 1921 to 1930, envisaged himself as "a master puddler of humanity" who had to "gather thousands of men into a melting-pot and boil out the envy, greed and malice as much as possible and purify the good metal of human sympathy."[379] In contrast to the *ding*, the American pot was constructed around the excess of negative human affects and parochial strife that had to be purified by boiling. But, like the Chinese cauldron, it had the function of making right the injustices of the past by mending divides, healing the wounds of conflicts, and calming the traumatic memories of massacres. That, at least, was the idea behind Israel Zangwill's play *The Melting Pot*, which was dedicated to Theodore Roosevelt and which lent its name to the American immigration policy.

The play's plot revolves around a love story between David, a young talented Jewish musician who survived the Kishinev pogroms and found refuge in New York, and Vera, a daughter of Russian aristocrats, who fled to the New World after engaging in subversive political actions against tsarist regime. As David confesses to his uncle Mendel, however, his love for Vera pales next to his love of America that melts distinctions between people and nourishes their peaceful coexistence. On American soil, Zangwill suggests, Jews should not fear assimilation, since the fire of this country's love is a singular event on the horizon of their long history:

MENDEL [*With prophetic fury*]
    The Jew has been tried in a thousand fires and only tempered and annealed.
DAVID
    Fires of hate, not fires of love. That is what melts.
MENDEL [*Sneeringly*]
    So I see.
DAVID
    Your sneer is false. The love that melted me was not Vera's—it was the love *America* showed me—the day she gathered me to her breast.[380]

The fire of the melting pot blends assorted ingredients because it emits the heat of love that softens, rather than that of hatred tempering metals. This softening heat buttresses the light of liberty as the other half of the phenomenon of fire, embodied in the promise of America that shines its torch all over the world.[381] Clinging to her breast, David repeats, in miniature, the projection of the hearth, which is the icon of the private dwelling, onto the public sphere: he transposes the intimate emotion of love onto the relation between a freshly minted citizen and the country that attracts immigrants toward itself while making romantic love between newcomers, David and Vera, possible. The softening heat of this love prepares the protagonist, who will later learn that his beloved's father was responsible for the massacre of his family members, to forget, if not to forgive, the atrocities he left behind in the Old World of Europe. The melting pot thus combines the three main functions of cooking: mediating between, blending, and perfecting the cooked ingredients.

The most thought-provoking part of the play is, in fact, David's vision of America as "God's Crucible" and of the model American as the new Adam, or, to keep to the alchemical framework, so obvious here, a homunculus:

VERA
    So your music finds inspiration in America?
DAVID
    Yes—in the seething of the Crucible.
VERA
    The Crucible? I don't understand!
DAVID
    Not understand! You, the Spirit of the Settlement!
    [*He rises and crosses to her and leans over the table, facing her.*]
    Not understand that America is God's Crucible, the great Melting-Pot where all the races of Europe are melting and re-forming! Here you stand, good folk, think I, when I see them at Ellis Island, here you stand
    [*Graphically illustrating it on the table*]
    in your fifty groups, with your fifty languages and histories, and your fifty blood hatreds and rivalries. But you won't be long like that, brothers, for these are the fires of God you've come to—these are the fires of God. A fig for your feuds and vendettas! Germans and Frenchmen, Irishmen and Englishmen, Jews and Russians—into the Crucible with you all! God is making the American.[382]

Glaring in their absence from "God's Crucible" are Native Americans and African Americans, not to mention non-European immigrants from Asia and other parts of the world. The premise of the melting pot is that, to create a perfect mix, the right ingredients must be combined in a correct proportion and that what is not "right" or "correct" ought to be excluded from the interiority of the vessel. In 1892, for instance, less than two decades before the composition of Zangwill's play, the Anti-Japanese Movement first gained momentum on the West Coast of the US, culminating in the segregation of Japanese students in Chinese schools the following year.[383] By the 1920s, the champion of the melting pot, Secretary Davis, advocated (as Trump would nearly a hundred years later) "selective immigration or none" and lamented the decline of the American stock and standards of living due to the influx of immigrants from Southern and Eastern Europe.[384] His intolerance toward certain European ethnicities evinced still more xenophobia than Zangwill's theologically tinged fantasy of perfecting ("melting and re-forming") Europe in the American Crucible.

The fire of love, above which the melting pot is boiling, is imbued with a redemptive potential for those lucky to gain admittance into the mix. Everything that torments Europe, from "blood hatreds" to crime and subversive politics, is supposed to be cleansed, to grow innocuous, and to melt away soon after immigrants from the continent land on Ellis Island. A comical dialogue between Vera's father (the baron) and his American host illustrates this point well:

BARON [*Points to window, whispers hoarsely*]
    Regard! A hooligan peeped in!
QUINCY [*Goes to window*]
    Only some poor devil come to the Settlement.
BARON [*Hoarsely*]
    But under his arm — a bomb!
QUINCY [*Shaking his head smilingly*]
    A soup bowl.[385]

Zangwill's joke is entirely pyropolitical: the bomb that should have unleashed the fire of destruction turns out to be a cooking implement, mounted over the same transformative fire as the melting pot itself. The desired erasure of cultural differences among the ethnicities that join in the Crucible is accompanied by the neutralisation of political differences on the new continent. If the sharp distinction Vera makes between herself and her father — "His life and mine are for ever separate. He is a Reactionary, I a Radical"[386] — is unresolved, that is because her father does not enter the melting pot but, instead, makes manifest everything that is wrong with Old Europe.

On a more serious note, the redemptive power with which love blazes does much more than just give warmth to the lover; to effect a transformation in "raw" ingredients, it cannot avoid causing suffering. As David spells it out to Vera, "Those who love us *must* suffer, and *we* must suffer in their suffering. It is live things, not dead metals, that are being melted in the Crucible."[387] Coming from the mouth of a Jewish character, this patently Christian association of suffering with redemption is a sure indication that the melting pot has been effective. More than that, David's statement shatters the illusion that "America" is a shining idyll, a pyropolitical utopia of easy coexistence. Transformative suffering, as opposed to the useless and continuing anguish of Europe, is the fee one pays for being admitted into the Crucible. What its fire transforms, David reminds us by way of introducing culinary references into alchemical discourse, are "living things."[388] The suffering one experiences in the melting pot is that of being boiled alive, of losing one's insular natural belonging in exchange for a shared, though arduously acquired, civic identity. That is the sense of the American *panspermia*.

## 6.4. In Search of Perfection: The Arts of Cooking and Politics

Besides the pragmatic improvements it has ushered in, including easing digestion and providing a more nutritious diet, cooking is also an art that appeals to the palate by deftly making distinct flavours coalesce. No less sophisticated than the combination of colours in painting, the mix awakens in the eaters (as well as in the chefs) a profound feeling of pleasure, an agreeableness that is subjectively more significant than usefulness.[389] Culinary mediation among divergent tastes and ingredients relies on the analytic and synthetic powers of fire, while perfection demands a perfect timing of, and control over, the intensity of the flame that neither burns nor leaves the dish raw. Classically conceived, the art of the political, in the sense of a practice of good governance, similarly entails situating the "golden middle" between two extremes. But, speaking more generally, what does the nexus of cooking and perfection hold in store for pyropolitics?

Both in the East and in the West, the culinary art embarks on a bittersweet quest for perfection, which is different from the utopian ideal. The truly perfect state is that of the Golden Age, when food was abundant and did not require human intervention, be it in the shape of agriculture or of cooking. After the Fall, on the other hand, perfectibility calls for hard work, as a human mediation of nature necessary for bare survival. In *Works and Days*, Hesiod relates that "gods keep hidden from men the means of life [*bion*]" (42-4) by maintaining food scarce and by hiding the fire (50), which is used for cooking and which Prometheus subsequently steals from Zeus. The Delian myth of *Oinotropoi* illustrates the contrast between post-Fall scarcity and the Golden Age, replete with nutritious products springing out of the earth on their own accord (*autophuēs*) and "perfectly 'cooked'" so that humans could "eat [them] directly without using fire to prepare them."[390] According to a medieval Jain narrative, "wishing-trees" supplied abundant food that obviated the need to toil; only later did the trees we are familiar with today grow in their stead. The supplanting of trees is construed as the origin of evil, of anger that the loss of plenitude ignited in human beings, and of fire, which "arouse from the branches of trees rubbing together" and upon which "people began to cook their food."[391] Fire flares from a deficiency and points a way toward overcoming this very deficiency. Its redemptive potential notwithstanding, the human search for perfection through the exercise of their skills is but a shadow of the original and forever lost faultless condition.

In addition to evil, anger, fire, and cooking, scarcity also gives rise to an entire social and political order, with laws governing human conduct and dispensing appropriate punishments.[392] Politics not only emerges together with the culinary arts but it also responds to the same need of regulating human life that unfolds against a persistent backdrop of limited resources. Virtually all the implications of this regulation have to do with fire, which must not get out of hand if analogous goals of refashioning "uncivilised" beings into the subjects of civilisation and raw materials into delicious fare are to be achieved. That is probably why, in ancient China, culinary talent was "a fine qualification for a ministerial appointment."[393]

A milestone in interrelating politics and cooking in the Chinese context was the appointment of Yi Yin, who rose from his lowly origins (as a foster child taught by his parents how to cook) to the post of Prime Minister in the second millennium BCE. As Lu Jia, a minister and political writer, expressed it with admiration, Yi Yin's culinary expertise ("shouldering a tripod [*ding*]") was invaluable: "[i]f one wishes to pass down great renown across a myriad generations one must first put it into practice in subtle and small things." "Within the confines of his humble residence," Lu Jia continued, "his ambitions were set on planning the layout of the eight extremities [i.e., governing the world]. Therefore, he abandoned his ambitions in the kitchen to become an advisor for the Son of Heaven [...]."[394] Cooking, political advising, and governing the world are of a piece; what varies is the type of the materials and the magnitude of fire each activity engages with. From the "subtle and small" ingredients for cooking to the grandeur of the governable universe, something is handed over to a transformative blaze that, within carefully delineated limits, ennobles the contents of the cauldron. And only a cook, an advisor, or a ruler knows how these materials are to be prepared and when an adequate amount of heat has been imparted to them.

The classical reading of Yi Yin's transition from cook to Prime Minister is very much in line with the wisdom of Lao-Tzu, who, in *Tao Te Ching*, opines that "Ruling a great state / is like cooking a small fish / when you govern the world with the Tao / spirits display no powers."[395] Various commentators have disagreed on the message of Lao-Tzu, but two main hermeneutical possibilities are prominent among a vast array of interpretations:

- On the one hand, from the cosmic vantagepoint of the Tao, the difference in scales between cooking and political governance is so negligible that the "great" and the "small" merge into one. This argument is attributed to a twelfth-century Taoist master Li Hsi-chai, who thinks that "[f]or a sage, ruling the state is a minor affair, like cooking a small fish."[396] Assisting in a proper preparation of phenomena, fire facilitates the becoming-small of what is great, and vice versa. For the sage, even fateful political matters are as trivial, mundane, and easy to handle as cooking small fish.
- On the other hand, the words of Lao-Tzu have been taken as an advice to minimise the ruler's interference in the lives of the ruled. Han Fei, a philosopher born in the late "Warring States" period and spanning the transition to the Han dynasty (280 – 233 BCE), says that in "cooking small fish, too much turning ruins it. In governing a great state, too much reform embitters the people. Thus, a ruler who possesses the Way

values inaction over reform."³⁹⁷ The elucidation ascribed to Ho-shang Kung, a legendary figure from roughly the same period,³⁹⁸ echoes that of Han Fei: "If you cook small fish, don't remove its entrails, don't scrape off its scales, and don't stir it. If you do, it will turn to mush. Likewise, too much government makes those below rebel."³⁹⁹ A certain extinguishing of ceaseless activity (and, with it, of the fire that underlies all change) is recommended to a good ruler and a skilful cook of small fish. Letting the ruled and fish be, providing the right conditions for their self-transformation without burning them to charcoal, is the exact opposite of equalising the relative magnitudes of great and small fires. Letting-be compels one to pay utmost attention to the singularity of what is cooked, or who is ruled, and to be aware of the limits, beyond which fire and violent interference destroy this singularity.

To return to the Indian milieu, the semantic links between cooking, ripeness, and perfection are at their strongest in Sanskrit, where "*āma* purely and simply means 'raw' and 'non-ripe' in all the direct and metaphorical senses these terms can bear, in the same way as *pakva* means 'cooked', 'ripe', 'digested'."⁴⁰⁰ As a result, the funeral hymns in the *Rig Veda* implore Agni not to burn the corpse he consumes entirely but to "cook him perfectly" and "then give him over to the fathers."⁴⁰¹ The perfection of the early Christian martyr Polycarp, who "baked" in the centre of a fire that was kindled in order to kill him, obliquely belongs to this tradition, as do, much more explicitly, Hindu nuptial rites that must render the bride "*saṃskṛtā*, 'brought to perfection'—a term that might also be translated by 'well-cooked'."⁴⁰²

The relation between the cooking and the cooked belongs under the umbrella of igneous elemental sovereignty. The imbalance of power between the living and the dead, as well as the groom and the bride, ordains a strict allocation of roles, according to which the disempowered are nothing but materials for the practice of culinary arts. Add class dynamics to this hierarchy, and, in no time, you will arrive at the precept, according to which *brahmin* members of the highest caste are in a position to cook the world (*lokapakti*) with the view to its improvement.[403]

Cooking responds to the evil of injustice and privation at the same time that it lends a voice to an irresistible desire for justice, for adjusting, refining, and perfecting the world, for instance, by conquering the finality of death. The Hindu notion of ripening beings in fire, similar to Taoist minimal interference with the cooked "small fish," implies that thermal force is not imposed from the outside, but only expedites these beings' ownmost growth and permits them to reach their highest potential faster. We must tread with caution around assertions of this kind. They can either lead us on the promising path of *pyr phronimon* — discerning fire and its singular justice — or entangle us further in the ideological ruse of a hegemony, which convinces those it dominates that its interests are identical to theirs, as it happens in *satī* rituals. Be this as it may, the reference to the vegetal world and its processes with regard to *pakva* makes it plain that fire is vital to life itself and that cooking imitates the self-preparation, say, of a fruit as it ripens and ferments thanks to the external and internal emission of heat.

## 6.5. Revolutionary and Post-Revolutionary Political Kitchens

Revolutions have historically set their sights on smelting the structures of the *ancien régime* and quasi-alchemically creating a new *body politic*, but their goal was at times expressed in the more prosaic terms of cooking. At Château-Porcien, during celebrations of the Festival of the Supreme Being, which Robespierre had instituted, orators declared that "the Revolution is a boiling pot of which the guillotine is a skimming ladle."[404] If the foment of revolutionary change parallels boiling raw ingredients in the same pot, then the undesirable by-products of this political-culinary procedure are comparable to the foam that periodically comes up to the surface of the mix. The skimming ladle purifies the concoction by removing this foam; the guillotine sanitises the nascent political subject by ridding it of the perceived enemies of Virtue.

All this, however, was much more than an allegory. The political revolution in France provided the pretext for a revolution in cooking, "as food writers and chefs realized that their texts and cuisine would need to be altered in order to appeal to a new nationwide population."[405] The formation of modern citizenry as a relatively levelled and homogeneous political subject spurred the tendency to bring *haut cuisine* down to the masses and spread it far and wide together with, and thanks to, the ideology of *égaliberté*. Political homogenisation led, through more or less circuitous routes, to a homogenisation of tastes that were, in equal measure, honed on the fires of the revolution (unless the very notion of taste, applicable to any person whatsoever yet variable according to individual preferences, issued from these fires). The dynamic was circular: while "French cuisine was an indelible national phenomenon that turned into an exemplar for revolutionary action,"[406] the outcomes of the Revolution quickly transformed all "things culinary."[407]

No one has sensed more acutely the mutual influence of the revolution and French cuisine than the author of the eight-volume *Almanach des Gourmands*, Grimod de la Reynière. As he bluntly writes, "*la Révolution a tout changé en France, jusqu'aux estomacs* [the Revolution has changed everything in France, all the way to stomachs]"[408] that, as we know, house the inner fire of digestion. As to whether revolutionary change has been beneficial, de la Reynière is ambiguous. Early on in the *Almanach*, he laments the "revolutionary torrent" which has "invaded and ruined everything."[409] But, rather than offer a straightforward narrative of decline, the author salutes the democratisation of more refined tastes, made possible by the eradication of *ancien régime*.[410] Far from being ruined by political upheavals, gourmandise, which de la Reynière believed to be the backbone of being-human, emerges as a national feature crowning the general purification of tastes and the adoption of a more varied diet in post-revolutionary France.

If, in the celebrations of Supreme Being, the French revolution was compared to a boiling pot, Chinese revolutionaries were prudent enough to adjust their political-culinary techniques depending on the circumstances and the desired degree of change. Xie Juezai, Mao's first Minister of Domestic Affairs and, later on, the President of the Supreme People's Court of China, recommended a combination of boiling on "high fire" and steaming on "low fire" among a variety of tactics extended from cooking to revolutionary activities and reforms.[411] His rhetoric is clearly in keeping with the Chinese representation of the state as a tripod cauldron, the *ding*. Compared to the French "boiling pot" of the revolution, this approach is more nuanced, in that it meticulously regulates the procedure by selecting the right approach and correct intensities of fire beforehand, instead of boiling everything on the strongest flame and adjusting the mixture from the outside, by "skimming" it. Shifting gears, or switching between various kinds of fire and cooking, becomes a crucial skill for revolutionary leaders.

Moreover, in Xie Juezai's view, under no circumstances should what is cooked be limited to existing state institutions and practices; above all, one must totally transform *oneself* as though one were "slowly boiling raw meat until it was well-done."[412] Drawing upon a deeply entrenched cultural correlation between consuming cooked food and a higher degree of civilisation, Xie Juezai hints at the need for a revolutionary self-cultivation proceeding in tandem with the cultivation of external reality. He selects a low-intensity fire for the transformation of subjectivity, which has to boil gradually for the desired change in oneself to take place. Otherwise, one may surmise, a rapid conversion impelled by a high flame would not take root in the labyrinthine life of the psyche.

Similar to the French situation, the Chinese revolution could not leave dietary practices unaffected. To fulfil official production quotas, the population was ordered to hand over for smelting many quotidian iron and steel implements, "including cooking pots, iron doors, and in one North China Commune even the heating pipes of a secondary school. The population resentments generated by such measures were intensified by the fact that, with poor quality food and service in the public mess-halls, many who would have preferred to eat at home were unable to do so for lack of cooking implements."[413] Melting individual cooking pots down to one common alloy is symbolic of the formation of a common, communist state that would finally live up to the essence of the *ding*. The same holds for the cultivation of a new political subjectivity. So long as people have no other choice but to eat in public dining halls, they stop gathering as disparate families around their respective hearths and, instead, join with countless others. Probably more momentous than the abolition of private property, the unmooring of cooking from the domestic sphere allows the authorities to combine disparate hearths into a single fire, shared by all.

In his 1938 address before the students of the Lu Xun Academy of the Arts, Mao Zedong acknowledged the exemplary status of culinary activity in the aesthetic realm. Departing from the premise that artistic products must both please and serve the masses, he concluded that "[l]ike a good meal, a work of art must be both nutritious and flavourful."[414] "After skilful cooking," he continued, "a wonderful flavour emerges, and the nutritional value is preserved. Great chefs learn how to cook well through a long period of practical experience, not simply after studying for one day. When they cook, they use the same ingredients as other people but are able to create marvellous flavours. To achieve this, one must master blending spices, cooking time, and cooking temperature."[415]

Mao encouraged the students of the Lu Xun Academy to make their work relevant to the people by treating the considerations of utility as paramount as those of formal enjoyment. Nothing could be further from Kant's aesthetic philosophy than that! Moreover, with the figure of Li Lin looming in the cultural background, he links culinary skill to the art of the political, which similarly demands long years of practical experience, the ability to create the right blend, sensitivity to the needs of the people, and knowledge of the optimal temperature and timespan for revolutionary change. His advice to art students encapsulates, at bottom, Mao's political aesthetics, itself a blend of sensibilities shared with socialist

CHAPTER 6. *AROUND THE HEARTH* 211

realism and with the pre-communist Chinese tradition of governance.

The other great revolutionary of the twentieth century, Lenin, also associated the art of cooking and the practice of governing a communist polity. Mind you, he has been terribly misquoted, with the statement imputed to him being: "under communism, even a simple woman-cook would be able to run the state." In fact, Lenin never actually uttered such words, but he did mention the woman-cook at an important junction of the post-revolutionary period, in a speech titled "Will Bolsheviks Hold onto State Power?" There, Lenin insists: "We are not utopians. We know that no manual labourer or woman-cook [*kukharka*] is capable of taking the reins of the state right away. [...] But [...] we demand that statecraft *be taught* [...] and that this teaching start immediately, i.e., that all the workers, all the poor immediately take part in this teaching. [...] What we need is *revolutionary* democratism, *revolutionary* measures of precisely this sort."[416]

Upon successfully instituting the democratic education of the masses, even a woman-cook will be able to run the state. For the time being, however, she appears side-by-side with a manual labourer as a female personification of the poor and the uneducated. It is significant that Lenin singles out a cook and not, say, a cleaning lady as his preferred example. Isn't a woman-cook, who is practically acquainted with the appropriate intensities of fire in the kitchen, a good model for revolutionary leaders who are aware of the right measures to be taken and the degree of the masses' own "readiness"? Still, a transition from the culinary familiarity with natural fire to pyropolitical expertise will not be immediate, Lenin suggests, and, in the same breath, he implies that the political education of the poor, their training in "*revolutionary* democratism," is a variation on the activity of cooking, of bringing the political subject to the state of preparedness.[417]

So, when will a simple cook-woman be finally allowed to take the reins of the state? An ironic response, consistent with Lenin's vision of the communist future, is: when the revolution is fully "cooked" and there is no longer any need for maintaining the state. In that future, briefly outlined in *State and Revolution*, "we ourselves, the workers, will organize large-scale production on the basis of what has already been created by capitalism [...]. Such a start, on the basis of large-scale production, will of itself lead to the gradual 'withering away' of all bureaucracy, to the gradual creation of an order, an order without quotation marks [...], an order in which ever simpler functions of control and accounting will be performed by each person in turn, will then become a habit and will finally die out."[418]

Elsewhere, I have commented at length on the intricate economy of this passage,[419] which foretells a certain end of politics in the self-administration of communist economy. Once the "ever simpler functions of control and accounting" are "performed by each person in turn," even a manual worker and a woman-cook will be efficacious enough to govern a state, but the state itself will "wither away" and collective self-governance will become a matter of habit. Lenin has in mind a two-pronged process, in the course of which the political preparedness of the masses would match the creation of an "order without quotation marks." Participation in and administration of this new order would be the prerogative of a woman-cook as much as of an engineer or an architect. It is no wonder, then, that the bland economicism of a fully prepared (or cooked) post-revolutionary society will extinguish the fire of the political by domesticating its functions and turning them into "habits." The genuine order Lenin is after is a collective *habitus* and habitat, a common hearth, or, in a word, *communism*.

## 6.6. Consuming Ourselves: Pyropolitical Cannibalism

Individually and collectively, human beings eagerly consume themselves. We do so in distinct ways—for instance, by depleting our own energy in a burnout, converting the environment we depend upon into sources of fuel, or passing from the "raw" uncivilised state to that of being "cooked" and cultured. A coherent and more or less unitary *body politic* comes into existence as soon as, mediated by the transformative power of fire, diversity is dissolved into a homogeneous mix and symbolically eaten up, following the prototype of the Greek *panspermia*. "We" do not predate the act of our self-consumption; "we" come to be ourselves in this very act, of which we are both subjects and objects. (In a similar sense, as I put it in the Introduction, the world *as a totality* becomes itself when, engulfed in fire, it is on the verge of non-being.) The birth of the Hegelian self-consciousness at its most material and concrete is indebted more to the self-consumption of the subject than to a life-and-death struggle, which is a type of that self-consumption.

Much has been written on the issue of cannibalism in colonial and postcolonial experiences. In "Notebook of a Return to the Native Land," twentieth-century poet from Martinique Aimé Césaire appeals to the coloniser with the words, "Because we hate you / and your reason, we claim kinship / with dementia praecox with the flaming madness / of persistent cannibalism."[420] Pyropolitical "flaming madness" burns to the ground the structures of reason imposed by Europeans.

Nothing but bodies remain, those of the colonisers and those of the colonised, the former swallowed up by the latter—and, from the self-relation of the cannibal body, another reason germinates. The kinship of the colonised with dementia praecox is, at the same time, their corporeal affinity to the coloniser, physically assimilated into the budding collective subject (the "we") in the act of eating, aided by the "fire" of digestion. Though they emanate from burning hatred, the flames of madness do not simply annihilate the hated object but prepare it for consumption, roasting the Europeans who are ready to be eaten up by those they subjugated.

That, *mutatis mutandis*, is the message of the Brazilian tragicomedy *How Tasty Was My Little Frenchman* (Nelson Pereira dos Santos, 1971), which depicts the tribulations of a Frenchman, first captured by the Portuguese and later on by the local Tupinambás in the Guanabara Bay region in 1594. Despite marrying into the tribe and adapting the Tupinambá way of life, the "little Frenchman" is ceremonially killed and eaten at a communal meal in the film's tragic finale. Not until he is physically assimilated into the bodies of the colonised does the coloniser become a part of them, next to an enormous bonfire. Material incorporation is a token of spiritual assimilation, upon which the continued existence of the postcolony is contingent. Or, as Césaire's wife, Suzanne, succinctly put it, "*La poésie martiniquaise sera cannibale. Ou ne sera pas* [The poetry of Martinique will be cannibalistic. Or it will not be at all]."[421]

Cannibalising otherness exemplifies the general dynamics of political subject-construction. "We" are not really "we, ourselves" before our collective interiority is consumed and consummated, and the most palpable mode of its consummation is the act of eating. But, just as before ingesting food one must prepare it, mediating—often with the help of fire—between the raw things of nature and the human organism, so the consummation of *body politic* requires a fair amount of work on its ingredients.

In this chapter, I have listed some of the tactics used in this pyropolitical operation, such as "the melting pot," or revolutionary steaming and boiling. Whatever the tactics, the "we" who, in devouring ourselves, become ourselves are simultaneously constituted and annihilated in the dialectical movement of political life-process. Coextensive with life itself, the hunger of a living being cannot be satisfied once and for all;[422] analogously, pyropolitical self-cannibalising must repeat the sequence of constitution and destruction until the life-process is finally exhausted. In other words, we must periodically eat ourselves up in order to keep becoming ourselves. The outer fire of cooking and the inner fire of digestion are the catalysts in the synthesis and analysis of political identity that can feed on itself, as much as on an external other, until its time is up, its resources depleted. Better than a purely formal performative gesture of subject-formation, the two fires (the external and the internal) cast light on how "we" are brought to life as a unity in the "crudely" material act of roasting and cannibalising ourselves.

# Extinguishing
*The Politics of Ashes*

\*

In the twenty-first century, the myth of the Phoenix continues to bewitch us. We still think of ashes as fertilisers, nourishing new growth. After destructive flames have done their work, the sun's creative blaze will give a sign of resurrection to the plants it will call forth from the residues of past burning. Between the two fires, life and hope will resume. Vegetation will spring from the earth and strive skywards afresh.

In its vegetal configuration, the "Phoenix complex,"[423] of which we are suffering, underpins the destruction of forests in the Amazon, where slash-and-burn agriculture aimed to convert dense forests into fertile farmland at an increasing pace since Jair Bolsonaro's election to the presidency in 2018, the pace slowed down but still catastrophic after Luis Inácio Lula da Silva's return to power in Brazil. But while "crops planted after slash-and-burn benefit from the nutrients in the ash," "rapid nutrient depletion takes place" immediately afterwards.[424] "Fire follows fire," as the heat of the tropical sun is no longer deflected or absorbed by the lush green of the destroyed forest.[425] Short-term rejuvenation is but a prelude to the long-term destitution of the earth and affirmation of fire's reign.

Much of the same happens on the global scale, with governments, corporations, and individuals disregarding the disastrous implications of the planetary burnout and putting their blind trust in the self-renewal of the environment still romantically viewed as natural. The Phoenix forces us to forget death and finitude, even as we stare them in the face. On its wings, it carries a surplus of ideality and the empty promise of redemption after the fire has already gone out. A political "rebellion against the Phoenix"[426] is well overdue.

Having materialised from ash and having reawakened past ideals, the Phoenix bears lethal force, while auguring a new life; it spreads the seeds of death (whence it has issued) all around itself, while affirming that life is eternal, or, at a minimum, eternally recurrent. Every return to metaphysical unity from the dispersed plurality of the ashes must contend with this quandary, as does every project of gathering and returning from the diaspora—for example, Israel's self-representation as a polity resurrected from the ashes of Auschwitz. The triumphalist renaissance of this Middle Eastern Phoenix betrays the memory of past suffering, at best paraded before the rest of the world in a perverse spectacle of victimhood. At its worst, the incessantly replayed spectacle serves to legitimate its death-bearing politics.

"The Phoenix's privilege," writes Bachelard, "is to be reborn of its own self, not of the 'ashes' of others."[427] The Phoenix is averse to a community of and in ashes; it carries the ridiculous principle of autonomy and self-sufficiency through to its logical conclusion in death, and even beyond death. But precisely this community devoid of hope for another life or another fire, one where my incinerated self is mixed with "the 'ashes' of others," is badly needed today. The Phoenix's sunny optimism is deadlier still than the deepest, darkest nihilism, which wells over is as we soberly overview the panorama of the earth ravaged by the great fires of metaphysics. The ashes themselves are witnesses. They testify to what has singularly been and will not be repeated in exactly the same way (or in any way) ever again. They are *of* the other, even if one's impression is that they belong to the self, from which the Phoenix is reborn.

The obscure testimony of the ashes is a record of defeats, the record that forms the underside of history written by the victors. As he gives a messianic twist to pyropolitics, Walter Benjamin concludes that "[t]he only writer of history with the gift of setting alight the sparks of hope in the past is the one who is convinced of this: that not even the dead will be safe from the enemy, if he is victorious. And this enemy has not ceased to be victorious."[428]

It is too late to speak of fire and of "the sparks of hope" *after* the victims have been reduced to ash in the blaze of progress and world history. Assuming that the dead, who are neither "safe from the enemy" nor, more generally, protected from further violence by the fact of their having already died, could speak—assuming that they could voice and present themselves on the historical scene, if only to affirm their essential non-appearance on it—, they would do so in the voice of Shakespeare's Cleopatra, who, in her confrontation with Caesar, eschews being illuminated by the victor's light. From the depths of her "wounding shame," she withdraws her presence from triumphant Caesar. There is, for her, something worse than defeat ("It smites me / Beneath the fall I have"), namely the spectacle of the defeated, where the victim would "show the cinders of my spirits / Through th'ashes of my chance."[429]

The economy of this unthinkable violence, more devastating than death itself, is unfathomable. Standing in the victor's light, the victim is victimised again, in excess of the initial trauma, by being forced to show cinders *through* ashes, to present the remains of extinguished spirit, along with the totality of the past that has led to defeat, in the ashen light of the future in ruins, the "chance" already reduced to ashes.

Victims are forced to affirm, silently, that they will have (would have, must have...) always been victims, including before and after their actual victimisation. Through the filter of ashes, whatever is left of life (its cinders) is reconstructed as if it has, from the outset, teleologically pointed toward and culminated in the victor's accomplishment. Not even past possibilities of victims' lives prior to their victimisation are spared this reconstruction. The spectacle of the defeated, dragged into the sphere of visibility, speech, and phenomena, is the ultimate historical violence that befalls every modality of the victims' time, reducing it, too, to ashes.

When Cleopatra prohibits the spectacularisation of her defeat, she also affirms the fiery nucleus of her being, as much as the political meaning of her suicide. Her words gravitate toward the Platonic politics of truth, with its embrace of ideal spirit as fire: "I am fire and air; my other elements / I give to baser life."[430] It seems, *prima facie*, that death plays its usual metaphysical role of purifying Cleopatra's spirit by ridding it of its material substratum ("baser life"). But, on closer reading, it becomes obvious that the space for transcendence within elemental immanence is shut and that there is only one gap left: between the ideal elements of fire and air and the "other elements" that belong to the material sphere. This division takes place within life itself, divorcing its "baser" from its "nobler" modalities following an onto-political logic whereby "life struggles not with death, spirit not with spiritlessness; spirit struggles with spirit, life with life [...]."[431] Or, in the words of St. Gregory of Nizianzus that have surely inspired this Schmittian formulation, *to hen stasiāzon prōs heautōn*, "the One is in revolt against [and static within] itself" (*Oratio Theologica* iii.2). An internal separation is kept in place as long as spirit, or the One, is burning and, divided against itself, maintains the tension of oppositionality that defines the political. If Cleopatra rejects her own appearance in the glorious light of Caesar, it is because she can still muster spiritual strength aplenty to be the principle of her own light and meaning, of the heat of motivation and truth that resist those of Caesar.

"I am fire and air" reclaims the sovereignty of the speaker, who, like the Sun King, embodies the solar blaze and interiorises the prerequisites for appearing and truth, or, like a self-immolator, takes phenomenality into her hands for a brief flash of a terrifying instant. Cleopatra's simple statement translates the Christian "I am the truth; I am the light" into the language of the elements and rebels against the vision of cinders through ashes, the finality of victimisation, and the extinguishing of antagonisms that keep the spirit of the political intact. Despite her victimhood, she is not ready to say, "Ashes to ashes, dust to dust." At least, not yet...

*

The leitmotif of fire in Heidegger's reading of Georg Trakl's poetry in *On the Way to Language* has provided Derrida with ample materials for deconstruction. It is in Trakl (and in the wake of Heraclitus) that Heidegger comes across the notion of spirit as a flame, that is, as the luminous and thermal source of phenomenality, of the totality of all that is present, and of concrete life experienced as pain: "Spirit is flame. It glows and shines. Its shining takes place in the beholding look. To such a vision is given the advent of all that shines, where all that is, is present. This flaming vision is pain [...]. The spirit which bears the gift of a 'great soul' is pain; pain is the animator [...]. Everything that is alive, is painful."[432] In contrast to theoretical sight, which surveys eidetic fields flooded with transcendental light, a "flaming vision," *flammende Anschauen*, is inseparable from the corporeality of those who see. This vision is almost tactile, so palpable that it provokes pain, *Schmerz*. As distances between the seer, the seen, and the animating vision collapse, fire burns in us and burns us, threatening to reduce the sentient body to ash.

We would not be amiss if we detected in the foregrounding of pain the influence of Ernst Jünger on Heidegger. Nevertheless, the dangerousness of spirit lies not so much in pain per se as in the convergence of spiritual luminosity and burning, in the synthesis of the two powers of fire, which Origen and other Church Fathers craved so much: "[…] flame is the ek-stasis that lightens and calls forth radiance, but which may go on consuming and reduce all to the white of ashes [*alles in das Weiße der Asche verzehren kann*]."[433] The possibility that everything, i.e., the totality shining and glowing in the flaming vision of spirit, would be destroyed is inseparable from the radiant self-presentation of this totality. Once materialised, the possibility of total destruction would resolve the brilliance of spirit into the whiteness of ashes, where the "all" is "nothing" or next to nothing, a trace of past flames that falls apart.

The modal verb *kann* (may) is highly significant here: for Heidegger, as for Trakl, reduction to ash is only a coming event that may happen, given the "internal duplicity of Geist" that "affects all the thinking up to and including that of ash."[434] But for the other pair of thinker-poets, namely Celan and Derrida, the catastrophe of Geist has already occurred, leaving behind a trail of ashes from the past inflammations of spirit. In Celan's dense language, the past, that which is behind our shaken being, is enveloped in an ash-aureole, *Aschenglorie*: "Ash-aureole behind / your shaken knotted / hands at the Threeways."[435] This "aureole," or literally this "glory," surrounding and haunting every act and every gesture of "your shaken knotted / hands," is the white of ashes Heidegger had anticipated with some degree of anxiety. It is an aftereffect of metaphysical burning brilliance that illuminated, brought into being, and despoiled whatever fell in its spotlight.

In line with the pyropolitical theology of the preceding chapters, glory is the mark of sovereignty, and its gleaming — a necessary attribute of divine and monarchical power. In the burning light of sovereign presence, everything comes into being, is allowed to show itself as itself, but also runs the risk of being ruined. Power and phenomenological ontology, making be and letting appear, are virtually indistinguishable from one another in the pyropolitics of glory. And both fade away once glory has been reduced to ash.

How to interpret "glory in ashes"? Does it not make manifest the proliferation of meanings after the blazing politics of truth with its life-giving and death-bearing flame enters the phase of decline, its flames nearly extinguished? Yet, does this manifestation not border on the nonmanifest, its singular testimony unaligned with any formal authority? By the end of "*Aschenglorie*," the paradox of this secret testimony of the ashes themselves (emitting a light that does not bedazzle, is shorn of lustre, and claims to have broken the spell of metaphysics) reaches its crescendo: "No one / bears witness for the / witness."[436] There is no higher light nor a fire to illuminate the testimony of the witness; the evidence of victimhood can be rendered only in the non-sovereign glory in ashes that, as a weird aureole, surrounds the victim.

At this point, we must part ways with Derrida's reading of both Celan and Heidegger on the ashes for two reasons.

- First, the otherwise perceptive and patient analysis of Celan's poem in "The Poetics and Politics of Witnessing" still finds itself under the sway of a metaphysical construction of testimony and truth. Writing that "[a]sh [...] annihilates or threatens to annihilate even the possibility of bearing witness to annihilation,"[437] Derrida ties witnessing to the politics of truth, for which ash and its obscure light amount to almost nothing. The lack of uniform, evenly spread, and brilliant luminosity of ideas does not imply a complete absence of light, dim as the circumstances may be. The aureole of ash is far from an absolutely idiosyncratic testimony that isolates each surviving victim, let alone those no longer alive, in the solipsism of its unique, interminable suffering. The ashes in and of themselves (which is to say: outside of themselves), in their sheer non-identity with themselves, are shared in their multiplicity, falling apart into a plurality of traces. Only in such a barely describable condition do they non-communicatively transmit their secret testimony.

- Second, with regard to Heidegger's terror in the face of "white of ash," Derrida plausibly concludes that "[e]vil is not on the side of matter or of the sensible matter generally opposed to spirit. Evil is spiritual, it is also Geist [...]." This insight into an inner division within spirit, reminiscent of Schmitt's statement "spirit struggles with spirit, [etc.]" leads Derrida, in the conclusion of this intriguing paragraph from *Of Spirit*, to a somewhat misguided question, "Is ash the Good or the Evil of spirit?"[438] The question is inapposite, considering that a system of valuations from the vantage point of spirit no longer matters when ash is not only a destiny that "awaits us," a catastrophe infinitely deferred and different from world history, but the event that has always already happened and constituted the innermost aspects of this history. As Shakespeare's Cleopatra and Celan's poetry convey, one commits a violent act by casting ash into a light not its own and by observing the victim in the glorious brightness of its triumphant opponent. Prospective (if still sorrowful or apprehensive) contemplation of ash as the future of spirit's flame is impossible at the close of metaphysics; for us, the conflagration of spirit belongs to a now distant past. Given this fundamental shift in temporal orientation, the differences of ashes are to be transvalued in such a thorough fashion that the categories "good" and "evil," as well as the "one" and the "many," may themselves become outmoded.

\*

Whatever does not fit the rigid format of calculative rationality is disdainfully rejected as "obscurantism" and "mysticism." Novalis puts his finger on this hyperrational filtering in "Christendom or Europe": "If somewhere an old superstitious belief in a higher world and such-like reared its head, the alarm was sounded at once on all sides, and whenever possible the dangerous spark was suffocated in the ashes of philosophy and wit."[439] There is but one caveat: rationalism is not in a position to ascertain that philosophy and wit are the ashes of the superstition they suffocate. Unbeknownst to it, "pure reason" belongs among the remains of theological fire — secularised, rationalised, distilled to frigid light.

William Blake poetically explains: "Satan divided against Satan resolvd in open Sanhedrim / To burn Mystery with fire and form another from her ashes [...] / The Ashes of Mystery began to animate they calld it Deism / And Natural Religion as of old so now anew began."[440] If the power of rationality is the ash of mystery, then the limits of critique are not set by the unknowable thing-in-itself, but by fire. The same goes for power without sovereignty. Sovereignty in ashes is highly mysterious, rather than demystified, transparent, open to universal scrutiny. Split against itself, non-sovereign power copies Blake's Satan, who "is divided against Satan." What does this new mystery hide? Liberal "division of powers"? Technocratic dissolution of politics in managerial practices? An inexpressible demand the victims of past injustices place on us?

*

To reiterate a set of questions, which we have been surveying from various angles in *Pyropolitics*: is the eclipse of the Platonic sun a temporary occurrence, obeying the rhythmic movement of being's donation and withdrawal, self-presentation and retreat, or is it a sign of what might be called "the absolute extinguishing"? Does it exceed or is it inscribed in the calculative and sacrificial logic of metaphysics? How does the ensuing depoliticisation, expressed, first and foremost, in the de-idealisation of politics, dovetail with a certain end of metaphysics, on the one hand, and the replacement of fire with the residues of the combustion process, on the other?

In a preliminary response to these questions, it will be necessary to come to grips with a complex alignment of the history of being, the history of the political, and the natural-artificial history of fire. The regular and rhythmic kindling and extinguishing of cosmic blaze in Heraclitus, the donation and withdrawal of being in Heidegger, and the intensification and retreat of the political in Schmitt ought to be considered together, under the same conceptual roof. But inquiries into meaning of being, fire, and the political today ought to focus on the second moment of these movements, abstracted from their cyclical course. In other words, they are to commence from the brink of an irrecoverable loss.

A juxtaposition of ontology, politics, and the elements returns to the pre-Socratics after the completion of Western metaphysics. In the thought of Heraclitus, *kosmos* was an ever-lasting fire, kindling in measures (*metra*) and going out in measures (Fr. 30).[441] Political order and apparent being coincided: *kosmos* connoted, at once, an ordered arrangement and a shining-forth, a just and adjusted, well regulated, harmonious, "measured" order, which handed itself over to sight. Treating *kosmos* as a kind of fire, Heraclitus chanced upon its phenomenal character, as well as on its dialectical nature, especially pronounced in the unity of opposites—kindling and quenching, need and satiety—that similarly governs the lives of animal and vegetal organisms.

In accordance with this cosmology, are we living through the measured going out of cosmic fire that, obeying its rhythmic vacillations, will be re-kindled soon? Or, conversely, has fire lost its metaphysical quality "ever-lasting," and so, too, its uncanny capacity for self-regeneration, which is also the renaissance of the world and of life itself? If the latter, then what happens to the measures inherent to fire and, above all, to solar fire as the measure of time?[442] Does the invalidation of metaphysical measures leave us with what is by definition immeasurable, excessive, and extreme? Or, does it hold out the promise of other standards that, after a long passage through nihilism, could germinate from our own finitude, from the immanence of human existence?

There is, after all, nothing either measured or orderly about the ashes, their inescapable dispersion supplying deconstruction with an equivalent to dissemination.[443] There is, moreover, no justice for all those and all that served as fuel for the pyre of world history; neither satiety nor the quenching of need after the process of combustion has fizzled out; no bright light radiating from the remains that challenge the power of the spectacle. In the closure of metaphysics, when everything has been consumed, the light of the ashes themselves replaces the shining-forth of phenomena, and the fading afterglow of fire gives way to the obscure trace of its victims.

*

Every time the blazing politics of truth has tried to melt and to mould material existence in conformity with its ideals, the unintended consequence has been an upsurge in in solidarity among the non-idealisable residues of its activity.[444] The leftovers of the fire that was world history proved to be ineliminable, more obstinately enduring than the ideal itself. Among victims already reduced to ash, power imbalances and all other political differentiations lose their significance. It is, perhaps, in this vein that we should revisit the Marxist notion of communism as a "classless society" (*klassenlos Gesellschaft*), or, better yet, the "unclassifiable society" of difference without oppositionality, where conceptual and hierarchical distinctions have been burnt beyond recognition; in short, the society of and in ashes.

The unclassifiable society is the horizon of our present and of the future, in which, in the words of Derrida, "ash awaits us."[445] The collapse of conceptual and hierarchical distinctions, be they quantitative or qualitative, in the unclassifiable society does not occasion the levelling of its members to particles that are essentially the same, homogenous, or interchangeable. As Derrida notes in *Archive Fever*, ash is "this irreplaceable place, [...] where the singular imprint, like a signature, barely distinguishes itself from the impression." "And," he continues, "this is the condition of singularity, of the idiom, of the secret, testimony."[446] Ash, then, is the figureless figure of singularity, a product or a by-product of concrete judgments rendered by "discerning fire," *pyr phronimon*, and untranslatable into the language of predication.

Keeping themselves secret, the ashes do not present themselves in logos and so invalidate phenomenology at its root. Although their own light is indiscernible to the eyes that have grown accustomed to the glow of metaphysics, it is consistent with a singular testimony, the register of unspeakable destitution, inevitably betrayed the moment it is expressed or illuminated from the outside, with a light foreign to it. Cinders and ashes are not absolutely nothing but, rather, "nothing that can be in the world,"[447] provided that the "world" is understood in its phenomenological sense either as the world of (appropriated and made familiar by) spirit or as the structures of meaning we build all around ourselves. Nothing "in the world," ashes are meaningless within the everyday matrix of sense, unpresentable and unrepresentable on the grounds of logos. But they are, at the same time, the only things that survive, that outlive life itself, and that persist outside the bygone world consumed by fire. Ashes embody the anarchy of the unclassifiable society, where the flame is neither quenched nor ready to be reignited again, where fire fails to establish another identity across its difference to itself, where everything has been burnt beyond recognition and has slipped away from the reach of metaphysical hierarchies.

\*

At the end of a book, the author and the readers part ways, the words on a page ready to become the ashes of memory and — so one hopes — to fertilise further thinking. As a parting gift, then, a piece of Hasidic wisdom from Reb Moshe-Leib of Sassov, handed down to us courtesy of Elie Wiesel: "You who wish to find fire, look for it in the ashes."[448] The saying invites a wealth of interpretations. Perhaps, in a proto-Hegelian fashion, Reb Moshe-Leib proposes that fire fully becomes itself when it is about to be extinguished, dying in the ashes; paradoxically, one can find and identify it only when it is at the point of no longer being. Or, he implies that fire may be known only through its traces and effects, obliquely. Or, he recommends that we discern the nature of fire at very low intensities, not in the raging of a blaze but in the smouldering of what remains. Or, he is convinced that the ideality of fire expresses itself in the materiality it reduces to ash. Or, he insinuates that its ostensibly accidental and secondary by-products are more crucial for conceptualising fire than its intended outcomes. Or, figuratively, he notes that the strength of fiery spirit may be gauged only in the depths of suffering and destitution, as Wiesel himself tends to think. Or...

Equally rich, from a hermeneutical perspective, is the relation between the political and depoliticisation, the politics of fire and of ashes. Does the political fully become itself on the verge of disappearing? Is it known solely through its effects on the victims of the world-historical blaze? Is its nature discoverable on the hither side of intense friend-enemy oppositions, in the nearly extinguished *agon* of the unclassifiable society? Do political ideals appear as what they are not under the steady light of truth but flickering in dim glimmer and emitting the low-grade heat of finitude? Does the singular flame of victim's sovereignty—concealed by extreme abjection and occasionally flashing before our eyes in the figures of Tenzin, Moshe, Plamen, David, Sahar, and Aaron—maintain fire alive among the ashes? Whatever the response, depoliticisation does not simply discontinue political processes, in the same sense that postmetaphysical thought does not cut loose from metaphysics and ash does not negate the fire, whose memory it preserves. Instead, their negative (or negational) mode contains more truth than their positive (or affirmative) dimension.

*

When the world is, it is ablaze. But, in its materiality and finitude, it cannot sustain the conflagration of creative destruction by fire indefinitely and turns, instead, into a smouldering pile. In the midst of the ashes, to which it will have been reduced, who will testify to the time when the world *was* ablaze?

# Appendix

## *Fiery Words:*
## *Against the Literal / Metaphorical Divide*

Fiery words, incendiary speech, the discourses of incitement... Can they really set anything alight? Do these figures of speech exceed the bounds of speech, their effects disfiguring (symbolically *and* physically) their scapegoated targets? Incitement obviously culminates in violence, while fiery addresses can impart the speaker's yearning for justice or, more generally, her vision of another world, believed to better than that of the present, to the listeners. Regardless of their repercussions, we might sense that we are dealing here with words that are not only words: with words that scorch, reduce to ash, make people come to blows, and bring to ruin, or that awaken, impassion, electrify and empower those who are receptive to them to seek the good. But is all this accomplished *through* words or *with* them? Under what circumstances, if ever, does a word serve as a match, a lighter, or a torch?

Almost automatically, without giving the matter much thought, we tend to rationalise the element of fire so prominently featured in descriptions of extraordinary speech as a nifty rhetorical instrument, a metaphorical device, which renders the potency of the word more vivid. When in the 2016 US Presidential elections Hillary Clinton accused her then-opponent Donald Trump of "political arson," was she being cryptically allegorical? Or — assuming that we are willing to probe a little deeper than the usual distinction between literalness and metaphoricity would allow — did Clinton's precise expression glimmer with the politics of fire capable of actually constituting or, more often still, hastening the destitution of reality?

If we refer back to the theological sphere, where the sources of contemporary politics lie hidden, we will espy a precursor to the language of fire in the sermons that were supposed to impart the divine spark through the prophet or the priest to the masses of believers, whose souls would be thus set ablaze. In religious metaphysics, corporeal ardor is secondary to the burning of spirits inflamed with divine love or faith. Something of this attitude survives in Cartesian rationalism, unconditionally privileging the mind over the body in the infamous "split." The other, empiricist part of modernity, however, valorises body over spirit, which it considers to be an ingenious invention. With physicality converted into the site of of utmost gravitas and ultimate reality, everything else is categorized as "just metaphor." The same way that art is sidelined and brushed off as "mere art" when, having ceased to perform the cult function, it is relegated to the sphere of imagination, fancy, and, at its utilitarian best, pure decoration.

In the transition from one *meta-* to another, from metaphysics to metaphor, we witness a nearly symmetrical inversion of values: palpable, experientially accessible phenomena and their effects come to the center-stage, whereas matters of spirit retreat into the vapors of archaic obfuscation and unscientific abstraction. Given this state of affairs, "metaphor" is a convenient technique of accounting for the latter from the standpoint of the former, that is, a technique (indeed, a sleight of hand or of the mind) for capturing non-literal, non-physical significations in the disenchanted discourse of modernity.

It goes without saying that for us, moderns, fire is a chemical process of combustion, releasing heat and light thanks to the rapid oxidation of a material. Absent oxygen, let alone a material substratum to be burnt, there is no fire, and unless souls or spirits are air-based (a hypothesis that is not so outlandish in light of their ancient association with breath, the Greek *pneuma* or the Hebrew *neshamah*), they cannot, in truth, go up in flames. As a result, the only mould their conflagration fits is that of metaphoricity. In turn, the notions of the soul and spirit themselves are explicable in term of the more or less individuated metaphors of vitality, the principles of life endowed with an identity yet irreducible to the corporeal extension of living beings.

So long as the division between the literal and the metaphorical is preserved, the two hierarchically organised orders of being that have originated in the metaphysical worldview will remain intact. Its protest against metaphysical mystification notwithstanding, insistence on pure literalness is a faithful inheritor to what it dismisses as frivolous metaphor. Particularly unscathed by the modern revalorisation of old values is a rift in meaning, whereby certain *types* of signification are assumed to have a closer relation to truth, to what really and truly is the case, than others. This proximity has nothing to do with their content; fire, for instance, may pop up on either side of the literal/metaphorical barricades. In lieu of content, the form of meaning makes all the difference, provided that the pivotal question is: does the signification at hand point directly at the thing it encodes, or does it indicate the thing obliquely at best (and, at worst, leads through a labyrinthine path to yet another signification)?

A direct form of signifying and communicating appears to be superior, more efficient and economical than the oblique. Metaphor, viewed through this lens, is waste of breath or ink, a diversion, an obstacle on the highway of information sharing. Unnecessary noise clogging the vacant medium that connects us, it is an annoyance, out of place in consequential, solemn exchanges of words.

Consequently, a formal semantic division runs in front of and through us, with one of its sides infinitely more attractive than the other. We are seduced by the utopia of total transparency. And, blinded by the intense light of literalness that, like the Platonic sun leaves no space for shadows, we forget to linger on the meanings of transparency, of *clara et distincta perceptio*, when the metaphorical tinges of the clear and the transparent have been all but expunged. In the pyrological scheme, absolute literalness is the shining of light devoid of heat and, therefore, separated from fire—meaning oblivious to its provenance from the minimally transparent opaqueness, out of which the world of sense and of the senses is woven.

I see only one justifiable rendition of literalness, namely L I T E R A L N E S S, the word and the thing itself trimmed down to letters, to the *literae* that lend it meaning. Except, of course, that a purely literal literalness flips into non-sense, the body of the text in its dense materiality failing to gesture beyond itself (not toward an otherworldly, supersensible domain but toward relations, connections, associations: first, among the letters themselves; then, among words, objects, ideas…) Unless metaphor carries us elsewhere—always elsewhere—, there is no smooth connectivity we envision for the ideal medium of communication. In fact, there is no connectivity at all, because a completely literal world is a place of "blooming, buzzing confusion," as William James would have it, where the atomic particles of matter, sense, and signification chaotically move about, colliding and shifting apart again.

To establish relations, including those of being and life itself, fire and metaphor are in order. Or, better, fire *as* metaphor and metaphor *as* fire, each defined by the act of transposing, transporting, effecting transformations—from the literal to the metaphorical (and back again) and from the combustible to the combusted... We are left with little more than a strange afterglow of both: the shadow-free, cold light of literal meaning, which will not rest until it has enveloped and neutralised-depoliticised everything in existence. But the chaos born from the desire for a rigidly crystalline order is not the end of the road. Under the aegis of information so salient in the paradigm of literalness (note the difference in the prefixes of information and transformation: the *trans*formative movement of carrying-beyond comes to a halt in *in*formation), *literae* become digits. Enamored of these figures for fingers or toes, we are ready to supplant a numeric code for language and do away with the spoken or written word altogether, as well as with heat, with the life it gives, and with a dimmer light our bodies and minds are capable of receiving within the limits of our finitude.

In response to the hyperinflation of literalness, I do not wish to place undue stress on metaphoricity with the opposite thesis: *everything is metaphorical*. One or another version of this statement tends to emerge in parodies on deconstruction that, in a twist on the Platonic world of appearances, announce: *nothing means what it seems to mean*. (From there, it's a small step to the absurd affirmation: *nothing means anything*.) I am cautious not to endorse the other extreme of total literalness above all because I believe that doing so would merely displace and replicate, in a distorted fashion, the very thing I am reacting against. I prefer not to be embroiled in the a priori rigged contest between the text's body and spirit, the contest that has for its main objective, still folded into the vast fabric of metaphysics, an overarching claim relevant to "everything." I want to test, instead, various methods for softening, melting, deliquescing, and finally making the literal/metaphorical divide evaporate.

In its non-caricaturised iterations, deconstructive thought has pursued a similar goal in an effort to show the cross-contamination of literalness and metaphoricity. The problem is that these efforts have been married to practices of reading (Derrida used to term them *protocols*) that, however broad their scope, did not venture outside the textual frame and on to the territory of that which they designated as "the undeconstructible" — for instance, the demand for justice underlying the mechanisms of legality. The undeconstructible also includes, I would argue, the entire non-, pre- or post-individuated elemental universe and, especially, the element of fire.

It is not by chance that I have focused on the possibility of melting rather than, say, on demolishing the literal/metaphorical divide, since a catalyst is required for the inner (and, thus, a reliably radical) transformation to happen. That catalyst is, precisely, a flame. Now, the place where such a possibility might be fleshed out is politics, its fires no longer identifiably allegorical or actual, real or imagined, rhetorical or carnal. Let us, then, try to imagine the contours of a political chemistry, if not of political alchemy, drawn in blazing brushstrokes that leave the demarcation lines between literalness and metaphor in ashes.

The cynical view of politics prevalent in the West is that it is the native turf of barefaced lies, of words turned instruments for no other purpose than to get elected or to continue holding an office. The critique of opportunistic political reason in which rhetoric prevails over veracity has long roots, reaching back to the bitter standoff between the sophists, proud of their prowess in making any argument appear plausible, and the philosophers, who cared about and for the truth. More recently, the charge of relying on empty words has been leveled against parliamentary democracy: in

Weimar Germany, the weariness of the population with the perceived ineffectiveness and protracted nature of democratic discussions and procedures played a role in Hitler's rise to power.

Eliminating the mediations that the word provides is now a political desideratum not only in blatant authoritarianisms, where discussion and dialogue are discouraged to say the least, but also in the contemporary, technocratic permutations of democracy, with their own standard of literalness that literally invalidates words. Without prospects for a meaningful debate on the substantive aims and aspirations befitting a polity, technocrats labor to convince us to take directives from market forces, whose messengers they feign to be. If vacuous words were the messengers of political light bereft of heat, then the virtually wordless technocratic decrees extinguish the last glares of luminosity along with the memory of how motivation and sense, meaning and intense commitment once belonged together.

Unfulfilled promises aside, political words are not only words, and extreme phenomena, such as revolutionary or incendiary speech, put this quality—their excess over and above themselves—into sharper relief. In the political sphere, words are either catalysts or anticatalysts; they either fan or douse fires. Which fires? Those of acrimony and division alongside those of the desire for justice and equality; those of carpet bombings and scorched earth, as much as those of the revolutionary barricades and of self-immolations protesting political and economic oppression. If there is an unmistakable continuity between, and a blending of, the literal and metaphorical dimensions of the blaze here, that is because the matter of politics, the material wherein it sets itself to work, is immediately spirit. The entire conservative-progressive axis ought to be replaced with a classification, according to which some political programs dispirit the people to prevent resistance, and others inspire to act, based on a shared vision for a different future.

Politics, we might say, is a set of tactics, methods, and procedures for the deployment (and often the minimization, the extinguishing) of fire in all its modalities, be they figurative or tangibly "real." As such, politics operates with the model of incitement-excitement: it incinerates the public by spreading hatred toward minorities (religious, ethnic, sexual, and so forth) *or* by propagating the love of others, all equally deserving of a dignified life. Conversely, the politics practiced in the shape of technocratic business-as-usual and, indeed, any acts geared toward the preservation of the status quo strive to lower the level of public engagement and go as far as to induce apathy, stomping out the spark of rebellion, to cool the polity down. Their energy is poured into fire prevention, management and control, which often amounts to a repression of collective desires and fantasies.

The empirical fires that flare up (or fail to flare up) from these contrasting approaches are an expression of political work on its exceptional prime matter—*materia prima*: typically, *hulé* (wood) and, hence, a common substratum for incineration—which is spirit or, rather, spirits. In an endless loop disconnected academic reading practices, literal and metaphorical blazes pass into one another and, with every passage, spawn a plethora of effects, both symbolic and imprinted on the actuality of human and non-human living beings, landscapes, climates, geographies, the planet as a whole. Flaming bodies become indistinguishable from inflamed spirits—of a community, a nation, for sure, but also of trees and crops destined to become biodiesel, of animals thrown onto the pyre of global warming, of the earth.

And words—words burn, too. More than semantic channels between bodies and spirits alight, they are burnt to a crisp and ignite emotions and actions. What does their conflagration reveal? What is hidden from view by the fumes they are shrouded in? We already have some preliminary indications for an answer. Fiery words bespeak the irreducibility of affect and of everything deemed irrational in Enlightenment politics, even as they conceal the differential valuations of "good" and "bad" incitement-excitement, the one caring for and the other murderous toward outsiders. Still, the concealment is a revelation of sorts: it lifts the curtain on the limits of political visibility that retrace those of our finitude and on the impossibility of absolute transparency in the light of a fire that, emanating together with heat, clothes its source in smoke.

## A Shadow Sun

The unmitigated disaster that is Western metaphysics, responsible for the global environmental crisis, may be neatly summarized in the following statement: *for over two thousand years, we have been living with a shadow sun for our guiding star.* We have not been living in the shadows, the penumbra impenetrable to sunlight. Nor even in the sun's shadow. But in the orbit of a shadow sun.

Plato, who systematized and gave philosophical credence to extant myths of the Sun God, prevalent in the Near East and Asia Minor, was clear on this point: the other sun is the analog (*analogon*) of an idea, namely the idea of the good (*Rep.* 508c). Reasoning by analogy draws a proportion—that is the sense of *analogon*—between things that are, for all intents and purposes, disparate. In this case, the sun makes vision possible, while it is itself impossible to look at with unprotected eyes; the idea of the good makes all other ideas possible, while it cannot itself be thought, beheld with the mind's eye directly. Strict proportionality governs the relation between the hidden and the revealed, causes and effects, the potentiating and the actual, in sensuous and intellectual domains alike. There are really two suns, Plato implies: the one illuminating the world accessible to our ocular sense and the other showering light on the world of ideas. The true sun, the sun of truth, is the second of the two, more original still than the celestial body, which gave rise to the Platonic analogy. His take-home lesson is that we must stop trusting our senses and learn how to see reality otherwise, orienting ourselves not by the physical but by the metaphysical sun.

What should we make of metaphysical luminosity, converted in early modernity into *the light of reason*? Since the dawn of the European Enlightenment, the goal of philosophy has been to spread the nets of understanding and reason that conceived themselves as universal: the same for everyone, in any part of the world at any time, indifferent to particular contexts, lived experiences, and identities, all of them lumped together as unhelpful biases. The light of reason was, consequently, even and uniform, with human progress indexed to how widely it shone on various parts of the earth. It had no phases, periods, or cycles; instead, its development was linear, progressive, and ever-expanding. Time itself, which was originally measured by tracking the course of the sun in the sky, changed in keeping with the light of the Modern Age that was meant never to go out. The other sun—that of metaphysics—established a system of coordinates, to which the experience of a rational human being would belong.

The shadow sun is bizarre, and so is everything that unfolds under it. Whereas eyesight relies on a constant play of light and shadow to do its work properly, the vision of the ideas or of abstract reason is supposed to transpire in a true, shadowless luminosity. When it comes to bodily sight, the shady areas of an object and its shadow are the enabling limits of ocularity, the edges that define, by way of contrast that sharpens our focus, what is visible and give it perspectival depth. Shadows are the finitude of light; hence, their appropriateness to our finite existence. Depending on the angle at which a ray falls, as well as on the variable standpoints of the object and the spectator, shadows will dance, though always in unison with the entire visual field. Longer or shorter, they will indicate the time of day based on the position of the sun vis-à-vis the earth, with each being—whether animate or inanimate—for a sundial. Events in the everyday hustle-and-bustle we call *life* will be, in this way, encrusted into a cosmic drama, pointing back to the alignment of planets and stars, senses and experiences, each with the others and amongst themselves.

For Plato, and in his wake, all theater is the appearance of mere shadows, and all appearance is the shadow theater of true being. The underground realm of the cave is not qualitatively distinct from the cosmic theater; only the scale and extent of their respective fires and moving shadows vary. The non-sensuous luminosity of metaphysics, in turn, is shadowless, detached both from shadows and from the objects that cast them. Given this double separation, the play of light and shadow (a kind of theater before theater, provided that we take various semantic aspects of *play* into account) also ceases. One can no longer tell what time it is on the clock of existence, and for a good reason: there are no shadows, short or long, emanating from eidetic objects. Does shadowlessness not account, if only in part, for Plato's designation of ideas as unchangeable, atemporal, eternal?

The act of freeing shadows from objects and from light spawns chimeras and threatens to transform the world herebelow into a vast collection of phantoms. The insubstantial becomes substantial and begins to lead a life of its own. To paraphrase Hegel, non-substance becomes subject (which we tend to associate with spirits or specters). Metaphysics, in effect, uses the hypostasis of the shadows to consolidate its stature. Its key moments, including the ideas, the unmoved mover, God, the thing-in-itself, will-to-power, and even being, are shadows unglued from, and presumed more genuine than, portions of actual existence. The non-substantial subject is deemed truer than mere substance. And palpable objects are viewed as the shadows of their former shadows. That which appears before the senses—a sensory appearance—is interpreted as an apparition, a confounding and mendacious ghost. Our fragile, ever incomplete, finite reality turns out to be a lie so long as it is illuminated by the shadow sun.

In the name of true being, unperturbed by any empirical occurrences, philosophers have not hesitated to sacrifice the entire world. Their theoretical desire has received the practical tools for accomplishing such a feat from technological development and from economics, in particular from the logic of capital. I could say that capitalism is the continuation of metaphysics by other means, because the value of anything and anyone whatsoever is a shadow that grows more significant than the valued being itself. It trades in shadows and the shadows of shadows, in firm belief that they are the emanations of absolute brightness.

An economic system stemming from metaphysical ideation, capitalism manages to bring the livable planet to naught, having ushered in the geological epoch of the Anthropocene. Besides unofficial shadow economies, also known as the black markets, capitalism as a whole is a monstrous shadow economy that keeps growing whilst the majority of the global population is impoverished. Indifferent to material existence and, in fact, to anything unrelated to the project of capital's augmentation, it replicates the untethering of shadows from light and from the objects that happen to be in the ray's path. For, here, too, everything visible and tangible is a lie. The truth of capitalism is in the non-sensuous workings of abstract, quantitatively determined value.

The shadow sun of metaphysics, not least in its economic instantiation, has overshadowed the earth and the sun our planet orbits. How to emerge out of the shadow that claims for itself the status of pure light? How to come back to the world woven out of an interplay of lights and shadows?

Nietzsche recommends transvaluing all values hitherto posited, a project that, instead of stopping at a simple revaluation, puts in question the very value of value. It would be insufficient to invert the scale and to put the shadow sun in its rightful place *below* that of astronomy. We ought to question the hierarchical mode of valuation, presupposing the vertical axis of what is above and what is below.

In a fragment titled "How the 'True World' Finally Became a Fable. The History of an Error" and featured in *Twilight of the Idols*, Nietzsche writes: "The true world is gone: which world is left? The illusory one, perhaps? But no! *we got rid of the illusory world along with the true one!* (Noon, moment of the shortest shadow; end of the longest error, high point of humanity; INCIPIT ZARATHUSTRA.)"[449] The illusory play of lights and shadows was only an illusion from the standpoint of the now-demolished static and luminous conception of truth. The conclusion that both worlds disappear corroborates not the decimation of real and ideal being, but the ineluctable necessity of learning to see and to think anew, with and from the shadows.

Nietzsche is reluctant to equate the moment of truth, when the "true world" is revealed as the biggest lie, with the illumination a particularly clever insight would offer. The "high point of humanity" corresponds to noontime, the "moment of the shortest shadow," which is still a shadow. However energetically hypercritical reason smashes the old idols, however bright its light, such reason will belong together with what it incinerates, unless it admits obscurity and scorching heat into its midst, or, more exactly, recognises their unavoidable presence within itself.

With his thesis, Nietzsche provides the first answer to our questions about the shadow sun of metaphysics. The shortest shadow conveys the doubling at the heart of a being we still dare name *human*. As long as there is meaning, as long as we make sense of the world, this meaning and this sense will be the world's shadows. The point of a consistent philosophy is not to get rid of them, but to live as though it is always midday, keeping semantic shadows as close as possible to the things that cast them: keeping them short. In the most recent history of philosophy, this has been the mission of phenomenology. There are, of course, metaphysical tinges to always seeing the same hour on the clock of being: to do so, one would have to eschew the daily and nightly movements of the celestial body and the corresponding rhythms (e.g., those called "circadian") they stimulate in the living. It would entail following the other sun that does not budge from its fixed non-physical, metaphysical spot, despite the acknowledgement of that, in its pure identity, it does not coincide with itself.

The metaphysical tradition has not only lengthened the shadows of meaning beyond belief and has not only caused these shadows and the objects that cast them to switch places. It has also distorted the doubling of human reality by granting independent existence to the double. Metaphysics is the name of a spatiotemporal dissociation, above all from physical space and time: it ensures the reign of permanent daylight in one hemisphere of being (above) and a never-ending polar night in the other (below), so much so that this darkness passes in its eyes for non-being. The adherents of the shortest shadow, for their part, refrain from choosing between meaning and reality, thought and the world. They track two-in-one and one-in-two, observing and participating in the play of lights and shadows staged in the theater of being.

If the shortest shadow on the plains of thinking is the inexorable doubling of reality with signification, then in the visual field it is a shadow pierced with light. Translucent, nearly transparent shadows are really so many transitory passages from the Western metaphysical obsession with pure luminosity to a desire for dwelling in and on the obscure. Bordering on shadowlessness, more insubstantial still than the umbra of a dense object, they are in fact the instances of the becoming-shadow of shadows stripped down to their (fleeting, inessential, superficial) essence. They lead the gaze, imagination, and insight toward emancipation from the metaphysical shadow sun.

In and of itself, the shadow sun is much older than metaphysics; indeed, it is older than humanity itself. It may equally refer to solar energy released millions of years ago, giving life to the plants and animals whose remains have by now been converted into oil, coal, and natural gas. Not by accident, the economic arm of metaphysics that is global capitalism owes its origins to, and still clings onto, these nonrenewable, highly polluting and deadly sources of energy. Material and intellectual dynamics grow from and in the same shadow. Just as the shadow sun prevents us from seeing and thinking the world around us, so it curtails the development of present and future—rather than past—*non-extractive* solar energy—i.e., solar energy not reliant on environmentally harmful panels; photosynthetic in its vegetal essence—and blocks the return of our minds, imagination, and the senses to the earth, the atmosphere, and the astronomical sun. Today, more than ever, this return is vital to the preservation, continuation, and thriving of life. That is why we cannot afford to ignore the voices and visions of the thinkers-artists capable of charting the paths back to the actual earth, the sky, and everything in-between.

## Burning Ourselves to Death

In the early hours of Saturday, April 14, 2018, charred remains of a prominent New York lawyer, David S. Buckel, were found in New York City's Prospect Park. According to the note he left behind, Buckel committed an act of self-immolation to draw attention to the noxious effects of burning fossil fuels on human health and on the planet as a whole. "Pollution ravages our planet, oozing inhabitability via air, soil, water and weather," he wrote. "Most humans on the planet now breathe air made unhealthy by fossil fuels, and many die early deaths as a result—my early death by fossil fuel reflects what we are doing to ourselves."[450] In the microcosm of his own mortality, Buckel recreated the macrocosmic consequences of continued reliance on coal, oil, and natural gas for energy production. We are, he implied, collectively burning ourselves to death, while dragging numerous other species and the very conditions for liveability along.

Beyond a strong emotional reaction to such an extreme act of protest (which the protestor himself locates in a long tradition of self-immolations, for instance, by Tibetan monks), the event ought to serve as a wakeup call to thinking. More precisely, it should impel us to rethink the meaning of natural environment and of life, whether human or not, at an age when these are not only polluted but have been reshaped by the centuries-long blaze of energy derived from fossil fuels.

When we burn ourselves to death, who or what is burnt? And who or what ignites the fire?

The act seems to be an exercise in elemental sovereignty, in which the subject and the object of burning is one and the same. Yet, we are unconscious sovereigns: when we set the world around us alight (above all, by using fossil fuels, but also by resorting to such "renewable" sources of energy as biodiesels) we feel as though we are incinerating something separate, something outside ourselves. We implicitly frame our natural environment as a milieu, to which we are only incidentally related and in which we are not at all embedded. Our will and intention are to fire what this background existence is to flammable materials. What we fail to realise, however, is that the world we burn is not set apart from us in the same way the mind is not split from the body. That is to say, we overlook our own ecopsychosomatic constitution whereby we "ourselves" are comprised of the body, the mind, and the environment.

The axiom of ecopsychosomatics is simple: bring a match to any one of its three intertwined components, and the other two will catch fire as well. Past theological and metaphysical systems postulated that the psyche (or, at least, its portions situated at a distance from the material world) would survive the death of the body. More than that, if the body were to be disposed of in a ritually prescribed way (for instance, by cremation), the soul would enjoy an easier passage to its afterlife (for example, thanks to the cleansing power of fire). For a Gnostic, death is a moment of liberation, the soul discarding the prison-house of the body that had pulled it down and had forced it to engage with the messy realm of matter.

In secular modernity this set of beliefs has been transposed, in a modified shape, onto the body-mind complex. Even the staunchest materialists who debunk the myth of an otherworldly reality would agree that to extract a human being from her environment is not tantamount to terminating her life. But "only" two and a half millennia ago, the opposite conviction prevailed. Exile was equivalent to death, and the latter in many cases (such as that of Socrates, who was given a choice between the two) was preferable to the former.

Nowadays, the consensus is that, so long as one flees from a disaster zone (be it environmental, military, or a mixed variety), one would be safe and sound. Whereas this approach might not work for other kinds of organisms deeply embedded in their ecological niches, human resilience and adaptability allow us to change the physical contexts of our existence at will, or so the argument goes. The bottom line is that, by analogy to the theological narratives of old where the soul outlived the body, the psychosomatic unit survives its extraction from its lifeworld and is highly capable of learning to make sense of another environment. Succinctly put, the individual survives the end of *its* world.

A cardinal premise of the secular argument is that there is a difference between individual human worlds and *the* world, the difference that permits those suffering the destruction of their immediate environment to re-establish themselves in other parts of the common living realm, in other worlds vouchsafed by *the* world. It shares this premise with phenomenology and, increasingly, with political forces that, on the right, endeavour to police the boundaries of destroyed worlds so as to stem population flows from the affected areas, and, on the left, affirm their commitment (more theoretical than practical) to the concept of open borders for climate and other refugees. Indeed, a difference between worlds and *the* world remains, but what does it really mean today? Isn't the predominant meaning of *the* world, as a shared horizon of worlds, that of world-devastation? This is the backdrop against which all worlds are to be seen—the sinking and the desertified, the bombed and the eroded, the fracked and the depleted, as well as those apparently still thriving.

With regard to world-devastation, the corners of the earth that are still liveable provide no more than a temporary reprieve from the disastrous tendency, in which the sweep of actual world-destruction approximates the sense of world-devastation. On the planetary scale of pollution Buckel mentions in his note, the rule, to which humanity is thought to have been the exception, applies to us, too: the destruction of the ecological context, wherein a psychosomatic unit exists, cannot but destroy this very unit. Local destruction is contingent upon the much wider world-devastation, which goes hand-in-hand with world-transformation. And the element enabling the confluence of devastation and transformation is fire, through which we change our surroundings and are, ourselves, changed.

So, by burning the world around us, we burn ourselves to death. But, in keeping with the metaphysical and theological luggage we unconsciously haul with us, the deadly conflagration blazes a path to a higher life. A life ranked higher than lives is not biological, nor is it that of divinity, as traditionally understood. Supranatural, the vitality in question is the life of self-augmenting value, also known as capital, or of an idea, such as progress. We are not spared the fate of the world that is given as a burnt offering to that other life, which is the other *of* life. While we burn and are burnt unbeknownst to ourselves, Buckel consciously delivered himself to fire in what might be thought of as a counter-sacrifice. He inverted the dynamics of our secular theology, as he burnt to death in the name of *this* life, in an act that did not ripple out from destructive energy production but emanated from a movement opposed to the hegemonic sacrificial paradigm.

It is tempting to gear efforts toward individual suicide prevention, while conveniently overlooking the fact that humanity is head over heels in a drive toward a collective, intergenerational suicide. This psychologizing of the problem, which is thereby depoliticized, is precisely what has happened. David Buckel's death will not have been in vain if it were to trigger political action against the ongoing use of fossil fuels as much as a sustained reflection on what happens to the "outside" world, to our bodies, and to our minds before they are sucked into the vortex of devastation. In other words, on the different ways, in which we are burning ourselves to death.

## The Implosion of History

As philosophers, we are supposed to comprehend events and phenomena in the world from a rather detached standpoint, keeping in mind useful theoretical models and precedents. Thinking is, perhaps, this minimal detachment from existence, which nonetheless engages with existence across a gap that thinkers either interpose or highlight between themselves and reality.

With Russia's full-scale invasion of Ukraine in February 2022, it was difficult for me to keep such detachment for two reasons. First, more than half of my family comes from Ukraine. Second, the issues of nuclear and radioactive threats, centering on the Chernobyl power plant and the use of nuclear weapons, have been preoccupying me for years from a philosophical as much as from a personal point of view. Nonetheless, thinking must proceed, if only under the sign of the simultaneous necessity and impossibility of detachment.

Looking back at a chapter titled "The Unfinished Collapse of the Soviet Union," from my 2021 book *Senses of Upheaval*,[451] I cannot help but think about today's world, in which we need to develop, more urgently still, "a robust philosophy of history" capable of accounting for historical "gaps, protracted subterranean processes, and time lags between causes and effects." It becomes even more painfully obvious in 2022 that what we are witnessing is an outcome of the time lag between the official end of the USSR in 1991 and its unresolved

legacies, responsible, following the example of the collapse of Yugoslavia, not only for the war in Ukraine, but also for the simmering conflict between Armenia and Azerbaijan in the Nagorno-Karabakh region (since "resolved" by the forcible removal of a large Armenian population that lived there), or the fate of Belarus. Added to this is Soviet nuclear arsenal, which, based on international agreements, Ukraine gave up upon becoming independent and which was inherited by the Russian Federation.

At the same time, the knots tied or untied in Putin's war in Ukraine are much more complex than the as-yet indeterminate legacy of Soviet collapse. To European observers, the invasion of Ukraine is redolent of the actions of Nazi Germany in 1939. To the Ukrainians themselves, it invariably brings to mind the national catastrophes of the recent past, from the 1932-33 Holodomor to enormous losses suffered in WWII and the nightmare of the 1986 Chernobyl disaster. To the Russians, the tightening of censorship and other internal repressive measures undertaken in the aftermath of the invasion awaken the memory of Stalinism. Whatever the perspective, an old, tired adage "History repeats itself" seems to apply.

I do not think, however, that history is merely repeating itself. Repetition entails cyclicality and definite temporal rhythms, not to mention the completion of whatever is being repeated. Yet, many of the issues at play in Putin's war are, precisely, the comet tails of incomplete events, from the dissolution of the Soviet Union to the effects of radioactive fallout that take thousands of years to wear off.

So, what is happening if not a repetition of history? I would like to suggest that history implodes, tumbling unto itself in a vortex of events that give off an appearance of repetition. One indication for the implosion of history is the convergences of different timelines in a single event of the Russian invasion of Ukraine: the timeline of Soviet collapse thirty years ago, that of the Chernobyl disaster, which happened thirty-six years ago and points toward an indefinite future of environmental contamination, that of the two world wars, of the Ukrainian genocide and Stalinist repressions of the 1930s... All this is concentrated and condensed in the current war, much as fissionable material "is suddenly compressed into a smaller size and thus a greater density" in an implosion-type atomic bomb.[452] The explosion of hostilities is, at its core, a historical implosion.

The three classical models that explain the movement of history have included the conservative Fall, bemoaning the loss of past greatness; liberal Progress, celebrating the opposite upward vector of ever-improving life conditions and ever-expanding markets; and cyclical repetition (sometimes combined with the first or the second model in a spiral) of world destruction and rejuvenation "by water or fire," as in Plato's Timaeus. Implosion is the fourth option that similarly borrows from physics to describe how history caves in and buckles if not under the weight of its inner contradictions, then because of an amassing of unresolved legacies. In a sense, the fourth model combines elements from the other three, pitting conservative against liberal visions and exhibiting aspects of repetition due to the centripetal forces unleashed in an implosion. Which is why we hear echoes of "the restoration" of the glorious past of the Russian empire, of the "irrepressible" march toward market freedom and democracy in Ukraine, and, last but not least, of the tirelessly repeated mantra "History repeats itself."

The implosion of history is also palpable in the global environmental crisis, where the sixth mass extinction that is now underway is not merely a repetition of the previous five mass extinctions but also the collapse of human species-history, along with those of countless other species. In the geological epoch of the Anthropocene, this collapse is self-provoked, as far as agriculture and the Industrial Revolution are concerned, and, therefore, bears all the marks of an implosion within the framework of the natural-cultural history of Homo sapiens. The centrality of fossil fuels to environmental degradation and to the possibilities of funding Putin's regime holds a clue to their co-belonging within the paradigm of the implosion of history. And here President Zelensky emerges as a new Greta Thunberg-like figure vis-à-vis the West, speaking truth to power, but to no avail.

The perennial question of political action—"What is to be done?"—cannot be raised seriously without at least a rough understanding of the historical context, in which such an action hopes to be effective. Is the war in Ukraine a temporary setback on the road to freedom, spreading around the world? Is it an equally temporary obstacle to the atavistic, colonial restoration of Russia's imperial greatness? Does it repeat WWII in reverse, with the defenders of their homeland now in the position of occupiers? Or is something else afoot on Ukrainian soil in 2022?

One characteristic of the implosion of history is that it draws everything and everyone into its vortex. If, indeed, the war in Ukraine is a telltale sign of this implosion, then it is naïve to think that, though it is still early to talk about WWIII, the hostilities taking place on Ukrainian soil are limited to the territory, on which they are unfolding. The imbrication of the nuclear issue in the conflict, including nuclear power plants and atomic weapons, is symptomatic of the temporally and spatially unlimited effects of these hostilities. Just as, at the outset of the COVID-19 pandemic, which adds another brushstroke to the portrait of history's implosion, Europe and the United States considered the SARS-CoV-2 virus a regional health problem in China, so now the "defensive" position of the NATO block overlooks the transnational threats of nuclear fallouts, or biological or chemical weapons, which crop up with greater and greater frequency in the war in

Ukraine. The sooner the logic or the illogic of the implosion is grasped, the better we will be able to respond to the urgent question, "What is to be done?"

For, we are living not only at the end of an era with an acute sense of the end of history, but also, and more significantly, at the end of how we see history itself.

## Kant's Fire

It is tempting to read Kant through Hegel even when it comes to the triad of texts, written in Latin, which Kant submitted in the span of a single year (between April 1755 and March 1756) in order to fulfil the requirements of teaching at a university.[453] In keeping with a simple dialectical scheme, the first "dissertation" titled "Succinct Exposition of Some Meditations on Fire [*Meditationum quarundam de igne succincta delineatio*]" deals with an objective phenomenon from the physical world, the world of natural science. The second essay, "A New Elucidation of the First Principles of Metaphysical Cognition [*Principiorum primorum cognitionis metaphysicae nova dilucidatio*]" turns away from the world of nature to consider the laws of cognition, the *prima philosophia* of the subject, rather than that of the object. The third essay, on "Physical Monadology [*Metaphysicae cum geometrica iunctae usus in philosophia naturali, cuius specimen I. continet monadologiam physicam*]" returns to the philosophy of nature modified by the metaphysics of the subject to produce a synthesis that is a *Kantian* monadology.

Should we accept this view, the textbook narrative about Kant as the one who bridged the gap between radical empiricism and strict rationalism by inventing transcendental idealism would no longer hold. If the first submission is a tribute to Newtonian physics (filtered through Euler, as well as Voltaire's and Émilie du Châtelet's studies of fire in their respective 1737 entries to an essay competition organized by the Académie des sciences), then the second is an allusion to Descartes' metaphysics of the subject, and the third — an amalgam of Leibniz and Spinoza, who have passed through the crucible of Newton and Descartes. Fire, cognition, and monadology (conceived as a physical metaphysics) would then be the triad of Kant's pre-critical approach, which nonetheless surpasses the rigid limits of the critical project.

Schematic as it is, I am not quite satisfied with this preliminary reading of the early works Kant submitted to obtain a teaching and (unsuccessfully) an extraordinary professorial post at the university. I am skeptical for the most part because fire already contains all three moments of what seems to be a dialectical triad, and it does so not in a merely abstract, potential, or formal mode typical of a fledgling dialectical beginning. How so?

*First*, Kant stresses the negativity of fire, its force (*vis*) "manifested principally in the rarefaction of bodies and in breaking down their combination [*in rarefaciendis corporibus et ipsorum nexu solvendo*]."[454] The starting point has nothing to do with the unmediated positivity of matter or nature; rather, fire is already imbued with negativity, which is its very force (*vis*). That said, fiery negativity is not pure either. Kant will, from the outset, reject the Cartesian approach to matter (above all, to liquid matter), which is not mechanically divisible: "The fluidity of bodies cannot be explained by the division of matter into smooth minute parts that loosely cohere, as most physicists, following the teachings of Descartes, think" (Prop 1).[455] Instead, what liquid matter has in common with fire is its elasticity: "elastic matter [*materiam elasticam*], which is present between the elementary parts of a fluid body, is nothing other than the matter of heat" (Prop. 2).[456] The negative force of fire is, thus, already a mediation between an elastic positivity and a rarefying negativity, synthetic and analytic; in other words, fire is both matter and force. Descartes and his followers, however, privileged the negative aspect of fire and of matter as such, conceived in terms of its infinite divisibility.

*Second*, ever since its pre-philosophical—mythical—origins, the metaphysics of cognition has operated with two fundamental processes: analysis and synthesis. In Plato's dialogues (notably in *Phaedrus*), Socrates professes to be the lover of both synthesis and analysis that, jointly, comprise a dialectic. From Heraclitus to Novalis, fire has been not a metaphor but the embodiment of a cosmic or material mind, thinking the world into being by means of the two processes of breaking things up and joining the bits together. In this tradition, to which Freud also belongs with his recovery (in *Beyond the Pleasure Principle*) of *eros* and *thanatos* as the drives toward congregation and segregation, thinking and being are indistinguishable from one another in the heat and light of fire. Hence, a certain "physical monadology"—the subject of Kant's third submission to the University of Königsberg is also folded into the ontology of fire.

Particularly fascinating in this respect is Kant's main contribution to theorization of fire, which is the hypothesis that fire is comprised of "elastic matter." The notion of elasticity includes the positive and the negative vectors of force. On the one hand, it implies a drive, a propulsive action; on the other hand, it entails a reaction as a response to pressure or compression in one of the parts: "Matter that when pressed anywhere endeavors with the same force to expand in a different direction, is commonly called an elastic matter [*materiae cuidam elasticae ipsis intermistae incumbant, cuius ope, quicquid desuper premit virium, versus latera eadem quantitate agat*]" (Prop 2).[457] This formulation will have been recognizable as a restatement of one of Newton's laws of motion (viz. that for every action in nature there is an equal and opposite reaction), except that elastic matter allows Kant to de-formalize the Newtonian law, or better, to shift the categorial understanding of the relation between action and reaction from quantity to quality. More tellingly still, the same phenomenon of elasticity should apply to the domain of cognition, implied in the concept of fire. If there is pressure or contraction in one area of that domain, then it will strive "to expand in a different direction." And doesn't Kant's critical project induce precisely such pressure, aiming at a contraction, upon finite human reason in order to put it within its proper boundaries? The elasticity of cognition is crucial here. Conceivably, the pressure of critique keeping the flight of reason in check would then result in its expansion with the same force "in a different direction," thereby rendering the work of critique interminable.

When Kant postulates "elastic matter" as the common denominator of fire and of liquid bodies (which can maintain their liquid state thanks to their warmth), he is combining elements that are, physically and symbolically, taken to be mutually opposed. Elasticity performs the function of a *complexio oppositorum*, the immediate union of opposites. A further step is taken when Kant adds solid bodies to the mix; according to Proposition 3, "Solid bodies, like fluid bodies, are held together not by the direct contact of their molecules but by the mediation of an elastic matter [*materia elastica pariter mediante cohaerentibus*]."[458] Elastic matter (which is none other than heat or fire) becomes a universal mediator, the in-between that makes possible the coherence of molecules not touching one another directly. While, in theology, the universally mediating role of fire raises it to the status of spirit, this step allows Kant to forge a shortcut to the physical monadology, with which he aims to complete his early draft of a metaphysical system.

The mediation of elastic matter varies depending on the degrees of heat and the corresponding distances between molecules. Kant observes that "metals and other bodies of this kind, when they solidify out of fluids, occupy smaller and smaller volumes as they become less and less hot."[459] The expansiveness of a body permeated by fire is then due to the greater distance between its molecules, at the same time separated and drawn together by elastic matter, whereas the withdrawal of heat is responsible for the contraction of a body, with the spaces occupied by elastic matter becoming smaller. The first pyropolitical implications of Kant's conjectures come through in this very moment: fire not only mediates a multiplicity of semi-autonomous entities, drawing them together into a single body (here: body politic), but it also drives the rhythms of this body's expansion and its inevitable contraction when heat diminishes. But what does this actually mean? It means that individual actors (represented by separate molecules) are *further apart* from one another, when the body politic they participate in is inflamed by revolutionary fervor, war, tumult, and the like. And, vice versa, the solidity and compactness of the cooled down body politic is due to the shrinking of fire's elastic matter between individuals. Kant himself notes this inversion of common sense in Proposition 5: "What is ordinarily called compression in a solid body is more truly called by the name dilatation or extension [*quae in corporibus duris compressiones vulgo vocantur, dilatationis verius s. extensionis nomine nuncupandae sunt*]."[460]

That said, elastic matter (hence, heat and fire) never evanesces entirely; every single body, for Kant, contains residual heat, which accounts for its resilience. The main effect of this perseverance is that solid bodies can stretch, when, for instance, extra weight is affixed to them, rather than tear. Hence, "it is clear that the elements of solid bodies, not being in immediate contact, attract each other at a definite distance by means of some mediating matter [*elementa corporum durorum non immediato contactu, sed mediante materia quadam in definita etiam distantia semet attrahere]*" (Prop 4).[461] When it comes to attraction, elastic matter plays the role of another universal force, that of gravity. However weak, fire still articulates the multiplicity of bodies, without letting them either fuse with one another (nor even to be in immediate contact) or fall apart. Its function harkens back to the principle of reason, or the idea of reason, which Kant will later elevate to, among other things, the principle of the right governing our outer freedom—i.e., that no person can invade the space of the other, seen in light of the synthetic *a priori* axiom that two bodies cannot occupy the same space at the same time—and the foundations of the social contract.

The intermediate position of elastic matter does not make it inherently moderate, however. When elastic matter is extremely expansive—that is, when heat is increased beyond the fragile limits within which it can draw together molecules and hold them apart—then the burning body disintegrates. When it nearly fades, then the exceptionally cool body loses its elasticity and, becoming brittle, suffer a similar fate. That is why, if there is a Kantian pyropolitical art, it is that of moderating the fire of body politic, albeit not by controlling the intensities of revolutionary fire, in the manner of Lenin or Castro, but by seeking guidance from reason and *its* transcendentally indifferent heat (within the limits of its critique) for peaceful coexistence. In the concluding proposition of the first part of his treatise on fire, Kant expresses the variability of elastic matter in terms of its compression and distension.[462]

The immoderate character of elastic matter becomes apparent in the transition to Part II of Kant's study on fire. If, in the general corollary to Part I, Kant claimed that "upon increase of the quantity or even of the elasticity of the matter, the body can increase in volume and the particles recede from each other without loss of cohesion in the body as a whole,"[463] then in the opening salvo of Part II, he observes that "fire shows its presence first by rarefying a body, whether fluid or solid, in all directions, then, the cohesion of the body being weakened, by breaking down its structure, and, finally, by dissipating it in the form of vapor [*debilitata sensim cohaesione, corporum compagem solvendo, postremo partes in vapores dissipando*]" (Prop 6).[464] The same elastic matter, which *is* the matter of fire ("*materia ignis non est nisi [...] materia elastica*" [Prop. 7][465]), is supposed to account for the cohesion of other kinds of matter it interrelates *and* for the loss, or the weakening, of that very cohesion. The instability of elastic matter is its conceptual and effective undecidability, its oscillations between the extremes of keeping and losing the cohesion of what it interrelates.

The loss of cohesion in particular is a return to the negativity of fire—indeed, the return of fire as a negative force, rather than a special kind of matter. Though perhaps surprising, given the study's previously reached conclusions, it is also understandable in light of what will have become a signature term of Kantian philosophy: the limit. Fire, writes Kant, "cannot grow without limit in any body [*in nullo corpore in immensum crescere potest*]; in growing hot to the point of seething, a body can never exceed its boiling point."[466] More precisely, Kant negates the negation of a limit to fire, which can*not* grow *im*mensely within any body. Such a gesture will become crucial to the entire critical project with its assertion that human *reason* cannot grow immensely, reaching out to areas, to which it has no legitimate access.

Despite fire's undeniable negativity and analytic effects, it is, for Kant, a great material synthesis of matter and energy, as well as of heat and light. The "elastic matter" of fire is heat and the latter, in turn, is light "compressed" (*compressus*), as Proposition 8 makes clear: "The matter of heat is nothing but the ether (the matter of light [*lucis materia*]) compressed by a strong attractive (adhesive) force of bodies into their interstices."[467] For Kant, heat is light compressed and absorbed by dense bodies, while light is heat reflected or refracted, scattered. In the proof of the proposition, he goes so far as to assert that "the matter of heat and the matter of light agree so closely as possible or, rather, that they are not different [*nihil differre*]."[468] Should this conclusion not hold for the light of reason, as well, which must "agree so closely as possible" with reason's heat? Within the budding physical monadology of fire, another enlightenment is discernible, one that does not fetishize the cold and indifferent light of reason, in the manner of Kant's later philosophy.

At the same time, though again doubly negative, material resistance to fire's elastic matter is what defines the possibility of measuring heat, according to Kant's reinterpretation of Guillaume Amontons' principle. If "the force of fire is principally manifested in the rarefaction of bodies, one could correctly measure its quantity by the compressive force required to withstand the endeavor of rarefaction" (Prop 9, note).[469] Matter that is not elastic *is* "the compressive force required to withstand the endeavor of rarefaction"; it is this compressive force that lends matter its density, as the opposite of the expansive elasticity of heat. When the quantity of compressive force is insufficient, the matter of bodies is rarefied by fire's elastic matter, which acts as anti-matter *and* as the intermediate guarantor of cohesion with respect to the materials it permeates.

The concluding propositions of Kant's brief treatise on fire deal with vapors, air, and flames viewed from the perspective of elasticity. When it comes to vapor, its "wonderful elasticity" (*admirandam elasticitatem*) consists in its explosive potential: "aqueous vapor, activated by fire, breaks the strongest container, and all vapors, each according to its own nature, often exhibit a wonderful elasticity" (Prop. 10).[470] In Proposition 11, Kant defines air as such as "an elastic fluid, almost a thousand times lighter than water [*fluidum elasticum, millies fere aqua levius*],"[471] observing that fire extracts this elastic fluid from the bodies it incinerates, such that "the matter expelled from the interstices of the body, which was not then elastic, shows elasticity only when liberated."[472] In turn, following Proposition 11, the flame "consists of ignited vapor," which derives from elastic matter found within a material body.[473] In the ignited body, "only the surface burns [*nisi in superficie ardet flammaeque*]," but as the burning moves down to the surfaces beneath the enflamed surface, "the elastic ether no longer holds it [a material body] bound together,"[474] which explains the disintegration of the burnt in ashes and cinders and the radiation of light and heat in the form of the ether that has been liberated from its material confines.

Fire becomes, for Kant, a purveyor of elastic matter, the vehicle for transferring it from the interiority of a material body to the air outside, which is itself an elastic fluid, and therefore one that is flammable. That is why the surface becomes so important: it is the plane, on which the inside and the outside communicate; it is in the in-between position even at the outer limits of a body. What holds bodies together is what leads to their demise; the very elastic matter that binds together its molecules facilitates its disintegration. Animation and death, cohesion and breakdown, hinge on the vicissitudes of fire, which, rather than merely dematerialize material entities, draws *another matter* out of them.

Lest we forget, the dynamics of cognition and a broad monadological ontology are also at stake in Kant's notes on fire. One of the implications, for instance, is that instead of a deep analysis of reality, thinking ought to operate on the surfaces of the world, at the interfaces between the inside and the outside. Another is that to extract meaning from an entity is to destroy it, given that it has been internally interlaced by the very meaning, corresponding to elastic matter, extracted from it. Further, if fire is not only symbolically related to cognition but if it *is* material cognitive activity (according to a philosophical line extending from Heraclitus—via Kant—to Novalis and, perhaps, Nietzsche), then cognition, too, boasts "a wonderful elasticity," which prevents it from being confined in mental containers, not least in Kantian categories and schemata: it breaks through them. Finally, a pyrological and pyropolitical reading of the world and of thought focuses on the interstices within and between bodies and concepts. That is *where* thinking-being happens, not in static routines but in the animating and potentially deadening, dissipating and condensing, coherency- and incoherency-laden effects of fiery elasticity.

## A New Shape of Pyropolitics

In the twenty-first century, the prospects of the entire planet going up in flames are at their highest. Global heating, well in excess of internationally agreed-upon limits, and continued reliance on massive incineration of matter for energy production; the warming not only of the atmosphere but also of the oceans; hybrid warfare, now involving AI, and the recently reignited nuclear arms race; inflammatory rhetoric immediately going viral thanks to the pervasiveness of new information technologies are so many signs of a devastating fire swallowing up not (only) the world but the earth itself, with its atmosphere and ecosystems, habitable places and previously inaccessible fossil reserves.

We are no longer sensing the transformative, positive effects of fire, be it the flames of technology or be it a revolutionary conflagration capable of instituting another economic and political mode of existence. In combination, the recommenced global arms race and the non-enforceable nature of international climate treatises amount to a scorching heat devoid of any light.

The contemporary pyropolitical flames have a decidedly apocalyptic feel to them. This is the case, in part, because the ashes they produce are not fertile; they suffocate, rather than nourish, the very possibility of the future. The byproducts of mass-scale industrial activity and nuclear waste are just two examples of such death-bearing ashes. Devastating as they were, "scorched earth" warfare tactics still contained the promise of a new beginning in the future, bearing as they did a close resemblance to the myth of the phoenix, reborn from the smouldering remains of its previous life. Today's "scorched world" no longer sustains this hope.

The world comes into view as a whole precisely when it is ready to burn up all at once. And the technologies responsible for global heating as much as those that may result in a thermonuclear war are making this terrifying vision of the finite world sharper than the catastrophic history of the two wars in the twentieth century known as "world wars." The end of globalization is finds its cheerleaders in ultra-nationalist far-right movements that nonetheless maintain clandestine ties among themselves and represent the old-new face of global capital. Is it by sheer chance that this contrived end coincides with the technological potential to wreck the world as such in its planetary extent, rather than the separate worlds of particular civilizations or peoples?

Another cause for despair is the relation to matters fiery by politicians of every stripe. On the one hand, technocratic governments—mostly in the West, whatever this disoriented orientational term means, in light of the inclusion of Japan, South Korea, Australia and New Zealand—are all but resigned to their own incapacity to regulate the fires of global heating and public affect, the prospects of forest fires in monocultured forests and the future flames of a nuclear holocaust. Instead, they dedicate themselves to the futile task of temporarily putting out some local fires, while others are ignited and still others rage uncontrollably. Despite their managerial approach to governance, they ultimately deal with the unmanageable. On the other hand, right-wing populisms and neo-fascisms thrive on fanning the flames of every conflagration imaginable, from hatred toward the other and the foreigner to the blaze of global heating, given the unrestricted and indeed increased extraction and combustion of fossil fuels. Whether due to the incapacity or due to the unwillingness to regulate their intensities, fires of every kind imaginable rage and ravage the planet.

More than that, we live in an epoch when fire (or, more precisely, its use) comes into its own, dispelling the daydream that, once unleashed, it can be easily controlled. Political and ecological fires appear terrifying and overwhelming, their elemental nature coming to the fore. Perhaps, this is a final footnote to the Promethean endeavour, which was based on the desire to control fire, on harnessing its explosive potentiality and placing it within definite spatial or purpose-oriented constraints. From the steam engine to nuclear fission, industrial and postindustrial production (of energy, and much else) relishes its illusion of control, while spawning uncontrollable side-effects that range from $CO_2$ atmospheric pollution to runaway chain reactions and non-disposable nuclear waste. What is gradually changing is not the sudden irruption of uncontrollability itself, but awareness about it—though there is still plenty of hope around that technological solutions could be found to the multiplying crises, reinforcing one another in positive feedback loops.

In light (and in the heat) of the current outlines of pyropolitics, it is easy to succumb to irresistible despair. But necessity is the mother of invention—how to come to experience the necessity *as* necessity, however, saddled with freedom other than the freedom of choice?—and the turning point lies not so far from the point of sheer despondency and gloom. So, what if we did not have to burn anything, while still procuring enough energy? An apparent utopia, this disposition has been crucial to the life of plants for millions of years. In their practical relation to energy, they demonstrate an evolutionary realization that it is redundant to burn anything here on earth, because the daily blaze of the sun caters to all energy needs in abundance. Plants do not rebuff fire, but merely displace it in time and cosmic space. Vegetal receptivity to the sun, to its light and heat, is an alternative to igniting fires (with the proviso that a few tree species, such as eucalyptus, actually welcome an earthly fire as well). If necessity is the mother of invention, then there is no need to invent anything radically new—merely to learn from plants how to recalibrate our relation to energy and to fire.

Politically, plants are not the absolute sun worshippers they are made out to be; they are not the conduits of the cosmopolitical figure of the One (God, King, Star…). Even as heliotropes, or the flowers that follow the movement of the sun across the sky throughout the day, they stretch up, down, and sideways at the same time, anarchically dispersing the principle (and the political principal thing, the authority) among several elements.

The new shape of pyropolitics is, thus, as sharp and discernible as it is still vaguely unrecognizable, depending on whether the vegetal recalibration and moderation of fire is on the horizon. Much hinges on the plants' own relation to fire on the earth scale and on our relation to this relation. Will the living and the long-dead forests (those converted into oil, coal, and natural gas) be engulfed in the flames, burning up the entire planet? Or will the growing-metamorphosing-decaying plants lead the way in renegotiating the approach to, as well as the applications and implications of, fire for the sake of a liveable future?

# Notes

1 Michael Marder, "Compassionate Genocide," *The Philosophical Salon*, April 22, 2024. < https://thephilosophicalsalon.com/compassionate-genocide/>
2 Michael Marder and André Parise, "Extending Cognition: A Vegetal Rejoinder to Extensionless Thought and to Extended Cognition." *Plant Signaling & Behavior*, 19(1), 2024, e2345984.
3 See Peter Sloterdijk, *Prometheus's Remorse: From the Gift of Fire to Global Arson* (Los Angeles: Semiotexte, 2024).
4 Cf. Martin Heidegger, *Elucidations of Hölderlin's Poetry*, translated by Keith Hoeller (New York: Humanity Books, 2000).
5 Cf. Michael Marder, "The Ethical Ungrounding of Phenomenology: Levinas's Tremors." In Santiago Zabala and Michael Marder (eds.), *Being Shaken: Ontology and the Event* (Basingstoke & New York: Palgrave, 2014), pp. 41-62.
6 Ernest Roguin, *Traité de droit civil comparé: Les successions* (Paris: F. Pichon, 1908), p. xviii.
7 Henry Robinson Luce, "Italy: Financial Improvement," *Time Magazine*, 02/02/1925, p. 191.
8 Hilary Hinds & Jackie Stacey, "Imaging Feminism, Imaging Femininity: The Bra-Burner, Diana and the Woman Who Kills." *Feminist Media Studies* 1(2), 2000, pp. 153-177.
9 Nigel Clark, *Inhuman Nature: Sociable Life on a Dynamic Planet* (London & Thousand Oaks: SAGE, 2011), p. 164.
10 Clark, *Inhuman Nature*, p. 164.
11 Jacques Rancière, "Ten Theses on Politics." *Theory and Event*, 5(3), 2011, pp. 1-16.
12 Gaston Bachelard, *Air and Dreams: An Essay on the Imagination of Movement*, translated by Edith Farell and Frederick Farell (Dallas: The Dallas Institute Publications, 1988), p. 11.
13 For an overview of the elemental mythology of *nomos* in Schmitt, cf. Mitchell Dean, "Nomos: Word and Myth," in *The International Political Thought of Carl Schmitt: Terror, Liberal War, and a Crisis of the Global Order*, edited by Louiza Odysseos and Fabio Petito (London and New York: Routledge, 2007), 242-58.
14 "[Goethe's verses "All pretty things have trickled away, / Only sea and land count here"] steer attention too much away from international law, and to either a geographical-scientific or an elemental-mythological approach. That would not do justice to the essentially jurisprudential foundations of this book, which I have taken so much pains to construct" [Carl Schmitt, *The Nomos of the Earth in the*

International Law of Jus Publicum Europaeum, translated by Gary L. Ulmen (New York: Telos Press, 2003), p. 37].

15  Schmitt points out this connection in *Land and Sea* [translated by Simona Draghici (Washington, DC: Plutarch Press, 1997)], pp. 3ff. Likewise, in the Forward to *The Nomos of The Earth*, he acknowledges the influence of Johann Jacob Bachofen, whose texts introduced him to the mythical sources of jurisprudence (p. 38). In his own investigations of ancient mythologies, Bachofen [*Der Mythus von Orient und Occident* (München: C.H. Beck'sche Verlagsbuchhandlung, 1956)] came to the conclusion that the earth was the spring of all human artifacts, including the earliest versions of jurisprudence (p. 183). Instead of the dialectics of myth and enlightenment, theorized by Adorno and Horkheimer, we are thus facing the dialectics of myth and jurisprudence.

16  For the Babylonian creation myth *Enûma Eliš*, detailing the relation between the elements, see *Myths from Mesopotamia: Creation, the Flood, Gilgamesh, and Others*, translated by Stephanie Dalley (London & New York: Oxford University Press, 2008).

17  Lucretius, *On the Nature of Things*, translated by Martin Ferguson Smith (Indianapolis/Cambridge: Hackett, 2001), p. 49.

18  Cf. Martin Heidegger & Eugene Fink, *Heraclitus Seminar* (Evanston: Northwestern University Press, 1993), pp. 75ff.

19  Michael Marder, *Groundless Existence: The Political Ontology of Carl Schmitt* (London & New York: Continuum, 2010), *passim*.

20  This formulation of the question cropped up in my discussions with César Alcaya.

21  For environmental approach to the elements, consult David Macauley, *Elemental Philosophy: Earth, Air, Fire, and Water as Environmental Ideas* (Albany: SUNY Press, 2010).

22  "The terrestrial fundament, in which all law is rooted, in which space and law, order and orientation meet, was recognized by the great legal philosophers" (Schmitt, *The Nomos of the Earth*, p. 47).

23  Carl Schmitt, *Land and Sea*, translated by Simona Draghici (Washington, DC: Plutarch Press, 1997), p. 1. In this and all the subsequent quotations of this book, the English translation has been modified.

24  Carl Schmitt, *Glossarium: Aufzeichnungen der Jahre 1947–1951*, ed. by E. Freiherr von Medem (Berlin: Duncker & Humblot, 1991), p. 179.

25  I have explored the ethical consequences of the loss of ground in "The Ethical Ungrounding of Phenomenology" [in *Being Shaken: Ontology and the Event*, edited by Michael Marder & Santiago Zabala (Basingstoke & London: Palgrave Macmillan, 2014), pp. 41-62].

26  Carl Schmitt, *The Nomos of the Earth in the International Law of Jus Publicum Europaeum*, translated by Gary L. Ulmen (New York: Telos Press, 2003), p. 42.

27  Schmitt, *Land and Sea*, p. 2.

| | |
|---|---|
| 28 | Carl Schmitt, *Theory of the Partisan: Intermediate Commentary on the Concept of the Political*, translated by Gary L. Ulmen (New York: Telos Press, 2007), pp. 14, 21. |
| 29 | Schmitt, *Theory of the Partisan*, p. 12. |
| 30 | Schmitt, *The Nomos of the Earth*, p. 38. |
| 31 | Carl Schmitt, *Roman Catholicism and Political Form*, translated by Gary L. Ulmen (Westport, CT and London: Greenwood Press, 1996), pp. 10ff. |
| 32 | Schmitt, *Land and Sea*, p.4. |
| 33 | Schmitt, *The Nomos of the Earth*, p. 49. |
| 34 | Most recently, Peter Sloterdijk has explored this dimension of elemental politics in *Terror from the Air* [translated by Amy Patton and Steve Corcoran (Los Angeles: Semiotext(e), 2009)].) |
| 35 | Schmitt, *Land and Sea*, p. 58. Likewise, in *The Nomos of the Earth* Schmitt states: "Today, as a result of a new spatial phenomenon—the possibility of a domination of air space—firm land and free sea alike are being altered drastically, both in and of themselves and in relation to each other. Not only are the dimensions of territorial sovereignty changing, not only is the efficacy and velocity of the means of human power, transport, and information changing, but so, too, is the content of this *effectivity*" (p. 48). |
| 36 | Schmitt, *Land and Sea*, p. 58. |
| 37 | Jan-Werner Müller, *A Dangerous Mind: Carl Schmitt in Post-War European Thought* (New Haven: Yale University Press, 2003), p. 46. |
| 38 | Schmitt, *Land and Sea*, p. 58. |
| 39 | The same interpretation is advanced by Fink and Heidegger in the *Heraclitus Seminar*, p. 82. |
| 40 | Schmitt, *Land and Sea*, p. 58. |
| 41 | Schmitt, *Land and Sea*, p. 8. |
| 42 | Schmitt, *Land and Sea*, p. 29. |
| 43 | This dissolution itself is appropriate to the Schmittian concept of the political. For more on this, see my *Groundless Existence*. |
| 44 | Schmitt, *Theory of the Partisan*, p. 92. |
| 45 | Such, also, is the sense of Derrida's interpretation of Schmitt. In relative or relativized enmity, the enemy "would gain reassuring and ultimately appeasing contours, because they would be *identifiable*. The figure of the enemy would then be helpful—precisely as a figure—because of the features which allow it to be identified as such, still identical to what has always been determined under this name" [Jacques Derrida, *Politics of Friendship*, translated by G. Collins (London and New York: Verso, 1997), p. 83]. |
| 46 | Schmitt, *Theory of the Partisan*, p. 54. |
| 47 | Schmitt, *Theory of the Partisan*, p. 94. |
| 48 | Schmitt, *The Nomos of the Earth*, p. 49. |
| 49 | Schmitt, *Glossarium*, pp. 180-1. |

50   Cf. Reiner Schürmann, *Broken Hegemonies*, translated by Reginald Lilly (Bloomington and Indianapolis: Indiana University Press, 2003), *passim*.
51   "At that time, a spark [*ein Funke*] jumped from Spain to the North. It did not ignite the same fire [*denselben Brand*] that gave the Spanish guerrilla war its world-historical significance. But it produced an effect whose continuation today, in the second half of the 20th century, changes the face of the earth and her humanity" (Schmitt, *Theory of the Partisan*, pp.6-7).
52   Schmitt, *Theory of the Partisan*, p. 47, translation modified.
53   In a recent article, Banu Bargu goes as far as to consider the revolutionary spark as a symbol of constitutive politics: "In this light, we can better appreciate why Schmitt refers to the partisan as the 'spark' that ignites a fire. This fire represents the elemental forces of the people to shape the fate of their community. Popular intervention is instigated by crises, such as foreign occupation, outbreak of war or general strike. Extraordinary moments enable the activation of constituent power that, under normal conditions, remains an invisible support of the constitutional order" ["Unleashing the Acheron: Sacrificial Partisanship, Sovereignty, and History." *Theory & Event* 13 (1), 2010]. In pyropolitical terms, this implies that the volcanic and fiery activity of constituent power underlies and dislocates the static crusts of instituted law and order, akin to the outer layers of the earth.
54   Schmitt, *The Concept of the Political*, p. 62.
55   Heinrich Meier, *The Lesson of Carl Schmitt: Four Chapters on the Distinction between Political Theology and Political Philosophy*, translated by Marcus Brainard (Chicago and London: University of Chicago Press, 1998), p. 35.
56   Barrington Moore, Jr., *Soviet Politics: The Dilemma of Power* (New York; M.E. Sharp, 1950), p. 175.
57   Heidegger & Fink, *Heraclitus Seminar*, p. 11.
58   Carl Schmitt, *The Crisis of Parliamentary Democracy*, translated by Ellen Kennedy (Cambridge and London: MIT Press, 1986), p. 6.
59   Iraq and Afghanistan have long become the familiar designations for these margins, though the tensions repressed or displaced on the planetary scale can and do explode in the center as well, as soon as the margins announce themselves there.
60   For a detailed analysis of political risk in Schmitt, refer to chapter 2 of *Groundless Existence*.
61   See Schmitt's *Ex Captivitate Salus: Erfahrungen der Zeit 1945/47* (Berlin: Duncker & Humblot, 2002), p. 12; *Glossarium*, p. 66; and "Three Possibilities for a Christian Conception of History," translated by Mario Wenning, *Telos* 147, Summer 2009, p. 170.
62   Schmitt, "Three Possibilities," p. 170.
63   For an original reading of the myth of Epimetheus, see Bernard Stiegler's *Technics and Time 1: The Fault of Epimetheus*, translated by Richard Beardsworth and George Collins (Stanford: Stanford University Press,

1998), especially Part II of the book, titled "The Fault of Epimetheus." For Plato's recounting of the myth, see *Protagoras*, 320d-322a.
64  Schmitt, *Land and Sea*, p. 59.
65  David M. Levin, *The Philosopher's Gaze: Modernity in the Shadows of the Enlightenment* (Berkeley: The University of California Press, 1999), p. 15.
66  Jacques Derrida, *Margins of Philosophy*, translated by Alan Bass (Chicago: The University of Chicago Press, 1982), p. 251/299.
67  Derrida, *Margins of Philosophy*, p. 253.
68  *The Rig Veda: An Anthology*, translated and annotated by Wendy Doniger (London & New York: Penguin Books, 1981), p. 118.
69  Heidegger & Fink, *Heraclitus Seminar*, p. 37.
70  Origen, *Homilies on Genesis and Exodus* (Washington, DC: The Catholic University of America Press, 1982), p. 382.
71  Gaston Bachelard, *The Psychoanalysis of Fire*, translated by Alan Ross (Boston: Beacon Press, 1964), p. 106.
72  Luce Irigaray, *Elemental Passions*, translated by Joanne Collie & Judith Still (London: The Athlone Press, 1992), pp. 40-1.
73  Origen, *Homilies on Genesis and Exodus*, p. 383.
74  Origen, *Homilies on Genesis and Exodus*, p. 383.
75  Saint Bernard of Clairvaux, *Honey and Salt: Selected Spiritual Writings of St. Bernard of Clairvaux*, edited by John Thornton and Susan Varenne (New York: Vintage, 2007), p. 402.
76  Jürgen Habermas, *The Theory of Communicative Action. Volume 1: Reason and the Rationalization of Society* (Boston: Beacon Press, 1992), p. 75.
77  Novalis, *Notes for a Romantic Encyclopaedia*, Das Allgemeine Brouillon, translated by David W. Wood (Albany: SUNY Press, 2011), pp. 120-1.
78  F.W.J. Schelling, *Philosophical Investigations into the Essence of Human Freedom*, translated by Jeff Love and Johannes Schmidt (Albany: SUNY Press, 2007), p. 13. More recently, Terry Eagleton has made a similar point in *On Evil* (New Haven & London: Yale University Press, 2010).
79  Reinhart Koselleck, *Critique and Crisis: Enlightenment and the Pathogenesis of Modern Society* (Cambridge, MA: The MIT Press, 1988), p. 15.
80  Koselleck, *Critique and Crisis*, p. 33.
81  Thomas Hobbes, *Leviathan*, edited by Richard Tuck (Cambridge: Cambridge University Press, 1991), p. 9.
82  Hobbes, *Leviathan*, p. 128.
83  Cf. Mary Kaldor, *Global Civil Society: An Answer to War* (London & New York: Polity, 2003).
84  Cf. Richard Bernstein, *Radical Evil: A Philosophical Interrogation* (London & New York: Polity, 2002).
85  Eagleton, *On Evil*, p. 158.
86  Luis Garagalza, "La existencia mala," in *Claves de la Existencia: El Sentido Plural de la Vida Humana*, edited by Andres Oriz-Oses, Blanca Solares and Luiz Gargalza (Barcelona: Anthropos, 2013), pp. 330-347.

87 Gershom Scholem, *Major Trends in Jewish Mysticism* (New York: Schocken Books, 1974), p. 239
88 Jacques Derrida, *Acts of Religion*, edited by Gil Anidjar (London & New York: Routledge, 2001), p. 46.
89 *Mutatis mutandis*, everything phenomenology has taught us on the subject of the reactivation of the origins applies to the efforts of reawakening the founding principles of Western politics, provided that we make a switch from the geo-archaeological to the pyrological model. Instead of unearthing the origin, covered over by dead sediments of its own systematization, it is a matter of reigniting the revolutionary fire that made it so potent in the first place.
90 Cf., http://millercenter.org/president/speeches/detail/4540
91 Rasmus Ugilt, *The Metaphysics of Terror: The Incoherent System of Contemporary Politics* (New York & London: Bloomsbury, 2012).
92 Scholem, *Major Trends*, p. 237.
93 Scholem, *Major Trends*, p. 238.
94 Immanuel Kant, "Perpetual Peace: A Philosophical Sketch," in *Political Writings*, edited by H.S. Reiss (Cambridge: Cambridge University Press, 1991), p. 123.
95 Eagleton, *On Evil*, pp. 73, 76.
96 Koselleck, *Critique and Crisis*, p. 98.
97 Emmanuel Levinas, *Totality and Infinity: An Essay on Exteriority*, translated by Alphonso Lingis (Pittsburg: Duquesne University Press, 1999).
98 Koselleck, *Critique and Crisis*, p. 11.
99 On this point, see Alain Badiou's writings on St. Paul, especially *Saint Paul: The Foundation of Universalism*, translated by Ray Brassier (Stanford: Stanford University Press, 2003).
100 Origen, *Song of Songs: Commentary and Homilies*, translated by N.P. Lawson (Mahwah, NJ: Paulist Press, 2002), p. 112.
101 And, conversely, see Simon Critchley's *The Faith of the Faithless: Experiments in Political Theology* (London & New York: Verso, 2012): "Agamben tries to keep open a space between law and life [...]" (p. 163).
102 G.S. Kirk and J.E. Raven, *The Pre-Socratic Philosophers: A Critical History with a Selection of Texts* (Cambridge: Cambridge University Press, 1963), p. 201.
103 Origen, *Homilies on Genesis and Exodus*, p. 314.
104 Origen, *Song of Songs*, p. 112.
105 Søren Kierkegaard, *Either/Or: A Fragment of Life* (London & New York: Penguin, 1992), p. 552.
106 "And new philosophy calls all in doubt, / The element of fire is quite put out; / The sun is lost, and th' earth, and no man's wit / Can well direct him where to look for it." John Donne, "An Anatomy of the World," in *The Complete English Poems* (London & New York: Penguin, 1977), p. 276.

107 Ian Balfour, "Introduction," *South Atlantic Quarterly*, vol. 106 (2), a special issue on *Late Derrida*, Spring 2007, p. 211.
108 Some fine examples of the new political possibilities arising from blindness and darkness may be found in Patricia I. Vieira's study *Seeing Politics Otherwise: Vision in Latin American and Iberian Fiction* (Toronto: University of Toronto Press, 2011).
109 Act 5, Scene 1.
110 Refer to the final chapter of this book.
111 Sergei Davydov, "The Evolution of Pushkin's Political Thought," In *The Pushkin Handbook*, edited by David Bethea (Madison, WI and London, UK: Wisconsin University Press, 2005), p. 293.
112 Ludmilla Trigos, *The Decembrist Myth in Russian Culture* (New York and Basingstoke: Palgrave Macmillan, 2009), p. 9, translation modified.
113 Trigos, *The Decembrist Myth*, p. 9, translation modified.
114 V.I. Lenin, *The Birth of Bolshevism*, Volume I: *Lenin's Struggle against Economism* (Chipendale: Resistance Books, 2005), p. 268.
115 Novalis, *Philosophical Writings*, p. 48.
116 Novalis, *Philosophical Writings*, p. 135.
117 Jean-Louis Chrétien, *L'Intelligence du Feu* (Paris: Bayard, 2003), p. 45.
118 F.W.J. Schelling, *First Outline of a System of the Philosophy of Nature*, translated by Keith Peterson (Albany, NY: SUNY Press, 2004), p. 59.
119 Leon Trotsky, *History of the Russian Revolution*, translated by Max Eastman (Ann Arbor: University of Michigan Press, 1980), p. 517.
120 Trotsky, *History of the Russian Revolution*, p. 556.
121 Trotsky, *History of the Russian Revolution*, p. 593.
122 Chrétien's *L'Intelligence de Feu* compiles this genealogy.
123 Master Eckhart, *Et Ce Néant Était Dieu… Sermons LXI à XC* (Paris: Albin Michel, 2000), p. 103.
124 Eckhart, *Et Ce Néant Était Dieu…*, p. 166.
125 Franz Rosenzweig, *The Star of Redemption*, translated by William Hallo (Notre Dame: University of Notre Dame Press, 2002), p. 298.
126 Martin Heidegger, *Unterwegs zur Sprache* (Stuttgart: Verlag Günther Neske, 1959), p. 62, translation mine.
127 Karl Kautsky, *Foundations of Christianity: A Study in Christian Origins* (Routledge Revivals) (London & New York: Routledge, 2013), p. 324
128 Kautsky, *Foundations of Christianity*, p. 327.
129 Kautsky, *Foundations of Christianity*, p. 365.
130 Kautsky, *Foundations of Christianity*, p. 348.
131 On the pyropolitics of *thymos*, consult Peter Sloterdijk's *Rage and Time: A Psychopolitical Investigation*, translated by Mario Wenning (New York: Columbia University Press, 2012).
132 Fidel Castro, *Selected Speeches of Fidel Castro* (New York: Pathfinder Press, 1979), p. 17.
133 Castro, *Selected Speeches*, p. 107.

134 Refer to chapter 5 of this book for a close reading of the solar symbolism of the empire.
135 Chrétien, *L'Intelligence du Feu*, p. 77.
136 "Although the German workers cannot come to power and achieve the realization of their class interests without passing through a protracted revolutionary development, this time they can at least be certain that the first act of the approaching revolutionary drama will coincide with the direct victory of their own class in France and will thereby be accelerated. But they themselves must contribute most to their final victory, by informing themselves of their own class interests, by taking up their independent political position as soon as possible, by not allowing themselves to be misled by the hypocritical phrases of the democratic petty bourgeoisie into doubting for one minute the necessity of an independently organized party of the proletariat. Their battle-cry must be: *The Permanent Revolution*." [Karl Marx, *The Revolutions of 1848: Political Writings* (New York & London: Vintage Books, 1974), p. 330.]
137 Quoted in *Witnesses to Permanent Revolution: The Documentary Record*, edited by Richard B. Day and Daniel Gaido (Leiden: Brill, 2009), p. 450.
138 See Artemy Magun, *Negative Revolution: Modern Political Subject and its Fate after the Cold War* (New York & London: Bloomsbury, 2013).
139 There is nothing strange in this juxtaposition, since, in the grand dialectical system, nature *is* spirit that is other to itself and that has still not recognised itself as such. It follows that natural processes are only the processes of spirit not yet conscious of itself.
140 G.W.F. Hegel, *Hegel's Phenomenology of Spirit*, translated by A.V. Miller (Oxford: Oxford University Press, 1977), p. 359.
141 Hegel, *Phenomenology of Spirit*, p. 359.
142 G.W.F. Hegel, *Philosophy of Nature: Encyclopedia of the Philosophical Sciences, Part II*, translated by A.V. Miller (Oxford: Oxford University Press, 2004), p. 106.
143 In his speeches, Robespierre frequently decries the *"excés de la corruption humaine"* [Maximilian Robespierre, *Textes Choisis*, Volume III (Paris: Éditions Sociales, 1958), p. 60].
144 Hegel, *Philosophy of Nature*, p. 110.
145 Hegel, *Philosophy of Nature*, p. 106.
146 Hegel, *Philosophy of Nature*, p. 106.
147 Hegel, *Philosophy of Nature*, p. 105-6.
148 Hegel, *Philosophy of Nature*, p. 106.
149 Hegel, *Philosophy of Nature*, p. 107.
150 See Alexandra Cook *Jean-Jacques Rousseau and Botany: The Salutary Science* (Oxford: Voltaire Foundation at the University of Oxford, 2012).
151 Hegel, *Philosophy of Nature*, p. 111.
152 Hegel, *Philosophy of Nature*, p. 351.
153 Hegel, *Philosophy of Nature*, p. 354.
154 Hegel, *Philosophy of Nature*, p. 355.

155 Hegel, *Philosophy of Nature*, p. 110.
156 Hegel, *Phenomenology of Spirit*, p. 360.
157 Hegel, *Phenomenology of Spirit*, p. 358.
158 Stathis Kouvelakis, *Philosophy and Revolution: From Kant to Marx* (London & New York: Verso, 2003), p. 37.
159 Hegel, *Philosophy of Nature*, p. 111.
160 Hegel, *Philosophy of Nature*, p. 110.
161 Rolf Hellebust, *Flesh to Metal: Soviet Literature and the Alchemy of Revolution* (Ithaca, NY: Cornell University Press, 2003). The alchemical heritage of utopian and revolutionary thought is also at the forefront of Luciano Parinetto's *Alchimia e Utopia* (*Alchemy and Utopia*) [Milan: Mimesis, 2004], with its thesis of continuity between the critique of alienation in Rousseau, Hegel, Feuerbach, and Marx, on the one hand, and the alchemical dialectics of matter-nature and human-spirit, on the other.
162 P.G. Maxwell-Stuart, *The Chemical Choir: A History of Alchemy* (New York & London: Continuum, 2008), p. x.
163 Hellebust, *Flesh to Metal*, p. 11.
164 On the summary of the stages in the alchemical process, see Maxwell-Stuart, *The Chemical Choir*, p. xi.
165 Hellebust, *Flesh to Metal*, p. 22.
166 Mircea Eliade, *The Forge and the Crucible: The Origins and Structure of Alchemy* (Chicago & London: University of Chicago Press, 1962), p. 51.
167 Eliade, *The Forge and the Crucible*, p. 42.
168 Magun, *Negative Revolution*, p. 7.
169 Lois Schwoerer, "Introduction". In *The Revolution of 1688: Changing Perspectives*, edited by Lois Schwoerer (Cambridge: Cambridge University Press, 2004), p. 2.
170 Eliade, *The Forge and the Crucible*, p. 159.
171 Moses Hess, "The Philosophy of Action," in Socialist Thought: Documentary History, edited by Albert Fried and Ronald Sanders (Doubleday: Edinburgh, 1964), pp. 263-4.
172 Yinghong Cheng, *Creating the 'New Man': From Enlightenment Ideals to Socialist Realities* (Honolulu: University of Hawaii Press, 2008), p. 190.
173 Quoted in Hellebust, *Flesh to Metal*, p. 59.
174 Maxwell-Stuart, *The Chemical Choir*, p. 52.
175 Jean Paul Marat, *Oeuvres Politiques, 1789-1793*. Volume 7: April-August 1792 (Brussels: Pole Nord, 1995), p. 4354.
176 Jean-Paul Marat, *Recherches Physiques sur le Feu* (Paris: Cl. Ant. Jombert, 1780), p. 8.
177 Edmond Jabès, *Book of Resemblances II: Intimations and the Desert* (Middletown, CT: Wesleyan University Press, 1991), p. 66.
178 Karl Kautsky, "Revolutionary Questions (February 1904)", in *Witnesses to Permanent Revolution: The Documentary Record*, edited by Richard B. Day and Daniel Gaido (Leiden: Brill, 2009), p. 220.

179 All of the references in this paragraph at to Johann Gottfried von Herder, *Philosophical Writings*, translated and edited by Michael N. Forster (Cambridge: Cambridge University Press, 2002), p. 26.
180 The same is true for the ethics of Emmanuel Levinas, where actions undertaken for the sake of the other spark the need for further action, *ad infinitum*.
181 Eckhart, *Et Ce Néant Était Dieu...*, p. 178.
182 See Patricia Vieira, "Will 'The Hunger Games' Spark a Revolution?" *Al-Jazeera*, December 13, 2013 < http://www.aljazeera.com/indepth/opinion/2013/12/will-hunger-games-spark-revolution-2013121113542 6971134.html>.
183 Bachelard, *The Psychoanalysis of Fire*, p. 112.
184 *The Rig Veda: An Anthology*, p. 105.
185 *The Rig Veda: An Anthology*, p. 106.
186 *The Rig Veda: An Anthology*, p. 110.
187 *The Rig Veda: An Anthology*, p. 50.
188 *The Rig Veda: An Anthology*, p. 50.
189 Kirk & Raven, *The Pre-Socratic Philosophers*, p. 199.
190 Catherine Bell, *Ritual: Perspectives and Dimensions* (Oxford & New York: Oxford University Press, 1997), pp. 112-3.
191 Giorgio Agamben, *Remnants of Auschwitz: The Witness and the Archive* (New York: Zone Books, 1999), p. 29.
192 The Apostolic Fathers, *Early Christian Writings*, translated by Maxwell Staniforth (London & New York: Penguin Books, 1987), p. 130.
193 Cf., *Code noir* or *The Black Code*, in *Édit du Roi, Touchant la Police des Isles de l'Amérique Français* (Paris, 1687), pp. 28-58.
194 Gayatri C. Spivak, *A Critique of Postcolonial Reason: Toward a History of the Vanishing Present* (Cambridge, MA: Harvard University Press, 1999), p. 293.
195 Spivak, *A Critique of Postcolonial Reason*, p. 287.
196 Spivak, *A Critique of Postcolonial Reason*, p. 294-5.
197 Catherine Weinberger-Thomas, *Ashes of Immortality: Widow Burning in India* (Chicago & London: University of Chicago Press, 1999), p. 46.
198 Spivak, *A Critique of Postcolonial Reason*, p. 299.
199 Weinberger-Thomas, *Ashes of Immortality*, p. 23.
200 For more on this betrayal, see chapter 4, "The Generative Potential of the Elements" in Luce Irigaray and Michael Marder, *Through Plant Being* (New York: Columbia University Press, forthcoming in 2015).
201 Weinberger-Thomas, *Ashes of Immortality*, p. 43.
202 Lindsey Harlan, "Perfection and Devotion: Sati Tradition in Rajasthan," in *Sati, the Blessing and the Curse*, edited by John Stratton Hawley (Oxford & New York: Oxford University Press, 1994), p. 83.
203 "Miscellaneous Notices," in *The Quarterly Oriental Magazine Review and Register*, Vol. IV, No. 7-8, July-December 1825 (Calcutta: Thacker & Co., 1825), p. cxv.

204 Weinberger-Thomas, *Ashes of Immortality*, p. 42-3.
205 Pyotr Gennadyevich Deynichenko, *Rossiya: Polnyi Entziklopedicheskiy Illyustrirovannyy Spravochnik* (Moscow: OLMA, 2007), p. 135.
206 Deynichenko, *Rossiya*, p. 135.
207 Ekaterina Romanova, *Massovye Samosozhzheniya Staroobryadtsev v Rossii v XVII – XIX Vekakh* (St. Petersburg: The European University of St. Petersburg Press, 2012), p. 198.
208 Quoted in Romanova, *Massovye Samosozhzheniya*, p. 203, FN#3.
209 *The Encyclopedia of Eastern Orthodox Christianity*, edited by John Anthony McGuckin (New York: Wiley, 2011), p. 419.
210 Irina Praet, *Old Believers, Religious Dissent, and Gender in Russia, 1760 – 1850* (Manchester: Manchester University Press, 2003), p. 109.
211 Vladimir Molzinskiy, *Ocherki Russkoy Dorevolutzionnoy Istoriografii Staroobryadchestva* (St. Petersburg: St. Petersburg State University Press, 2001), p. 141.
212 Nikolai Berdyaev, *The Russian Idea* (Hudson, NY: Lindisfarne Press, 1992), pp. 23-4.
213 Curiously, the name of the main character in the novel, Raskol'nikov, alludes to the schism, *raskol*, the technical term for the conflict between patriarch Nikon and the proponents of "old faith.")
214 Berdyaev, *The Russian Idea*, p. 200.
215 Jeffrey William Lewis, *The Business of Martyrdom: A History of Suicide Bombing* (Annapolis. Naval Institute Press, 2012), p. 31; Mordecai Dzikansky, et al., *Terrorist Suicide Bombings: Attack Interdiction, Mitigation, and Response* (Boca Raton, FL: CRC Press, 2012), p. 25.
216 Quoted in Norbert Gossman, *The Martyrs: Joan of Arc to Yitzhak Rabin* (New York & London: University Press of America, 1996), p. 61. Cf. also, Avraham Yarmolinsky, *Road to Revolution* (Princeton: Princeton University Press, 1986), p. 276.
217 Ivan Strenski, "Sacrifice, Gift and the Social Logic of Muslim 'Human Bombers'", *Terrorism and Political Violence*, 15(3), Fall 2003, p. 16.
218 Strenski, "Sacrifice, Gift…", pp. 14-5.
219 Strenski, "Sacrifice, Gift…", pp. 15ff.
220 Talal Asad, *On Suicide Bombing* (New York: Columbia University Press, 2007), p. 45.
221 Asad, *On Suicide Bombing*, p. 51.
222 Quoted in V. G. Julie Rajan, *Women Suicide Bombers: Narratives of Violence* (London & New York: Routledge, 2011), p. 91.
223 Quoted in James Benn, *Burning for the Buddha* (Honolulu: The University of Hawaii Press, 2007), p. 170.
224 Quoted in Benn, *Burning for the Buddha*, p. 171.
225 Kalu Rinpoche, *The Dharma: That Illuminates All Beings Impartially Like the Light of the Sun and the Moon* (Albany, NY: SUNY Press, 1986), p. 155.
226 Bachelard, *The Psychoanalysis of Fire*, p. 19.
227 Quoted in Benn, *Burning for the Buddha*, p. 171.

228  Walpola Rahula, *What the Buddha Taught* (New York: Grove Press, 2007), p. 95.
229  Rahula, *What the Buddha Taught*, p. 96.
230  Ronald Wintrobe, "Leadership and Passion in Extremist Politics," in *Political Extremism and Rationality*, edited by Albert Breton, et al (Cambridge & New York: Cambridge University Press, 2002), p. 25.
231  Carl Schmitt, *Political Theology: Four Chapters on the Concept of Sovereignty*, translated by G. Schwab (London and Cambridge: MIT Press, 1985), p. 5.
232  "With priests *everything* simply becomes more dangerous, not only curatives and healing arts, but also arrogance, revenge, acuity, excess, love, lust to rule, virtue, disease; — though with some fairness one could also add that it was on the soil of this *essentially dangerous* form of human existence, the priestly form, that man first became *an interesting animal* [...]." Friedrich Nietzsche, *On the Genealogy of Morality*, translated by M. Clark and A.J. Swensen (Indianapolis & Cambridge: Hackett Publishing, 1998), pp. 15-16.
233  Manus Midlarsky, *Origins of Political Extremism: Mass Violence in the Twentieth Century and Beyond* (Cambridge & New York: Cambridge University Press, 2011), p. 5.
234  St. François de Sale, *Traité de l'Amour de Dieu* (Paris: Casterman, 1859), p. 516.
235  St. François de Sale, *Traité*, p. 618.
236  St. François de Sale, *Traité*, p. 617.
237  "Again, Christ is signified by the two altars of holocausts and incense. Because all works of virtue must be offered by us to God through Him; both those whereby we afflict the body, which are offered, as it were, on the altar of holocausts [*altari holocaustorum*]; and those which, with greater perfection of mind, are offered to God in Christ, by the spiritual desires of the perfect, on the altar of incense, as it were [...]." (Summa, IIa.102.4.6).
238  Cf. chapter 3, "Plotinus's Anonymous Great Tree," in Michael Marder, *The Philosopher's Plant: An Intellectual Herbarium* (New York: Columbia University Press, 2014).
239  Eagleton, *On Evil*, p. 125.
240  Quoted in Agamben, *Remnants of Auschwitz*, pp. 30-1.
241  Lest we forget, the other groups victimised by the Nazis, including disabled and gay people, were also in one way or another marked, in the eyes of the perpetrators, with the sign of bodily reality, be it their sexuality or a physical "defect."
242  Agamben, *Remnants of Auschwitz*, p. 31.
243  Agamben, *Remnants of Auschwitz*, p. 31.
244  Bachelard, *The Psychoanalysis of Fire*, p. 17.
245  Moshe Lazar, "Scorched Parchments and Tortured Memories: The 'Jewishness' of *Anussim* (Crypto-Jews)," in *Cultural Encounters: The*

*Impact of the Inquisition in Spain and the New World*, edited by Mary Elizabeth Perry and Anne J. Cruz (Berkeley & Los Angeles: The University of California Press, 1991), p. 178.
246 Quoted in Lazar, "Scorched Parchments...", p. 178.
247 Gretchen D. Starr-LeBeau, *In the Shadow of the Virgin: Inquisitors, Friars and Conversos in Guadalupe, Spain* (Princeton: Princeton University Press, 2003), p. 174.
248 Juan-Antonio Llorente, *Historia Crítica de la Inquisición en España*, Vol. II (Madrid: Hiperión, 1870), p. 7.
249 Gonzalo Martínez-Díez (ed.), *Bulario de la Inquisición Española hasta la Muerte de Fernando el Católico* (Madrid: Editorial Complutense, 1997), pp. 178-9.
250 Helen Rawlings, *The Spanish Inquisition* (New York: Wiley-Blackwell, 2006), p. 3.
251 In the original Spanish: "*impenitente, negativo, convicto.*" Cf. Rafael Gracia Boix (ed.), *Autos de Fe y Causas de la Inquisición de Córdoba* (Córdoba: Cajasur, 1983), p. 493, *et passim*.
252 Boix, *Autos de Fe y Causas*, p. 509.
253 Boix, *Autos de Fe y Causas*, p. 465.
254 Starr-LeBeau, *In the Shadow of the Virgin*, p. 174.
255 Martínez-Díez, *Bulario*, pp. 136-7.
256 Martínez-Díez, *Bulario*, pp. 162-3.
257 Martínez-Díez, *Bulario*, pp. 96-7.
258 Martínez-Díez, *Bulario*, pp. 448-9.
259 Martínez-Díez, *Bulario*, pp. 142-3.
260 Boix, *Autos de Fe y Causas*, p. 488.
261 Boix, *Autos de Fe y Causas*, p. 488.
262 Boix, *Autos de Fe y Causas*, p. 488.
263 Schelling, *First Outline*, p. 96.
264 Schelling, *First Outline*, p. 96.
265 For a further development of this line of thought, consult my *Energy Dreams: Of Actuality* (New York: Columbia University Press, 2017) and *Dump Philosophy: A Phenomenology of Devastation* (forthcoming in 2020).
266 Herbert Marcuse, *Negations: Essays in Critical Theory* (Boston: Beacon Press, 1968), p. 207.
267 Vladimir Bibikhin, *Energiya* (Moscow: St. Thomas Institute of Philosophy, Theology and History, 2010), p. 12.
268 Michelle Cederberg, *Energy Now! Small Steps to an Energetic Life* (Boulder, CO: Sentient Publications, 2012), p. 132.
269 Cederberg, *Energy Now!*, p. 132.
270 Robert North Roberts, Scott John Hammond, Valerie A. Sulfaro, *Presidential Campaigns, Slogans, Issues, and Platforms*, Vol. I: "Slogans, Issues, Programs, Personalities, and Strategies" (Santa Barbara, Denver & Oxford: Greenwood, 2012), p. 129.
271 Bibikhin, *Energiya*, p. 37.

272   Bibikhin, *Energiya*, p. 43.
273   Sigmund Freud, "Civilization and Its Discontents," in *The Future of Illusion, Civilization and Its Discontents and Other Works*, Standard Edition, Vol. XXI (1927-1931), edited by James Starchey, et al. (London: Vintage Classics, 2001), pp. 91-2.
274   Kierkegaard, *Either/Or*, p. 46.
275   Hegel, *Philosophy of Nature*, p. 306.
276   "The priests of Heliopolis spread the names of their gods throughout the country and found ways to assimilate many of the local gods from the rest of Egypt into the group worshipped along with Ra" [Robert A. Armour, *Gods and Myths of Ancient Egypt* (Cairo & New York: The American University in Cairo Press, 2001), p. 5].
277   —, *The Book of the Dead: Translation*, translated by Sir Ernest Alfred Wallis Budge (London: K. Paul, Trench, Trübner & Co., 1898), p. xcvii.
278   Sigmund Freud, "Moses and Monotheism," in *Moses and Monotheism, An Outline of Psycho-Analysis and Other Works*, Standard Edition, Vol. XXIII (1937-1939), edited by James Starchey, et al. (London: Vintage Classics, 2001), pp. 18ff. pp. 91-2. See for instance: "It remains possible that the religion which Moses gave to his Jewish people was nevertheless his own—that it was *an* Egyptian religion, though not *the* Egyptian religion" (p. 20).
279   "He is both their spiritual and their temporal chief, and all decisions terminate with him" [Tommaso Campanella, *The City of the Sun: A Poetical Dialogue*, translated by Daniel J. Donno (Berkeley & Los Angeles: The University of California Press, 1981), pp. 31-3].
280   Margaret Cavendish, *The Blazing World and Other Writings* (New York & London: Penguin, 1994), p. 134.
281   Robert N. Nicolich, "Sunset: The Spectacle of the Royal Funeral and Memorial Services at the End of the Reign of Louis XIV," in *Sun King: The Ascendancy of French Culture During the Reign of Louis XIV*, edited by David Lee Rubin (Washington & London: Associated University Presses, 1992), p. 58.
282   Ellen M. McClure, *Sunspots and the Sun King: Sovereignty and Mediation in Seventeenth-Century France* (Champaign: University of Illinois Press, 2006), p. 15.
283   Cavendish, *The Blazing World*, p. 126.
284   Cavendish, *The Blazing World*, p. 133.
285   Campanella, *The City of the Sun*, p. 69.
286   Thomas Northmore, "Memoirs of the Planetes, or a Sketch of the Laws and Manners of Makar (1795)," in *Utopias of the British Enlightenment*, edited by Gregory Claeys (Cambridge: Cambridge University Press, 1994), p. 158.
287   Thomas More, *Utopia*, edited by George M. Logan and Robert M. Adams (Cambridge: Cambridge University Press, 1989), p. 87.
288   McClure, *Sunspots and the Sun King*, p. 1.

289 Quoted in Alison Saunders, *The Seventeenth-Century French Emblem: A Study in Diversity* (Geneva: Droz, 2000), p. 77.
290 Pierre Le Moyne, *L'Art de Regner* (Paris, 1665), p. 355.
291 Le Moyne, *L'Art de Regner*, p. 100.
292 Sigmund Freud, "Psycho-Analytic Notes on an Autobiographical Account of a Case of Paranoia (Dementia Paranoides)," in *Case History of Schreber, Papers on Technique and Other Works*, Standard Edition, Vol. XII (1911-1913), edited by James Starchey, et al. (London: Vintage Classics, 2001), p. 81.
293 Freud, "Psycho-Analytic Notes," p. 54.
294 Freud, "Psycho-Analytic Notes," pp. 81-2.
295 Daniel Paul Schreber, *Memoirs of My Nervous Illness* (New York: NYRB Classics, 2000), p. 76.
296 Gilles Deleuze and Félix Guattari, Anti-Oedipus: Capitalism and Schizophrenia (Minneapolis: University of Minnesota Press, 1983), p. 2.
297 Georges Bataille, Visions of Excess: Selected Writings, 1927-1939, edited by Allan Stoekl (Minneapolis: University of Minnesota Press, 1985), p. 8.
298 Bataille, *Visions of Excess*, p. 5.
299 Irad Malkin, *Religion and Colonization in Ancient Greece* (Leiden: Brill, 1987), p. 120.
300 Stephen G. Miller, *The Prytaneion: Its Function and Architectural Form* (Berkeley & Los Angeles: University of California Press, 1978), p. 180.
301 Malkin, *Religion and Colonization in Ancient Greece*, p. 117.
302 —, The Portable Greek Historians: The Essence of Herodotus, Thucydides, Xenophon, Polybius, edited by M.I. Finley (New York & London: Penguin, 1977), p. 86.
303 Alain Peyrefitte, *La société de confiance: Essai sur les origines et la nature du devéloppement* (Paris: Édition O. Jacob, 1995), p. 115.
304 Francis Bacon, *The Works of Lord Bacon: With an Introductory Essay*, Volume 1 (London: William Ball, 1838), p. 524.
305 Sigmund Freud, "The Acquisition and Control of Fire," in *New Introductory Lectures on Psycho-Analysis and Other Works*, Standard Edition, Vol. XXII (1932-1936), edited by James Starchey, et al. (London: Vintage Classics, 2001), pp. 190-1.
306 P.J. Marshall, "Introduction," in *The Oxford History of the British Empire*, Volume II: The Eighteenth Century, edited by P.J. Marshall (Oxford & New York: Oxford University Press, 1998), p. 8.
307 Sigmund Freud, "Fetishism," in The Future of Illusion, Civilization and Its Discontents and Other Works, Standard Edition, Vol. XXI (1927-1931), edited by James Starchey, et al. (London: Vintage Classics, 2001), p. 154.
308 Patrícia Vieira, *Portuguese Film, 1930-1960: The Staging of the New State Regime* (New York & London: Bloomsbury, 2013), p. 184.
309 António Vieira, "Sermão da Dominga Vigéssima Segunda-Feira Post-Pentecosten," in *Sermões*, Vol. XI (Erechim: EDELBRA, 1998), § IV.

310 Alenka Zupančič, *The Shortest Shadow: Nietzsche's Philosophy of the Two* (Cambridge, MA: MIT Press, 2003), p. 27.
311 David Crystal, *English as Global Language*, Second Edition (Cambridge: Cambridge University Press, 2003), pp. 10, 75.
312 Randolph Quirk, "The English Language in a Global Context," in *English in the World*, edited by Randolph Quirk & H.G. Widdowson (Cambridge: Cambridge University Press, 1985), p. 1.
313 William Jennings Bryan, *The Old World and Its Ways* (St. Louis: The Thompson Publishing Company, 1907), p. 294.
314 John Winthrop, "John Winthrop Defines the Mission of Government Officials," in *Lend Me Your Ears: Great Speeches in History*, edited by William Safire (New York & London: W.W. Norton, 2004), p. 860.
315 Jacques Derrida, *The Truth in Painting*, translated by Geoffrey Bennington (Chicago: University of Chicago Press, 1987), p. 122.
316 St. Augustine, *The City of God Against the Pagans, Books 1-13* (Cambridge: Cambridge University Press, 1998), p. 49.
317 Craig Shirley, *Rendezvous with Destiny: Ronald Reagan and the Campaign That Changed America* (Wilmington: Intercollegiate Studies Institute, 2009), p. 73.
318 Campanella, *The City of the Sun*, p. 87.
319 Mario Cuomo, "New York Governor Mario Cuomo Challenges President Reagan's Portrayal of America as a 'Shining City on a Hill," in *In Our Own Words: Extraordinary Speeches of the American Century*, edited by Robert G. Torricelli & Andrew Carroll (New York & London: Washington Square Press, 2000), p. 355.
320 Immanuel Kant, *Political Writings*, edited by H.S. Reiss (Cambridge, UK & New York: Cambridge University Press, 1970), p. 238.
321 Michael Marder, "On Being Lost at Home: Disorientation between Economy and Ecology," in *Dis-Orientations: Philosophical and Literary Inquiries into the Lost Grounds of Modernity*, edited by Tora Lane & Marcia Sá Cavalcante Schuback, forthcoming in 2015.
322 Ray Allen Billington & Martin Ridge, *Westward Expansion: A History of the American Frontier* (Albuquerque: University of New Mexico Press, 2001), p. 2.
323 Schmitt, *The Nomos of the Earth*, p. 281.
324 Schmitt, *The Nomos of the Earth*, p. 284. Compare Schmitt's thesis to that of Spengler, who polemically states in a footnote, "'East' and 'West' are notions that contain real history whereas 'Europe' is an empty sound." [Oswald Spengler, *The Decline of the West*, An Abridged Edition (Oxford & New York: Oxford University Press, 1991), p. 12, FN 5.
325 Schmitt, *The Nomos of the Earth*, p. 285.
326 Friedrich Nietzsche, *The Gay Science, with a Prelude in Rhymes and an Appendix of Songs*, translated by Walter Kaufmann (New York: Random House, 1974), p. 181.
327 Nietzsche, *The Gay Science*, p. 279.

328 Spengler, *The Decline of the West*, pp. 13-4
329 Spengler, *The Decline of the West*, p. 14.
330 Pyotr Chaadayev, "Otryvki i aforizmy," in *Collected Works* (Moscow: Pravda, 1989), p. 186.
331 Already in his nineteenth century Chaadayev had no hope for a new pyropolitical synthesis of the East and West; "it remains to be proven," he wrote, "that, besides the two sides denoted by the words 'East' and 'West', humanity also has a third side" ("Otryvki i aforizmy," p. 186). There are, of course, two other general directions on the map and on the compass, namely South and North, but this is not what Chaadayev means. At issue is the politicisation of global humanity as essentially polarised around two extremes.
332 Freud, "Civilization and Its Discontents," p. 90.
333 Eliade, *The Forge and the Crucible*, p. 57.
334 Freud, "The Acquisition and Control of Fire," p. 192.
335 Freud, "The Acquisition and Control of Fire," p. 189.
336 Freud, "The Acquisition and Control of Fire," p. 189.
337 Quoted in Bachelard, *The Psychoanalysis of Fire*, p. 49
338 Bachelard, *The Psychoanalysis of Fire*, p. 49.
339 Luce Irigaray, *The Speculum of the Other Woman*, translated by Gillian C. Gill (Ithaca, NY: Cornell University Press, 1985), p. 243.
340 Irigaray, *The Speculum of the Other Woman*, p. 274.
341 Jacques Derrida, *Glas*, translated by John P. Leavey, Jr. and Richard Rand (Lincoln & London: University of Nebraska Press, 1986), p. 46, left.
342 Irigaray, *Elemental Passions*, p. 80.
343 Friedrich Max Müller, *Vedic Hymns, Part I: Hymns to the Maruts, Rudra, Vâyu and Vâta* (Oxford: Clarendon Press, 1891), pp. 216-7.
344 Prudence Jones and Nigel Pennick, *A History of Pagan Europe* (New York & London: Routledge, 1997), p. 35.
345 Jones & Pennick, *A History of Pagan Europe*, p. 34.
346 Patricia Monaghan, *The Encyclopedia of Celtic Mythology & Folklore* (New York: Facts on File, 2004), p. 195.
347 Malkin, *Religion and Colonization in Ancient Greece*, p. 114.
348 Jones & Pennick, *A History of Pagan Europe*, p. 36.
349 Malkin, *Religion and Colonization in Ancient Greece*, p. 116.
350 Anne Pippin Burnett, *Pindar* (London: Bristol Classical Press, 2008), p. 84
351 Marcel Detienne, *The Writing of Orpheus: Greek Myth in Cultural Context*, translated by Janet Lloyd (Baltimore: Johns Hopkins University Press, 2002), p. 67.
352 Detienne, *The Writing of Orpheus*, pp. 62-3.
353 Martin A. Mills, *Identity, Ritual, and State in Tibetan Buddhism: The Foundations of Authority in Gelupka Monasticism* (New York & London: Routledge, 2010), p. 156.
354 Detienne, *The Writing of Orpheus*, p. 64.
355 Bachelard, *The Psychoanalysis of Fire*, p. 101.

356 Detienne, *The Writing of Orpheus*, p. 66.
357 Detienne, *The Writing of Orpheus*, p. 68.
358 Mills, *Identity, Ritual, and State in Tibetan Buddhism*, p. 166.
359 Sloterdijk's *Rage and Time*, p. 11.
360 Jan N. Bremmer, *The Early Greek Concept of the Soul* (Princeton: Princeton University Press, 1987), p. 55.
361 Ole Martin Høystad, *A History of the Heart* (London: Reaktion Books, 2007), p. 38.
362 Cf. chapter 1.
363 Ian Budge, et al., *The New British Politics*, Fourth Edition (New York & London: Routledge, 2007), p. 104.
364 Richard Longaker, "Was Jackson's Kitchen Cabinet a Cabinet?" *The Mississippi Valley Historical Review*, 44(1), June 1957), p. 94.
365 Robert Remini, *Andrew Jackson: The Course of American Freedom, 1822-1832* (Baltimore: Johns Hopkins University Press, 1998), p. 326.
366 Matthew Warshauer, "Presidential Politics and Social Scandal," in *Jacksonian and Antebellum Age: People and Perspectives*, edited by Mark Renfred Cheathem (Santa Barbara: ABC-CLIO, 2008), p. 24.
367 William Safire, *Safire's Political Dictionary* (Oxford: Oxford University Press, 2008), p. 373.
368 Blema S. Steinberg, *Women in Power: The Personalities and Leadership Styles of Indira Gandhi, Golda Meir, and Margaret Thatcher* (Montreal & Kingston, ON: McGill-Queen's University Press, 2008), p. 184.
369 Steinberg, *Women in Power*, p. 184.
370 Dalia Gavriely-Nuri, The Normalization of War in Israeli Discourse, 1967-2008 (Plymouth: Lexington Books, 2013), p. 85.
371 Steinberg, *Women in Power*, p. 185.
372 Bachelard, *The Psychoanalysis of Fire*, p. 74.
373 Philippe Hecquet, *De la Digestion et des Maladies de l'Estomac* (Paris: François Fournier, 1712), p. 413.
374 Wendy Doniger, *The Hindus: An Alternative History* (New York & London: Viking-Penguin, 2009), p. 109.
375 Steinberg, *Women in Power*, p. 185.
376 David W. Pankenier, Astrology and Cosmology in Early China: Conforming Earth to Heaven (Cambridge: Cambridge University Press, 2013), pp. 142-3.
377 Bruce Rusk, "Artifacts and Authentication: People Making Texts Making Things in Ming-Qing China," in *Antiquarianism and Intellectual Life in Europe and China, 1500-1800*, edited by Peter N. Miller and François Louis (Ann Arbor: Michigan University Press, 2012), p. 183.
378 Mun Kin Chok, *Chinese Leadership Wisdom from the Book of Change* (Beijng: The Chinese University Press, 2007), p. 331.
379 James J. Davis, *The Iron Puddler: My Life in the Rolling Mills and What Came of It* (New York: Grosset & Dunlap, 1922), p. 137.

380 Israel Zangwill, *Works of Israel Zangwill: The Melting Pot; Chosen Peoples* (New York: Jewish Book Company, 1921), p. 96.
381 Hence:
"DAVID
To think that the same great torch of liberty which threw its light across all the broad seas and lands into my little garret in Russia, is shining also for all those other weeping millions of Europe, shining wherever men hunger and are oppressed—" (Zangwill, Works, p. 31).
382 Zangwill, *Works*, p. 33.
383 Kathleen R. Arnold (ed.), *Anti-immigration in the United States: A Historical Encyclopedia*, Volume 1 (Westport, CT: Greenwood, 2011), p. 49.
384 Hans P. Vough, *The Bully Pulpit and the Melting Pot: American Presidents and the Immigrant, 1897-1933* (Macon: Mercer University Press, 2004), p. 175.
385 Zangwill, *Works*, p. 105.
386 Zangwill, *Works*, p. 68.
387 Zangwill, *Works*, p. 146.
388 The complex imbrication of cooking, metallurgy, sexuality, and alchemy through their utilisation of fire did not go unnoticed by Eliade, *The Forge and the Crucible*, pp. 38ff.
389 Bachelard, *The Psychoanalysis of Fire*, p. 103.
390 Marcel Detienne, *The Gardens of Adonis: Spices in Greek Mythology*, translated by Janet Lloyd (Princeton: Princeton University Press, 1994), p. 46.
391 Wendy Doniger, *The Origins of Evil in Hindu Mythology* (Berkeley & Los Angeles: University of California Press, 1976), pp. 29-30.
392 Doniger, *The Origins*, p. 30.
393 Joanna Waley-Cohen, "The Quest for Perfect Balance: Taste and Gastronomy in Imperial China," in *Food: The History of Taste*, edited by Paul Friedman (Berkeley & Los Angeles: University of California Press, 2007), p. 101.
394 Quoted in Roel Sterckx, *Food, Sacrifice, and Sagehood in Early China* (Cambridge: Cambridge University Press, 2011), p. 67.
395 Lao-tzu, *Lao-tzu's Taoteching: With Selected Commentaries from the Past 2,000 Years*, Revised Edition (Port Townsend: Copper Canyon Press, 2009), p. 120.
396 Lao-tzu, *Lao-tzu's Taoteching*, p. 120.
397 Lao-tzu, *Lao-tzu's Taoteching*, p. 120.
398 Alan Kam-leung Chan, *Two Visions of the Way: A Study of the Wang Pi and the Ho-shang Kung with Commentaries on the Lao-tzu* (Albany, NY: SUNY Press, 1991), p. 90.
399 Lao-tzu, *Lao-tzu's Taoteching*, p. 120.
400 Charles Malamoud, *Cooking the World: Ritual and Thought in Ancient India*, translated by David White (Oxford: Oxford University Press, 1996), p. 51.
401 *The Rig Veda: An Anthology*, p. 49.

402 Malamoud, *Cooking the World*, p. 46.
403 Cf. chapter 2 in Malamoud, *Cooking the World*.
404 Mona Ozouf, *Festivals and the French Revolution*, translated by Alan Sheridan (Cambridge, MA: Harvard University Press, 1991), p. 114.
405 Lara Anderson, *Cooking Up the Nation: Spanish Culinary Texts and Culinary Nationalization in the Late Nineteenth and Early Twentieth Century* (Woodbridge: Tamesis, 2013), p. 21.
406 Priscilla Parkhurst Ferguson, *Accounting for Taste: The Triumph of French Cuisine* (Chicago & London: The University of Chicago Press, 2004), p. 81.
407 Parkhurst Ferguson, *Accounting for Taste*, p. 55.
408 Alexandre-Balthazar-Laurent Grimod de La Reynière, *Almanach des Gourmands*, Volume 3, Part 2 (Paris: Jean-François Coste, 1812), p. 62.
409 Lawrence R. Schehr & Allen S. Weiss, *French Food: On the Table On the Page and in French Culture* (New York & London: Routledge, 2001), p. 54.
410 Schehr & Weiss, *French Food*, pp. 54-5.
411 Cheng, *Creating the 'New Man'*, p. 69.
412 Quoted in Cheng, *Creating the 'New Man'*, p. 69.
413 Richard H. Solomon, *Mao's Revolution and the Chinese Political Culture* (Berkeley & Los Angeles: University of California Press, 1971), p. 372.
414 Mao Zedong, *Mao's Road to Power – Revolutionary Writings, 1912-1949: The Pre-Marxist Period*, Volume 1, edited by Stuart R. Schram, (Armonk, NY: M.E. Sharpe, 1992), p. 298.
415 Zedong, *Mao's Road to Power*, p. 298.
416 Vladimir Lenin, *Polnoye Sobraniye Sochinenii* [*Complete Works*], Fifth Edition, Volume 34 (Moscow: Izdatel'stvo Politicheskoy Literatury, 1967), p. 315.
417 In response to the exhortation, "Be prepared! [*Bud' gotov!*]," Soviet pioneers, or young party members in the making, had to respond at various ceremonies they participated in, "Always prepared! [*Vsegda gotov!*]." Curiously, the same word, *gotov*, also means that a meal is ready to be consumed, and a related noun, *gotovka*, translates as "cooking.")
418 Vladimir Lenin, *The State and Revolution*, translated by Robert Service (London & New York: Penguin, 1992), p. 45.
419 Michael Marder, "On Lenin's Usability, or How to Stay on the Edge," *Rethinking Marxism*, 19(1), January 2007, pp. 123ff.
420 Aimé Césaire, *The Collected Poetry*, translated by Clayton Eshleman and Annette Smith (Berkeley & Los Angeles: University of California Press, 1983), p. 49.
421 Suzanne Césaire, *Le Grand Camouflage: Écrits de Dissidence, 1941-45* (Paris: Seuil, 2009), pp. 66, 109.
422 On the nexus of hunger, time, and life see Juan Manuel Garrido, *On Time, Being, & Hunger: Challenging the Traditional Way of Thinking Life* (New York: Fordham University Press, 2012).

423 This term is inspired by Bachelard's *The Psychoanalysis of Fire*, where he discusses "The Prometheus Complex," "The Empedocles Complex," and "The Novalis Complex."
424 Pedro A. Sanchez, et al. "Alternatives to Slash and Burn," in *Slash-and-Burn Agriculture: The Search for Alternatives*, edited by Cheryl Ann Palm, Stephen A. Vosti, Pedro A. Sanchez, Polly J. Ericksen (New York: Columbia University Press, 2005), pp. 23-4.
425 http://earthobservatory.nasa.gov/Features/AmazonFire/ [last accessed on December 8, 2019].
426 Jacques Derrida, *Cinders*, translated by Ned Lukacher (Lincoln & London: University of Nebraska Press, 1991), p. 59.
427 Gaston Bachelard, *Fragments of a Poetics of Fire* (Dallas, TX: Dallas Institute Publications, 1990), p. 42.
428 Walter Benjamin, "Theses on the Philosophy of History," in *Illuminations: Essays and Reflections*, edited by Hannah Arendt (New York: Schocken Books, 1969), Thesis VI, p. 255.
429 William Shakespeare, "Anthony and Cleopatra," in *The Complete Works*, edited by Stanley Wells and Gary Taylor (Oxford: Clarendon Press, 1994), p. 1033.
430 Shakespeare, "Anthony and Cleopatra," p. 1035.
431 Schmitt, *The Concept of the Political*, p. 96.
432 Martin Heidegger, *On the Way to Language*, translated by Peter D. Hertz (San Francisco: HarperCollins, 1982), p. 181.
433 Heidegger, *On the Way to Language*, p. 179, translation slightly modified.
434 Jacques Derrida, *Of Spirit*, translated by Geoffrey Bennington and Rachel Bowlby (Chicago & London: University of Chicago Press, 1987), p. 97.
435 Paul Celan, "*Aschenglorie*", in *Selected Poems and Prose of Paul Celan*, edited and translated by John Felstiner (New York and London: W.W. Norton, 2001), p. 261. For a close reading of this poem see Derrida's "Politics and Poetics of Witnessing," in Jacques Derrida, *Sovereignties in Question: The Poetics of Paul Celan*, translated by Thomas Dutoit and Outi Pasanen (New York: Fordham University Press, 2005), p. pp. 65-96.
436 Celan, "*Aschenglorie*," p. 261.
437 Derrida, *Sovereignties in Question*, p. 69.
438 Derrida, *Of Spirit*, p. 97.
439 Novalis, *Philosophical Writings*, edited and translated by Margaret Mahoney Stoljar (Albany, NY: SUNY Press, 1997), p. 145.
440 William Blake, *The Complete Poetry and Prose of William Blake*, edited by David V. Erdman (Berkeley & Los Angeles: University of California Press, 2008), p. 386
441 Kirk & Raven, *The Presocratic Philosophers*, p. 199.
442 Heidegger & Fink, *The Heraclitus Seminar*, p. 37.
443 Derrida, *Cinders*, p. 39.
444 Vattimo and Zabala term these remainders "discharges of capitalism." Cf. Giannia Vattimo & Santiago Zabala, *Hermeneutic Communism: From*

*Heidegger to Marx* (New York: Columbia University Press, 2011), pp. 7, 64, 70.
445 Jacques Derrida, *Sovereignties in Question: The Poetics of Paul Celan*, translated by Thomas Dutoit and Outi Pasanen (New York: Fordham University Press, 2005), p. 20.
446 Jacques Derrida, *Archive Fever: A Freudian Impression*, translated by Eric Prenowitz (Chicago & London: University of Chicago Press, 1996), p. 99.
447 Derrida, *Cinders*, p. 73.
448 Quoted in Elie Wiesel, *Somewhere a Master: Further Hasidic Portraits and Legends* (New York: Summit Books, 1982), p. 114.
449 Friedrich Nietzsche, *The Anti-Christ, Ecce Homo, Twilight of the Idols and Other Writings*, edited by Aaron Ridley and Judith Norman (Cambridge, UK: Cambridge University Press, 2005), p. 171.
450 —, "Prominent Lawyer in Fight for Gay Rights Dies after Setting Himself on Fire in Prospect Park." *New York Times*, April 14, 2018. <https://www.nytimes.com/2018/04/14/nyregion/david-buckel-dead-fire.html>
451 Michael Marder, *Senses of Upheaval: Philosophical Snapshots of a Decade* (London: Anthem Press, 2021).
452 —, "Atomic Bomb." *Encyclopedia Britannica* < https://www.britannica.com/technology/atomic-bomb>, accessed on June 25, 2024.
453 Immanuel Kant, "Succinct Exposition of Some Meditations on Fire." In *Natural Science*, edited by Eric Watkins (Cambridge, UK & New York: Cambridge University Press, 2012), p. 309.
454 Kant, "Succinct Exposition," p. 312.
455 Kant, "Succinct Exposition," p. 312.
456 Kant, "Succinct Exposition," p. 313.
457 Kant, "Succinct Exposition," p. 313.
458 Kant, "Succinct Exposition," p. 313.
459 Kant, "Succinct Exposition," p. 313.
460 Kant, "Succinct Exposition," p. 315.
461 Kant, "Succinct Exposition," p. 314.
462 Kant, "Succinct Exposition," pp. 315-316.
463 Kant, "Succinct Exposition," p. 317.
464 Kant, "Succinct Exposition," p. 317.
465 Kant, "Succinct Exposition," p. 317.
466 Kant, "Succinct Exposition," p. 317.
467 Kant, "Succinct Exposition," p. 318.
468 Kant, "Succinct Exposition," p. 319.
469 Kant, "Succinct Exposition," p. 320.
470 Kant, "Succinct Exposition," p. 321.
471 Kant, "Succinct Exposition," p. 323.
472 Kant, "Succinct Exposition," p. 324.
473 Kant, "Succinct Exposition," p. 326.
474 Kant, "Succinct Exposition," p. 326.

***ibidem**.eu*